A Guide to

THE DATA
PROTECTION
ACT

Implementing
the Act

Dr. Nigel Savage
Department of Legal Studies, Trent Polytechnic

&

Prof. Chris Edwards
Cranfield School of Management

First published in Great Britain 1984 by Financial Training Publications Limited, Avenue House, 131 Holland Park Avenue, London W11 4UT

©N. Savage and C. Edwards, 1984

First edition 1984
Second edition 1985

ISBN: 0 906322 92 8

Typeset by Kerrypress Ltd, Luton

Contents

Preface   viii

PART 1   WHAT IS THE NEED FOR THIS ACT?   1

1   What is the existing law regulating the use and abuse of information?   3

1.1 Introduction   1.2 What is the legal framework regulating the
use of information?   1.3 What is the nature of the legal
protection?   1.4 What are the main elements of the action?
1.5 What is confidential information?   1.6 What remedies are
available in the case of unauthorised use or disclosure of
information?   1.7 What is the difference between the law regulating
breach of confidence and the new data protection legislation?

2   Why do we have a Data Protection Act?   9

2.1 Background   2.2 Who are the persons and agencies involved in
the DPA?   2.3 What are the major procedures involved in the
Act?   2.4 What are the principles underlying the Act?   2.5 Are
there any exemptions from the Act?

PART 2   WHAT IS THE SCOPE OF THE ACT?   19

3   Who is affected by the Act?   21

3.1 Introduction   3.2 Who does the Act affect?

4   What data are covered?   25

4.1 Introduction   4.2 What is automatic processing?   4.3 What
are personal data?

5   Are there any exemptions?   31

5.1 How can one be exempt?   5.2 Payroll, pension and accounting
data   5.3 Membership details of clubs and name and address
files   5.4 Data held for statistical and research purposes 5.5 Crime
and tax data   5.6 Statutory functions   5.7 Health and social work
data   5.8 Other exemptions

Contents

PART 3   WHAT PROCEDURES AND RIGHTS ARE INTRODUCED BY THE ACT?   47

6   What is the registration procedure?   49

6.1 What is the purpose of the register?   6.2 Who is responsible for maintaining the register?   6.3 Who must register and how is it carried out?   6.4 How is the registration application form structured?   6.5 How many register entries can a data user have?   6.6 What information must be provided by data users and computer bureaux—DPR.1 part A?   6.7 What information must be provided by data users—DPR.1 part B?   6.8 Where there are a number of companies in a group how should they register?   6.9 Can the registration be altered at any time?   6.10 In what circumstances can the Registrar refuse registration?   6.11 Can the applicant process data pending the outcome of an application?   6.12 How will renewal applications be dealt with?   6.13 What are the implications of non-registration for data users?   6.14 What are the implications of non-registration for a computer bureau? 6.15 What are the implications of undertaking activities not covered by a registration?

7   What are the powers of the Registrar?   76

7.1 What is the principal function of the Registrar?   7.2 What powers does the Registrar have?   7.3 Is there anything that the Registrar cannot inspect or seize?   7.4 What happens if the data user or bureau fails to assist the Registrar?   7.5 What action may the Registrar take after an inspection?   7.6 What penalties may be imposed by the courts?   7.7 Can individual directors be liable to a fine?   7.8 How can the Registrar ensure compliance with the principles?   7.9 What are enforcement notices?   7.10 What are de-registration notices?   7.11 What are transfer prohibition notices?

8   What duties does the Registrar have?   85

8.1 What are the Registrar's duties?   8.2 How is the Registrar accountable?   8.3 Does the Registrar fulfil any obligation in respect of the Convention?

9   Can data users appeal against the Registrar's decision and actions?   88

9.1 Introduction   9.2 Who comprises the Tribunal?   9.3 What rights of appeal do persons have to the Tribunal?   9.4 How are appeals heard?   9.5 What powers does the Tribunal have to deal with obstructive persons? 9.6 What are the possible decisions of the Tribunal? 9.7 Is there any appeal from the Tribunal?

10 What rights are introduced for data subjects? — the courts   92

10.1 Introduction 10.2 Access rights 10.3 Compensation for inaccuracy 10.4 Compensation for loss or unauthorised access 10.5 Rectification and erasure 10.6 Who will hear claims by data subjects?

11 What rights are introduced for data subjects? — the Registrar   102

11.1 Introduction 11.2 How does the Registrar deal with complaints?

PART 4 HOW WILL USERS NEED TO RESPOND?   105

12 What are the administrative implications of the Act?   107

12.1 Introduction 12.2 Policy matters 12.3 Preparation for registration 12.4 Maintaining a current registration 12.5 Processing requests for access 12.6 Updating records to reflect changes required by a data subject 12.7 Anticipating problems

13 Does the Act have international implications?   115

13.1 What is the objective of the Convention and which countries does it extend to? 13.2 Does the Act comply with the Convention? 13.3 What does the Convention say about transborder data flows? 13.4 What powers does the Registrar have to regulate transborder data flows under the Act? 13.5 What does the Act say about data held and services provided outside the UK?

14 What is the timescale for action?   122

Appendix 1 Text of the Data Protection Act 1984   124

Appendix 2 Data Protection Registration Notes and Application Forms   174

Appendix 3 Specimen registration application   234

Index   283

Preface

The Data Protection Act affects most persons who process, or have processed for them, personal information. Its provisions require such persons to consider the nature and scope of their processing operations in order to register, and to introduce procedures for monitoring compliance with the Act and handling requests for access to data.

The objective of this book is to explain the provisions of the legislation in straightforward terms, to consider the likely impact of such provisions on computer users, and to suggest how processing operations may be organised to meet the requirements imposed by the Act. In particular, this book explains in detail how an organisation will register. A specimen completed application form is included and pitfalls to be avoided in completing these forms are explained.

We should like to express our gratitude to Miss Brigitte Courtney, Cranfield School of Management, for her excellent efforts in handling the automatic processing of the manuscript; and to our wives, who have heard us nattering about 'transborder data flows' and 'subject access rights' in our sleep.

We should like to acknowledge the kind permission given by the Data Protection Registrar to reproduce guidance notes and specimen application forms, which have been made readily available to all interested parties. Applications for registration should be made on the official forms which will be available from Crown Post Offices and the Office of the Data Protection Registrar, Springfield House, Water Lane, Wilmslow, Cheshire, SK9 5AX.

The work is of course entirely that of the authors and we remain responsible for any errors or omissions.

N. Savage, Farnsfield, Nottingham
C. Edwards, Ravenstone, Milton Keynes

PART 1

What is the need for this Act?

Chapter 1

What is the existing law regulating the use and abuse of information?

1.1 Introduction

Prior to examining the implications of the Data Protection Act 1984 (DPA) it would be useful to consider the wider legal framework regulating the use and abuse of confidential information. Although the DPA is the first major piece of legislation concerned exclusively with data protection, it is not the only law concerned with the handling of information, using the term in its widest sense.

1.2 What is the legal framework regulating the use of information?

Most of the rights and remedies that exist in respect of the infringement of privacy are derived from the civil law rather than the criminal law. There are, however, a great many statutes that have, over the years, sought to impose criminal penalties where confidential information is disclosed. Indeed, the Franks Committee in 1972 identified more than 60 statutory provisions which make the disclosure of information a criminal offence. Such statutes are mostly concerned with information controlled by the government. The Official Secrets Act 1911, for example, makes it an offence for government employees to disclose confidential information. There are also statutory provisions dealing with taxation information, census information and certain medical records.

Although the DPA is the first British statute that imposes sanctions tailored specifically towards protecting individuals against abuses involving computerised data, it is not the first attempt at giving individuals the right to correct misleading information held by others. The Consumer Credit Act 1974 gives individuals the right to examine and challenge files relating to themselves which are kept by credit agencies. If the information is incorrect, then the individual can insist that it is corrected and supply a statement which gives his or her account of the matter. The provisions are supported by the powers and authority of the Director General of Fair Trading.

The civil law provides some protection against the unauthorised disclosure or use of information which is of a confidential nature. The information must have been entrusted to an individual in circumstances which, expressly or impliedly, impose an obligation to respect its confidentiality. The action for breach of confidence is a remedy, arising out of common law, developed as a result of successive judicial decisions.

In essence, the common law remedy may be used for protecting any kind of information, whether it relates to technical, business or personal matters. To date there is, however, no reported decision specifically concerned with information derived from the use of computers.

1.3   What is the nature of the legal protection?

The precise nature of the protection afforded by the law is a source of considerable debate. A number of cases have been explained on the basis of the protection of property rights. In other cases, where the parties are in a contractual relationship, the courts have treated the action as one based on breach of a contractual term. The range of the protection is, however, much broader, and under certain circumstances, a person may restrain a third party from the unauthorised use or disclosure of confidential information, even in the absence of any contractual relationship. Indeed, in recent decisions the courts have emphasised the wider concept of confidence and good faith.

Lord Denning observed in 1969 that 'the jurisdiction is based not so much on property or contract as on the duty of good faith'.

One of the most influential decisions was *Saltman Engineering Co. Ltd* v *Campbell Engineering Co. Ltd* (1948) 65 RPC 203. This case is significant since the court accepted that the obligation to respect confidence is not limited to instances where the parties are acting under a contract. It may arise in any situation where a person is in possession of confidential information for a strictly limited purpose and uses or discloses it without consent.

4

1.4   What are the main elements of the action?

The Law Commission in 1974 concluded that before an action for breach of confidence can succeed, it must be shown that:

(a)   There is in existence an obligation of confidence regarding information.
(b)   The information itself has the necessary quality of confidence about it.
(c)   There has been, or is in contemplation, an unauthorised disclosure or use of the information.

The information must be communicated in circumstances which create an obligation of confidence. If a document is marked, 'Private and confidential', persons into whose possession the document comes are immediately made aware of a potential obligation of confidence. Indeed, from a practical angle it is always desirable that there is some express recognition or acknowledgement of confidentiality.

As Megarry J said in *Coco* v *A. N. Clark (Engineers) Ltd* [1969] RPC 41 at 48:

If the circumstances are such that any reasonable man standing in the shoes of the recipient of the information would have realised that upon reasonable grounds the information was being given to him in confidence, then this should suffice.

Where there is a contractual relationship it is always prudent to protect the confidence of information passing under the contract by an express term forming part of the agreement.

Frequent abuses of confidence occur between an employer and an employee. Every contract of employment contains an implied term that the employee will not disclose his employer's trade secrets or reveal confidential information that he acquires in the course of his employment. By their very nature, such obligations continue after the employment relationship has ceased. As Farwell J stated in *Triplex Safety Glass Co. Ltd* v *Scorah* (1937) 55 RPC 21:

Whether bound by express contract or not, no employer is entitled to filch his employer's property, in whatever form that property may be, whether it is in the form of a secret process or goodwill or in some other form. Whatever is the property of the employer must not be wrongfully used by the employee in any way, but remains the property of the employer.

1.5   What is confidential information?

The action for breach of confidence is not simply confined to the protection of trade secrets and technical information; indeed, it may extend to details about one's personal life. In *Duchess of Argyll* v *Duke of Argyll* [1967] Ch 302, the Duchess obtained an injunction to prevent the Duke from disclosing marital confidence in a national newspaper. The decision is significant since the court decided that the restraint could be enforced against the third-party newspaper into whose possession the information had passed.

There can be no breach of confidence in revealing to others something which is already public knowledge. It is, however, possible to have confidential information which is the result of work completed by an individual using techniques available to anyone; the materials and techniques may be public knowledge but the work completed on them is not. Thus, a novel computer program, or a set of flow charts and decision tables, may have the character of confidentiality even though their precise nature and function is public knowledge. As Lord Green MR observed in *Saltman Engineering Co. Ltd* v *Campbell Engineering Co. Ltd* (1948) 65 RPC 203:

> It is perfectly possible to have a confidential document, be it a formula, a plan, a sketch, or something of that kind, which is the result of work done by the maker upon materials which may be available for the use of anybody; but what makes it confidential is the fact that the maker of the document has used his brain and thus produced a result which can only be produced by somebody who goes through the same procees.

1.6   What remedies are available in the case of unauthorised use or disclosure of information?

Once a person has acquired information in circumstances of confidence, he is under a duty not to use such information or disclose it without the consent of the person from whom he acquired it. The duty may even extend to someone who may use the information in good faith. Thus, in *Seager* v *Copydex Ltd (No. 2)* [1969] 1 WLR 809,

6

the defendants were held liable even though the court accepted that they believed that the product they were marketing was the result of their own developments and not derived from information passed on to them.

The principal remedies available on a successful action are: an injunction, an account of profits, an order for delivery up or destruction of the relevant article, or damages.

Whether an injunction is granted depends upon the extent to which the information in question has already become public knowledge. It may be that where information has become public knowledge damages would be a more appropriate remedy.

Such damages are assessed according to the value of the confidential information. Essentially, damages are based on the market value of the information, which, in turn, would depend upon the character of such information. If the information was of such a nature that it could be obtained from a consultant for a fee, then the damages would accordingly represent the fee payable. If, on the other hand, the information was in the nature of an original invention, such as a computer program, the damages might be based on the capitalised value of a royalty on the sale or licence of the program.

1.7 What is the difference between the law regulating breach of confidence and the new data protection legislation?

Both the common law, as developed by the courts through the action for breach of confidence, and the DPA are concerned with privacy in its broadest sence — that is, the handling of information. There are, however, significant differences between the common law and the DPA.

(a) The action for breach of confidence may relate to any information, disclosed in circumstances of confidence, no matter how it is processed. The DPA seeks only to regulate automatically processed data from which an individual can be identified, irrespective of its confidentiality.

(b) Actions for breach of confidence can only relate to information of a confidential nature, whereas the DPA controls all data.

(c) The DPA is in essence preventative. It is concerned to avoid the misuse of information held on computers in advance, although it gives data subjects some new remedies. The common law remedies

7

can only be invoked when there is either an actual disclosure or use of confidential information, or at least a threat of disclosure or use.

Chapter 2

Why do we have a
Data Protection Act?

2.1 Background

There are two main reasons why the government decided that it was necessary to legislate on data protection: first, in order to ratify the Council of Europe Data Protection Convention (the Convention). Without such ratification firms operating in the UK could be placed at a considerable disadvantage by comparison to those based in other countries with data protection legislation in accordance with the Convention. The Convention permits ratifying countries to refuse personal information to be transferred to other countries which do not have comparable data protection law. This would clearly pose a threat to UK firms with international interests, particularly the activities of British computer bureaux which process a great deal of data for customers overseas.

The Convention was opened for signature in January 1981 and was signed by the UK in May of that year. Twelve states have signed the Convention. These are: Austria, Belgium, Spain, Denmark, West Germany, Greece, Iceland, Italy, Luxembourg, Portugal, Turkey and the UK. Four states have already ratified the Convention. These are: Sweden, Norway, France and Spain. It will automatically enter into force when ratified by five states. It is expected that the UK will not ratify the Convention until the DPA is fully operational, that is, after November 1987.

The second reason why legislation was introduced was because of the threat to privacy posed by the rapid growth in the use of high speed computers, with their ability to process and link information about individuals.

The Younger Report on Privacy in 1972 (Cmnd 5012) had identified ten principles which were intended as general guidelines to computer users in the private sector. These principles form the basis

9

for many of the subsequent reports, proposals and the DPA itself. The report argued that the government should seek to ensure compliance with the following principles:

(a)   Information should be regarded as held for a specific purpose and should not be used, without appropriate authorisation, for other purposes.

(b)   Access to information should be confined to those authorised to have it for the purpose for which it was supplied.

(c)   The amount of information collected and held should be the minimum necessary for the achievement of a specified purpose.

(d)   In computerised systems handling information for statistical purposes, adequate provision should be made in their design and programs for separating identities from the rest of the data.

(e)   There should be arrangements whereby a subject could be told about the information held concerning him.

(f)   The level of security to be achieved by a system should be specified in advance by the user and should include precautions against the deliberate abuse or misuse of information.

(g)   A monitoring system should be provided to facilitate the detection of any violation of the security system.

(h)   In the design of information systems, periods should be specified beyond which the information should not be retained.

(i)   Data held should be accurate. There should be machinery for the correction of inaccuracy and the updating of information.

(j)   Care should be taken in coding value judgments.

The government's response to the Younger Report was to promise a White Paper, which was not published until 1975 (Cmnd 6353). In it the government agreed that: 'the time has come when those who use computers to handle personal information, however responsible they are, can no longer remain the sole judges of whether their own systems, adequately safeguard privacy' (para. 30). The White Paper listed five features of computer operations which pose a threat to privacy:

(a)   They facilitate the maintenance of extensive record systems and retention of data in those systems.

(b)   They can make data easily and quickly accessible from many different points.

(c)   They make it possible for data to be transferred quickly from one information system to another.

(d)   They make it possible for data to be combined in ways which might not otherwise be practicable.

(e)   The data are stored, processed and often transmitted in a form which is not directly intelligible.

The government proposed that legislation should establish a statutory agency, the Data Protection Authority, to supervise a new legal framework. In order to obtain detailed advice on the composition of the authority, a Data Protection Committee was established under the chairmanship of Sir Norman Lindop.

The Lindop Report (Cmnd 7341, 1978) proposed that the Data Protection Authority should have the major task of ensuring compliance with a number of data protection principles to be enshrined in legislation. A particular feature of the report was its emphasis on flexibility (para. 07):

a single set of rules to govern all handling of personal data by computers simply will not do. The legislation must provide a means of finding appropriate balances between all legitimate interests. The scheme of regulation must therefore be a flexible one: flexible as between different cases, different times and different interests.

Consistent with this approach the report proposed that the newly established authority should be specifically required to draw up codes of practice, after appropriate consultations with computer users and other interested bodies. The codes would be promulgated by statutory instruments, thus giving them the force of law, and failure to comply with a code would result in the imposition of criminal sanctions.

A further task of the authority would be the establishment and operation of a register of 'data processors'. The system of registration would not, however, involve any form of official approval by the authority: registration would be automatic upon application.

The government responded to the Lindop Report in a White Paper in 1982, but the subsequent legislation, was less rigorous. It rejected the idea of a Data Protection Authority in favour of a Registrar of Data Protection appointed by the Crown, who 'may need a staff of about 20': the Registrar being responsible for the creation and maintenance of a register of those that control the processing of data. The government also rejected the idea of codes of practice having the force of law. It saw (para. 8):

some value in codes of practice in this field and expects that some professional bodies, trade associations and other organisations may wish to prepare such codes as a guide to their members. But the Government does not consider that these codes should have the force of law or that it would be practicable, without imposing an unacceptable burden on resources, to cover the whole field of personal data systems with statutory codes of practice within any reasonable timescale.

2.2 Who are the persons and agencies involved in the DPA?

The DPA refers to seven individuals or bodies (Figure 1).

Figure 1

s. 1(4)   A 'data subject' is any living individual on whom personal data are retained. Notice that corporate bodies cannot be data subjects because the Act refers to 'individuals' not 'persons'.

The second important group, central to the Act, are termed 'data
s. 1(5)   users'. These are individuals, corporations or other agencies that control the automatic processing of data. The discussion of what

12

constitutes processing data 'automatically' is technical; suffice to say at this stage that data processed by a computer would fall within the meaning, and manually processed data would not. Note that data users do not have to carry out the processing themselves; they merely have to control the process. Employing a third party to undertake the processing does not in any way reduce one's obligations as a data user. A third party acting in such a capacity is known as a bureau and is itself subject to certain provisions of the Act. s. 1(6)

The third vital actor in this introduction is the Registrar. He is appointed by the Crown with a small staff to supervise the legislation, is given many powers and rights and is the primary actor central to the whole Act. In particular, he is charged with creating and maintaining a publicly available register of data users and persons carrying on computer bureaux, with promoting observance of eight data protection principles, and with disseminating information on the DPA. Mr Eric Howe was appointed Registrar with effect from September 1984. s. 3(1)

Of the other parties involved, the Secretary of State has certain powers to supplement the legislation by making orders by statutory instrument after consultation with the Registrar. Such orders must be approved by both Houses of Parliament. A Data Protection Tribunal provides a right of appeal for data users from decisions of the Registrar. In addition to the Tribunal the courts have powers to adjudicate disputes between data users and data subjects and to give rulings on points of law on appeal from decisions of the Tribunal. s. 3(1)

2.3   What are the major procedures involved in the Act?

The most important procedure for data users is the requirement to register. The DPA also introduces procedures by which data subjects can assert their statutory rights.

The requirement to register becomes necessary if a data user processes personal data automatically. It involves completing an application form (DPR.1) containing the following details: s. 4(3)

(a)   The name and address of the data user.

(b)   A description of the personal data held and a statement of the purposes for which the data are held.

(c)   A description of the sources from which the data are obtained, and persons to whom it may be disclosed.

(d)   The names of any countries to which the data may be transferred.

13

(e)   An address for the receipt of requests from data subjects for access.

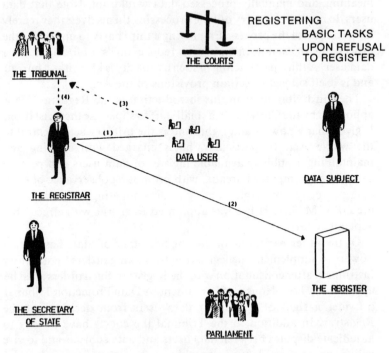

Figure 2

Registration does not involve listing every data field held by the data user as this would involve the Registrar in a volume of data too great to usefully record. If, after inspection the Registrar is satisfied with the application, it will be entered in a register which will be open to public inspection. Figure 2 summarises this point. Persons carrying on a computer bureau need only register their name and address.

ss. 5(1), (2)

If data users fail to register, or if the Registrar refuses to accept an application for registration subject to a right of appeal, data users commit a criminal offence if they continue to process personal data.

s. 21

Data subjects, having perhaps consulted the Registrar, have a right to request access to any personal data that a data user holds on them. This may necessitate the payment of a small fee to cover the data user's processing costs. The data user must supply the data within 40 days of the request and must interpret any codes into plain English. If any problems occur in this procedure the data subject has a right of appeal to the courts or a right to complain to the Registrar. These procedures are summarised in Figure 3.

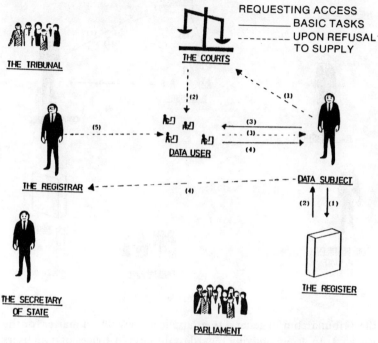

Figure 3

If data subjects suffer damage which is directly attributable to the inaccuracy, loss or unauthorised disclosure of data, they may claim compensation. This right is enforced through the courts. A data subject has a further limited right; namely to rectification or erasure of any erroneous data maintained by the data user. Once again this right is enforceable through the courts. Figure 4 summarises this procedure.

ss. 22, 23

s. 24

2.4   What are the principles underlying the Act?

The DPA is underpinned by eight data protection principles drawn from the Convention. They are expressed in very general terms and for that reason they are not directly enforceable through the courts, but only indirectly through the Registrar. The Act gives some guidance on their interpretation for the benefit of the Registrar and

sch. 1
Part I

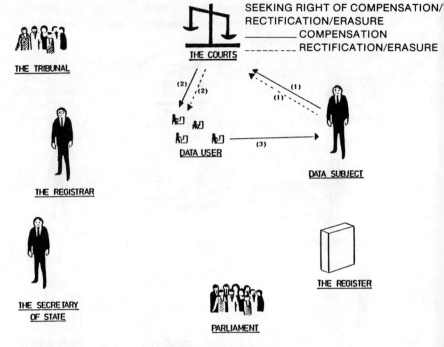

Figure 4

sch. 1
Part II
the Tribunal, but in general their application will be a matter for the Registrar to decide, having regard to the circumstances of data users and the interests of data subjects.

The first seven principles apply to personal data held by data users. The eighth principle applies to both data users and persons carrying on computer bureaux.

sch. 1
Part I
The first principle states that personal data shall be obtained and processed fairly and lawfully. Data would be said to be obtained unfairly if the data provider was deceived or misled about the purpose for which the data were obtained, held, used or disclosed. 'Lawfully' implies that the data should be obtained and processed in accord with the DPA, the common law and other relevant Acts of Parliament. If data are supplied or obtained under the authority of an Act of Parliament, or are disclosed under an enactment, they will be treated as having been obtained fairly. For example, a great deal of personal information is supplied by the data subject. It would be a breach of the first principle if the subject was not told the true reason for acquiring the information.

Data protection principle number two specifies that data shall only be held for one or more specified and lawful purposes. For example, a contravention of this principle would be for an organisation to register the holding of personal data for purposes of training and use it additionally for selection of staff for redundancy. The principle does not limit the processing of data, it merely requires such activities to be registered.

The third principle deals with data disclosure to third parties. It states that data shall not be disclosed to persons other than those described in the registration document, nor for any other purpose than that registered under the Act. Disclosure is not especially restricted; the change is merely that the details of such disclosures are public knowledge having being registered. For example, if an organisation collects information about its customers ostensibly to provide them with discounts, but then proceeds to sell that information to third parties, it will be contravening this principle to be registered.

Principle four relates to the adequacy and relevance of data kept in relation to the registered purposes. Data users will be contravening the principles if the data kept are inadequate, irrelevant or excessive in relation to what is required to satisfy the registered purposes.

The fifth principle embodied in the Act relates to the accuracy of the data kept by data users. In general, data should be accurate and, in appropriate circumstances, amended to meet changing situations. If, for example, an organisation purports to keep a list of undischarged bankrupts, but makes no effort to seek information on persons discharging themselves from bankruptcy, it will be contravening this principle.

Principle six states that personal data held for any purpose shall not be kept for longer than is necessary for the specified purpose or purposes. This principle suggests that data should be destroyed when the specified purpose for which they were collected has been achieved. For example, motor insurance companies take account of previous motoring offences of the applicant when fixing a premium. Under the law, ten years after an offence is committed that offence ceases to be legally relevant. Thus, under this principle the insurance company should delete details of the offence after ten years.

The seventh principle relates to a data subject's right to know if personal data is held on him and to have access to such data. Additionally, where appropriate, the data subject is given a right to have such data corrected or erased. Essentially, this principle provides the basis for the access procedure previously mentioned.

The last principle relates to the need for appropriate security procedures to be taken to avoid:

(a) unauthorised access to the data;
(b) unauthorised alteration of the data;
(c) unauthorised disclosure to third parties;
(d) accidental loss of personal data.

The extent of such security measures shall have regard to the degree of harm that would result from contravening the principle and to the ease with which security can be incorporated into the systems.

If the principles are breached, then the Registrar has powers of enforcement which he may exercise supported by criminal sanctions. Data subjects only have rights to compensation in relation to the fifth and eighth principles. However, if a data subject suffers damage arising out of breach of any of the other principles, the existing civil law relating to defamation, negligence, breach of contract and breach of confidence (see Chapter 1) should provide a remedy.

2.5 Are there any exemptions from the Act?

s. 1(2)   The DPA only applies to personal data processed automatically: manually processed data are totally excluded. In addition, there are a number of other exemptions from the Act which fall into two groups: firstly, some exemptions relate to the type of data being processed. For example, data that are vital to national security are fully exempt from the Act; secondly, some exemptions relate to other sundry matters that, of themselves are innocuous and pose no threat to data subjects. For example, personal data held for domestic purposes are exempt from the Act.

The extent of the provisions varies according to the exemption. For example, important national security matters are exempt from all parts of the Act, whereas other matters are exempt only from the prohibition on disclosure of data to persons not described in a registration entry. The list of exemptions and the extent of each exemption is most complex. They are discussed at length in later chapters.

PART 2

What is the scope of the Act?

Chapter 3

Who is affected by the Act?

3.1 Introduction

All legislation, whatever the area concerned, seeks to regulate a clearly defined set of activities performed by a clearly defined category of persons. In the case of the DPA the activity and the persons regulated are those who use automatic data processing equipment to process personal data. Unless falling within at least one of the exemptions, any person using automatic data processing equipment is therefore required to take appropriate actions.

It should be stressed at the outset that the Act does not seek to place substantial barriers in the way of the greater utilisation of computers. No business enterprise need be discouraged by the obligations that the Act creates from introducing or expanding the use of automatic methods of processing information. The Act simply seeks to give some protection to persons in respect of three potential dangers:

(a) The use of personal information that is inaccurate, incomplete or irrelevant.

(b) The possibility of access to personal information by unauthorised persons.

(c) The use of personal information in a context or for a purpose other than that for which the information was collected.

In general, provided that the operations of a business comply with generally accepted safeguards already fairly widely practised in industry and the operations are registered, evidence from other countries, whose data protection legislation has been operating for some time, suggests that the business will be largely unaffected by the DPA.

3.2   Who does the Act affect?

The DPA specifies three groups that will be affected: data users, data subjects and persons carrying on a computer bureau.

s. 1(5)   Persons will be 'data users' if they hold data in the sense of exercising control over it. A person is deemed to hold data where the following conditions exist:

s. 1(5)   (a)   The data form part of a collection of data processed or
(a)   intended to be processed by, or on behalf of, that person on equipment operating automatically; and

s. 1(5)   (b)   that person controls both the contents and the use of the data
(b)   in the collection; and

s. 1(5)   (c)   the data are in a form in which they are intended to be, or have
(c)   been, processed. Even if the data are not in such a form they are covered if they are in a form into which they have been converted after being so processed, and with a view to being further processed on a subsequent occasion. For example, payroll data which may be processed only once a month may be processed on a disk but copied to a magnetic tape when not in use. Such data continue to be 'held' within the terms of the definition, even though they are not in the form in which they have been processed in the past, as long as they are intended to be further processed in their original, or some other, form.

Thus, for example, an individual who keeps records of his professional contacts on a microcomputer floppy disk will be a data user, as the following conditions are satisfied. First, any single item of data is part of that data set to which it belongs and hence is part of a collection. Secondly, the equipment used for processing the data acts under the control of programs in an automatic mode. Thirdly, the individual controls both the content and use of the data as he decides who is to be represented on the file, and he accesses the file for use as required. Lastly, the data have been processed prior to arriving on the file. Hence, all of the basic conditions are satisfied and the individual is a data user subject to any specific exemptions that might apply.

The term 'data user' encompasses both individuals and any body of persons whether they are corporate bodies, such as companies registered under the Companies Act 1985 and public corporations such as nationalised industries, or unincorporated bodies, such as trade unions, partnerships, clubs and trade associations. Government

departments are subject to the same obligations and liabilities under s. 38
the Act as a private person. It is worth stressing that the Act extends
to the home computer user, unless their data is purely of a domestic
character or is otherwise exempt. An interesting question arises when
an individual processes data on behalf of his employer on his home
computer without the employer's knowledge. For example, an
efficient sales representative keeping customer contact lists on his
Sinclair QL. Will the law view the organisation or the individual as
the data user?

It should be understood from the outset that it is not necessary to
own or even see a computer in order to be a data user. It is merely
necessary to control the content and use of data. Such a relationship
may develop through the use of a computer bureau.

A 'computer bureau' is defined as either individuals or corporate s. 1(6)
bodies who provide another person (data user) with services in
respect of data. The services may be provided in the form of a
contractual agreement, whereby the bureau processes data for a data
user, or by the bureau allowing data users the use of the bureau's
equipment.

Thus, 'stand-by arrangements' which allow a data user to utilise
the facilities of others would mean the 'others' are classified as a
bureau. If reciprocal arrangements exist the data user would also be
acting as a bureau to the other user. In reality, most users of
minicomputers or mainframe computers will be acting occasionally
as bureaux to other users.

To illustrate and summarise, suppose that a company, Legal
Information Ltd, maintains a computer database of all legal authors
and articles written. This is accessed for their use by selecting a
subject or an author and all the relevant works are extracted and
printed. When they use this information themselves they are a data
user, and will need to register as such. As they expanded they started
selling this service to legal practitioners. The practitioners were
merely able to view information on screens in their offices. Legal
Information Ltd remain a data user and will need to register the
intended disclosures. The practitioners will not be data users as they
do not control the content of the database. Now suppose one of the
practitioners, to save communications costs, writes all his
information gleened from the database straight to a floppy disk. If he
processes this by say sorting the data prior to printing, he then also
becomes a data user and will need to register accordingly. Now,
further suppose Legal Information Ltd has become sufficiently large

for them to subcontract the processing of the data to a specialist computer company. In such circumstances the computer company is a bureau and Legal Information Ltd remains a data user.

s. 1(4) Any living individual to whom personal data relates is a 'data subject' and is given new rights in respect of access to such personal data and may seek, in certain circumstances, compensation for any damage suffered. Data subjects will therefore include persons who hold traditional relationships with the data user, such as:

(a) An employee, agent, officer or director.
(b) A shareholder, creditor, customer or supplier of the data user.

Indeed, potentially every individual anywhere in the world is a data subject. There is no minimum age limit for data subjects. For example, a list of company representatives in India held on a computer in the UK will be classed as a list of data subjects.

Because of the nature of the information that is being regulated, namely personal data, the new rights only extend to living individuals and not legal persons, such as coporate bodies. The DPA does not control the processing of data relating to companies, trade associations, trade unions, consumer groups or any other group of individuals. This contrasts with some European countries, notably Austria, Denmark, Iceland, Luxembourg and Norway, which have included legal persons within the scope of data protection legislation. In the UK it is generally considered that the protection of groups of persons is more appropriately dealt with in the context of company and commercial law rather than data protection law.

Chapter 4

What data are covered?

4.1 Introduction

For information to be covered by the DPA it must satisfy two criteria:

(a) It must be in a form that can be processed by equipment   s. 1(2)
operating automatically in response to instructions given for that
purpose; and

(b) it must be personal data, that is data relating to an identifiable   s. 1(3)
individual.

4.2 What is automatic processing?

As the long title of the Act states, the provisions only seek to regulate
the users of 'automatically processed information'. If data of any
kind are kept on manual files, whether they be card indexes or ledger
files, they are outside the scope of the DPA. Where, for example,
there is a computerised index to manual files the information on the
manual files is not automatically processed and the Act would not
apply to such files. It would, however, apply to the computerised
index, although access to the index by data subjects is of little value
without access to the manual files. It is considered that the speed of
computers, their capacity to store, combine, retrieve and transfer
data and their all-round flexibility justify confining the Act to
automatic methods of handling information. The omission of
manual files from the Act is a major consideration. If information is
held on individuals which would otherwise be caught under the Act
and the holders do not wish to give access to that information, or wish
to use the information for a variety of non-registered purposes they
may do so by transferring the data to manual files. Such information
may be inaccurate, incomplete, irrelevant or out of date, but neither
the subject nor the Registrar has any power to intervene.

25

What data are covered?

A question of the greatest relevance concerns the point at which manually processed information becomes 'automatically processed information' and hence subject to the Act.

The intention to limit the DPA to computing equipment was clearly conveyed in the parliamentary debates on the Bill. However, this is not conveyed in the Act: in fact, computing equipment is not mentioned in the Act, it simply makes reference to information processed by equipment operating automatically. Such a definition could cover a multitude of activities considerably less sophisticated than today's computing equipment. For example, edge-notched cards could be regarded as equipment operating automatically in that once the needle is inserted relevant cards are selected automatically.

s. 1(2)

It may reasonably be assumed that the enforcing authority will not pursue such non-computer applications but will confine their activities to electronically based equipment.

The absence of a clear definition and hence the subsequent vagaries and uncertainties are necessary consequences of swiftly changing technology. Any definition of a computer in 1984 will almost certainly be wholly inappropriate by 1994.

In simple terms, therefore, the DPA only covers those who hold and process personal data automatically. It is not the collection of data that gives rise to the legal requirements under the Act. Anyone who simply collects data is not a data user. It is the processing or intention to process data from a collection which designates a person a data user. It is considered that a collection of data is harmless unless it is processed or there is an intention to process it. As soon as the intention exists the provisions of the Act are triggered.

The Lindop Report talked of 'handling' data rather than processing, and agreed that there are many ways in which information can be 'handled' in a system. The report commented in relation to handling information (para. 18.11):

It can be assembled or combined by various means, or selections can be made from it. It can be altered; some or all of it can be deleted; or it can be destroyed. Finally, the resulting information can be displayed or communicated in some form to those who will use it, or it may be published generally. During or between any of these stages, the information may need to be transferred from one location to another, either within the information system or outside it.

The DPA, therefore, adopts a similarly wide view of the term s. 1(7) 'processing' in relation to personal data, as meaning amending, augmenting, deleting or rearranging the data, or extracting the information. All of these tasks need to be undertaken by reference to a data subject to be covered by the Act.

This phrase 'by reference to' is central to the Act. If a data user cannot access data by reference to the individual, then the data are not subject to the Act. For example, the names of referees will be contained on the personal records of individuals but it is unlikely that programs will have the facility to retrieve the data relating to a named referee. Hence, facilities do not exist to process by reference to the referee and therefore he does not have any rights to subject access. However, facilities will likely exist to examine the file by quoting the subject's name and hence he will have access rights. The importance is in deciding if the data user has facility to process by reference to the individual. If the facility does not exist, then those data are not subject to the Act.

It should be pointed out that although the mere collection of data does not attract the requirements of the Act, if the data are subsequently processed or an intention is developed to process the data then the collection would be subject to the Act.

It may be that information is in a form which is capable of being automatically processed; for example, some companies have 'optical character recognition' (OCR) equipment which allows a computer to read alpha-numeric information. If such a company intends to use the form read by the OCR equipment as direct input to a computer, then the company is covered by the Act. If the intention is only to store the data on manual files then the company is not covered by the Act. If the data are subsequently processed without a prior intention the fact of processing immediately subjects the company to the Act.

The use of word processing systems would fall within the scope of the Act so far described. However, the Act specifically excludes such activities. Word processing systems are viewed by the Act as s. 1(8) operations performed exclusively for preparing the text of documents. For example, a word processor used simply for preparing text, such as the production of standard letters to a firm's customers involving the equipment locating the name and address of the recipient and replacing it on each occasion with a new name and address, will not be subject to the Act. The key factor is, what is the purpose of the operation in question? If it is solely for preparing the text of documents then it is not processing within the meaning of the

Act. If it is for some other purpose, such as informing the operator whether someone is creditworthy, the Act will apply. Caution is required to be exercised as this provision is aimed at the nature of the operation rather than the description of the equipment.

4.3 What are personal data?

s. 1(3)

The second criterion that the information must satisfy in order to be covered by the DPA is that it is personal data, that is, data consisting of information which relates to a data subject who can be identified from the information, or from that and other information in the possession of the data user.

The aspect of identification is central to the definition of personal data. Clearly, a name or clock number identifies an individual but other items, such as address or telephone number may in effect identify the individual. Even to state that the individual lives in Ravenstone, Buckinghamshire, is a professor and drives a Morgan, may in effect identify just one individual.

If there is a statement on the computer that 'Mr X is a bad credit risk', that is personal data, since it identifies a living individual. If, however, all that appears on the computer is the statement that 'Reference 25 is a bad credit risk', an individual is not identifiable from the data. However, in such circumstances the data user will normally have information elsewhere which matches up references with names and addresses. If that is so, the information on the computer will fall within the definition of personal data because the

s. 1(3)

user is able to identify the subject from the data with the aid of other information in his possession.

The definition of 'personal data' extends to expressions of opinion about the individual but not any indication of the intentions of the data user in respect of that individual. Three categories of data are identified under the terms of the Act:

(a) Factual data. This category includes data covering a multitude of matters including, for example, names, addresses, ages, marital status, income and salary, religion, ethnic origin, number and ages of children and other dependants, membership of a trade union, political activities, examination marks, the results of aptitude tests. These are personal data in terms of the Act.

(b) Judgmental data. This category covers subjective judgments and expressions of opinion about a subject. This includes opinions of

28

the data user on a person's creditworthiness, employability, promotion prospects and appearance. Furthermore, it includes the opinions of third parties, for example, opinions forming part of an employee reference. These are personal data in terms of the Act.

(c) Intention data. This third category includes data indicating the intentions of the data user in respect of an individual subject. Such data are specifically excluded from the definition of personal data. In simple terms such statements as:

(i) 'We intend to promote Mr X'; or

(ii) 'We intend to dispose of the services of Mr Y at our earliest opportunity'.

are statements falling outside the definition of personal data. On the other hand, statements such as:

(i) 'Mr X is executive material'; or

(ii) 'Mr X is not up to our standard of performance'.

are statements of opinion and therefore personal data.

One might surmise that it would be possible to avoid giving access to sensitive data by careful use of language. Instead of recording: 'Mr Y is a trade-union trouble-maker', the data user may record: 'Given the opportunity we intend to select Mr Y for redundancy because of his trade-union activities.' In such circumstances the data user would probably be required to separate the two components of the material — the opinion and the statement. Thus, for example, the data subject would be entitled to have access to the statement that he is considered a trade-union activist, but the future intention to dismiss Mr Y would be concealed.

It may not, however, always be so simple to separate the opinion from the intention. It may even be wholly misleading to do so. For example, if the entry states: 'The credit control manager says that Mr Q is a bad credit risk; I intend to disregard this report' then what is revealed to the data subject is the statement of opinion that he is regarded by the credit manager as a bad risk. What need not be disclosed is that the data user intends to disregard the statement.

As an aside it is worth considering the relationship between statements of intention and statements of opinion. The former are very often arrived at after reviewing the latter. For example, a statement that the data user intends to allow credit for a particular customer up to £5,000 is clearly a statement of intention. But such a statement of intention is built upon the opinion of the customer's creditworthiness. Statements of intention and opinion are often closely related. Data users that desire not to reveal information to data subjects could seek to disguise opinion as intentions and hence avoid the need for disclosure of that item of information.

If, however, such a course of action was systematically adopted by a data user the Registrar might view it as a deliberate breach of the spirit of the seventh principle (access to personal data) and might take appropriate action against the data user.

There may be a number of legitimate situations where the data user's intentions are required to be held on a computer. To avoid any doubts and disputes such intentions should be clearly expressed as such. For example, it is common practice as an aid to management planning to plot senior staff changes some years ahead. A data user may hold on computer the information that he considers, in three years' time, Mr X should fill a particular post, Mr Y another post and Mr Z a new management post. At any time in the future the management plan could change because of staff turnover. Care should therefore be taken in such a situation to express the data clearly as intentions. Such data are outside the scope of the Act primarily because it was considered that to grant access to such data might have an adverse effect on the data user's business and, particularly in the case of management planning, seriously undermine staff morale and motivation.

If data users are in any doubt about whether a particular category of data is covered by the Act, they could always seek clarification from the Registrar. Alternatively, the data user could simply transfer the data to manual files.

Chapter 5

Are there any exemptions?

5.1 How can one be exempt?

The DPA allows certain data processing applications exemption
from some or all of its requirements. In general, exemptions are
granted for one of the following reasons:

(a) Because they do not pose a particular threat to the privacy of
data subjects and their inclusion in the scheme would be an
unnecessary burden on data users.

(b) Because the interests of the state and public agencies
necessitate exemption on grounds of national security, proper
administration of justice and detection of crime or the collection of
taxes.

The exemption may be from the registration and supervision
provisions, or from the subject access rights, non-disclosure rules, or
any combination thereof.

Where an exemption is granted in respect of the 'subject access'
provisions it means that: s. 26(2)

(a) The rights of access to data subjects in respect of personal
data will not apply to that particular activity.

(b) The exercise by the Registrar of any of his powers to enforce
the access rights of a data subject is curtailed. Thus, if a data user
processes data covered by one of the subject access exemptions he
may refuse to give subject access and the Registrar, provided the user
remains strictly within the terms of the particular exemption, may
take no action.

In the case of an exemption from the non-disclosure provisions: s. 26(3)

31

(a)   A data user may disclose data to a person irrespective of whether the person is described in the data user's registration entry.

(b)   The Registrar may not exercise any powers by reference to any data protection principle inconsistent with such a disclosure. For example, there may be circumstances where a data user is required to disclose to an outsider personal data held for the assessment or collection of a tax or duty. In such circumstances, provided that the disclosure was strictly within the terms of the exemption, the Registrar may not take action against the data user for breach of any of the data protection principles in respect of that disclosure.

5.2   Payroll, pension and accounting data

5.2.1   What is the scope of the exemption?
Exemptions are given to personal data which is held for the sole purpose of:

s. 32(1)   (a)   Calculating or paying amounts by way of remuneration or pension in respect of service in any employment or office, or making payments of, or of sums deducted from, such remuneration or pensions; or

s. 32(1)   (b)   keeping accounts relating to any business or other activity carried on by the data user, or of keeping records of purchases, sales or other transactions for the purpose of ensuring that the requisite payments are made by or to him in respect of those transactions or for the purpose of making financial or management forecasts to assist him in the conduct of any such business or activity.

In exempting payroll and accounting data the government has accepted that there are certain kinds of personal information that virtually every business in the country holds as part and parcel of everyday commercial activity. It is held as a necessary incident of a contractual relationship between data subject and the data user, be it an employment contract or supply contract. The data subject knows it is held and, more significantly, knows of what it consists and generally what it is used for. Indeed, it is only used in a way that is of direct benefit to the data subject: paying wages or pensions, deducting the correct tax, recording and regularising business transactions. Through the receipt of pay slips and the normal process of invoicing, the data subject is able to monitor the accuracy of the data. During the passage of the Bill the government accepted the need to include in this exemption management accounting information. Such information is commonly integrated with other aspects of accounts and cash-flow forecasts. Most of this will not be personal data, but at times it is inevitable that some personal data will be included: hence the exemption. s. 32(1) (b)

It must be emphasised, however, that the exemptions only extend to data held for payroll and accounting purposes. The data must not be used for purposes other than paying or calculating remuneration and pensions or keeping accounts, or disclosed except as permitted. A great deal of potentially sensitive data may be retained on payroll records in addition to the salary payable. This includes gross pay and tax data, personal tax code and National Insurance number. If any of the data are used for a purpose other than paying or calculating remuneration then the activity potentially comes within the scope of the DPA.

For example, to maintain data relating to the number of sick days taken will be exempt if this fact affects payment. However, if an employer keeps a cumulative record of sick days taken for the purpose of discriminating between employees this information becomes subject to the Act.

The government accepted in the parliamentary debates on the Bill that information required by the statutory sick pay regulations is information held as part of the general purpose of paying remuneration, and would thus be covered by the exemption.

The exemptions are in respect of registration and the provisions covering the rights of data subjects. It is an absolute condition of the exemption that payroll and accounting data are not used for any purpose other than that listed above, or disclosed, except as permitted under the terms outlined in 5.2.2 below. This means that s. 32(2) an entirely innocent breach of the precise terms of the exemption could result in loss of the protection of the exemption. The data user may then be holding data without being registered and thus commit an offence against which no defence is available. In order, therefore, to protect data users in such circumstances, the DPA provides that, although it is a condition of the exemption that the data are not used or disclosed for any other purpose, the exemption is not lost by any use or disclosure in breach of the condition if it is shown that the data user took such care as, in all the circumstances, was reasonably required. For example, breach of the condition may have been caused by a staff oversight or a technical malfunction resulting in disclosure of data. Provided that the data user has taken every reasonable care to ensure that such unpermitted disclosures do not occur and the disclosure was something beyond his control, the exemption will not be lost.

5.2.2 What are the permitted disclosures?

s. 32(4)   Disclosures of both payroll and accounting data may be made without loss of the exemption. These relate to data held for the purpose of audit where a disclosure is made for the purpose only of giving information about the data user's financial affairs. Auditors could not perform their functions properly unless they had access to both payroll and accounting data, in order to make the necessary checks which form part of the audit process. Similarly, it would be permissible to disclose details of payroll and accounting data where the disclosure is made as part of the process of presenting a picture of the data user's financial affairs to a bank or lending agency. It is perhaps worth reiterating that a great deal of accounting data will relate to corporate bodies which will therefore be totally outside the ambit of the legislation, since such bodies cannot be data subjects.

s. 32(3)   Payroll and pension data, but not accounting data, may be disclosed in the following circumstances:

(a)   To any person who is responsible for paying the remuneration or pensions. This will cover the situation where an employer has to disclose payroll details to a pension fund under the terms of a pension fund scheme for his employees.

(b)   For the purpose of obtaining actuarial advice.

(c)   For the purpose of giving information about the persons in any employment or office for use in medical research into the health of, or injuries suffered by, persons engaged in particular occupations or working in particular places or areas. This provision was added after approaches were made to the Home Office by bodies such as the DHSS, to safeguard a standard practice of medical researchers in the use of payroll data to identify people in particular occupations who may be at risk from certain diseases.

(d)   If the data subject (or a person acting on his or her behalf) has requested or consented to the disclosure of the data, either generally or in the circumstances in which the disclosure in question is made. For example, it may be that an employee is applying for a mortgage or other credit facility, and the lending body seeks confirmation of earnings. In such circumstances the employer (data user) should obtain the specific consent of the employee (data subject) concerned before a disclosure is made.

(e)   If the person making the disclosure has reasonable grounds for believing that the disclosure was made at the request, or with the consent of, the data subject. This provision is intended to protect data users where they reasonably believe that they are acting on the data subject's behalf, but have in fact been misled or deceived. For example, an employer may receive a request from a building society seeking confirmation of salary of a particular employee. If the employer responded to the request without reference to the employee it could possibly be argued that the employer has reasonable grounds to disclose the information by the very fact that the request came from a building society.

5.3   Membership details of clubs and name and address files

Also exempt from the requirements to register and the subject access provisions are:

(a)   Personal data held by an unincorporated members' club and relating only to the members of the club. This exemption includes, for example, a company staff/sports club or society using a micro-computer to hold membership lists for purposes of monitoring subscriptions.   *s. 33(2) (a)*

(b)   Personal data consisting only of names and addresses and other particulars necessary for effecting distribution or recording of articles or information held by a data user. This exemption will have a fairly limited application in a commercial context and will principally be of benefit to non-commercial bodies not able to claim the exemption in (a) above. For example, a local church may use a micro-computer to circulate a parish magazine and in such circumstances would be within the terms of the exemption, but not exempt by (a) above as the parishioners are not members of a club.   *s. 33(2) (b)*

The exemption extends beyond the traditional postal distribution system and covers not only information distributed in a written form but information distributed in less tangible forms, such as by electronic newsletter through a public or private mailing system. Such systems use 'addresses' more akin to telex numbers in order to define the location of both sources and destinations of messages carried, hence the reference in the exemption to 'other particulars necessary for effecting the distribution', in addition to names and addresses.

s. 33(3)   Neither of the exemptions will apply unless the data subject has been asked by the data user whether he objects to the data relating to him being held and he has not objected.

s. 33(4)   It is a condition of the exemption covering name and address data that the data are not used for any purpose other than distributing articles or information. Similarly, it is a condition of both exemptions that any data held under them is not disclosed, except as permitted within the terms of the exemption as noted below. However, as in the exemption covering payroll and accounting data, the exemptions are not lost by any use or disclosure in breach of the condition if it is shown that the data user took reasonable care to prevent the disclosure.

Data held under these exemptions may be disclosed in the
s. 33(5)   following circumstances:

(a)   If the data subject (or someone acting on his or her behalf) has requested or consented to the disclosure of the data, either generally or in the circumstances in which the disclosure in question is made. For example, if a sports club wishes to disclose its list of members to an insurance company or sports equipment supplier, they will have to seek the specific consent of all the members if they wish to retain the benefit of the exemption. It may be that in future such permission would be made a condition of membership of the club, or that consent will be sought and granted on behalf of clubs or holders of distribution lists by printed notices on appropriate items of stationery.

(b)   If the person making the disclosure has grounds for believing that the disclosure falls within (a) above. Thus, a disclosure is permissible if it is made in circumstances where the club or holder of the list genuinely believes that the data subject has requested or consented, even though in fact he has not.

When the Data Protection Bill was first published it was originally considered by some mail order companies that their trading lists would be exempt. Such a view is correct if such lists contain only names and addresses for the purpose of distributing or recording articles to data subjects. However, most commercial bodies holding trading lists will be subject to the Act because it is common for trading lists to carry much more information about data subjects than merely names and addresses: for example, records of previous sales to data subjects. If data covered by this exemption are used for any other purpose than that of distributing or recording articles or information to the data subject then the exemption will be lost.

5.4 Data held for statistical and research purposes

Where personal data are held only for the purpose of preparing s. 33(6) statistics or carrying out research, such data will be exempt from the subject access provisions. Unlike the two categories of exemption above, such data must still be registered, and thus be subject to the control of the Registrar.

It is an absolute condition of the exemption, however, that:

(a)   The data are not used or disclosed for any other purpose; and
(b)   The statistics or the results of the research are not made available in a form which identifies the data subjects.

Such statistics or research may be discussed amongst data users; it may even be 'made available' to other researchers, but if it is possible to identify data subjects from the statistics or the results of the research, then the exemption will be lost.

What is important under this exemption is not what range of statistics are being collected or what type of research is being undertaken, but whether, at the end of the particular endeavours, anyone is going to be identified. The exemption is aimed at protecting bona fide research. Provided such data is used and disclosed exclusively for research purposes and it is not possible to identify a data subject from the results, the data user may legitimately refuse access.

As a precaution, any organisation that processes statistical and/or research data should, as far as is possible in terms of the objectives of the research, seek to delete from the data the names and addresses of respondents, along with any other possible identifiers.

Since this exemption only relates to the subject access provisions, the Registrar retains his full powers to monitor the data user's operations in terms of compliance with the data protection principles, other than principle seven, i.e., the subject access provision.

sch. 1
Part II
para. 7

It is worth pointing out at this stage that where data are held for historical, statistical or research purposes, and are not used in such a way that damage or distress is likely to be caused to data subjects, the first and sixth data protection principles are modified. The information is not to be regarded as obtained unfairly (first principle) simply because its use for historical, statistical or research purposes was not disclosed when it was obtained. The data may, notwithstanding the sixth principle, be kept indefinitely.

5.5 Crime and tax data

s. 28(1)

Personal data held for the purpose of:

(a) the prevention or detection of crime;
(b) the apprehension or prosecution of offenders; or
(c) the assessment or collection of any taxes or duty,

are exempt from the subject access provisions in any case in which the application of those provisions would prejudice the matters in (a)–(c) above. For example, the police may obtain information that members of an extremist group are collecting materials for the assembly of bombs. Their sources may show that on a particular date all the materials will be assembled and could therefore be seized at a particular location. That information may well take the form of personal data relating to a member of the group and may well be processed automatically. Obviously, police activities would be seriously undermined if those individuals were allowed access to the data.

This exemption is available to data users not just the police and tax authorities. For example, supermarkets keeping records of till shortages to catch offending operators would use this exemption to deny access.

s. 28(2)

The subject access exemption explained above also extends to any person to whom the data is passed and who discharges statutory functions. For example, the Inland Revenue or Customs and Excise may pass data exempt from the subject access provisions to the Parliamentary Commissioner for Administration (the Ombudsman) to enable him to investigate a complaint. Indeed, the Commissioner has the power to compel production of documents so departments have no option but to disclose the data. Once the data are in the possession of the Commissioner, strictly speaking they would no longer be held for the purpose of assessing or collecting tax, and without the extension of the exemption the subject could gain access. The same would apply to data held by the police and passed to the statutory Police Complaints Board in the course of investigating a complaint about police conduct.

There may be cases where data which at one time could not have been disclosed for fear of prejudicing police or revenue work would no longer be prejudicial and hence are no longer exempt.

Data may also be exempt from the non-disclosure provisions if it is considered that the application of those provisions would be likely to prejudice any of the purposes mentioned in (a) to (c) above. For example, the police might have a tip-off that a man's life had been threatened and that an attack against him was planned. They may approach the man's employer to find out his address in order to protect him. If the employer kept the information on a computer but had not registered the police as the recipients of the data, it would be absurd not to allow the employer to disclose the personal data to the police in order to prevent a crime, or assist in the apprehension of offenders. `s. 28(3)`

Finally, in the context of this category of personal data, the Registrar's powers in respect of the first data protection principle (information obtained and processed, fairly and lawfully), to take action against data users, are curtailed if taking such action would prejudice any of the purposes mentioned in (a) to (c) above. `s. 28(4)`

It should be stressed that as a safeguard for data subjects who may, for example, be denied access under this exemption, it would be a matter for the Registrar or, ultimately, the courts, to consider whether the data were properly held for the exempt purpose. It is not sufficient for data users simply to deny access, they must be able to show that if they grant access that would be likely to prejudice one of the three purposes for which exemption is given.

5.6 Statutory functions

Personal data held for the purpose of discharging certain statutory functions are exempt from the subject access provisions where the application of those provisions would be likely to prejudice the proper discharge of those functions. `s. 30(1)`

The exemption only applies to those functions which the Secretary of State duly designates by an order. He may only make such an order where the statutory functions appear to him to be:

s. 30(3)   designed for protecting members of the public against financial loss due to dishonesty, incompetence or malpractice by persons concerned in the provision of banking, insurance, investment or other financial services or in the management of companies or to the conduct of discharged or undischarged bankrupts.

For example, the Director General of Fair Trading is charged under the Consumer Credit Act 1974 with the duty of granting licences to persons engaged in the credit industry. The Director must be satisfied that all licence holders are fit to be engaged in the activities covered by the licence and are not involved in unfair or improper practices. Should the Director build up a file on a computer covering the activities of a trader which contains some personal data, without this exemption he would have to grant access and thus possibly frustrate his investigations.

Like the exemption for law enforcement, it must always be shown that subject access would be likely to prejudice the proper discharge of the functions that Parliament has legislated for in the interest of protecting individual citizens.

Other examples of authorities charged with the appropriate statutory functions include:

(a)   The Bank of England — the supervision of banks under the Banking Act 1979.

(b)   The Chief Registrar of Friendly Societies — the supervision of building societies and friendly societies.

(c)   The Secretary of State — responsible for licensing and supervising insurance companies, for determining who are fit and proper persons to be dealers in securities under the Prevention of Fraud (Investments) Act 1958, and responsible for inspections and investigations under the Companies Act.

(d)   The Official Receiver with responsibilities under the Bankruptcy Act 1914, Insolvency Act 1976 and Companies Act 1985.

5.7   Health and social work data

The Secretary of State has authority to exempt three categories of
s. 29(1)   data. First, personal data concerning the physical or mental health of a data subject. Second, personal data held in respect of social work if
s. 29(2)   it is considered that to grant access under the DPA would be likely to prejudice carrying out social work. In both these cases the Secretary

40

of State may grant a total exemption or simply modify the operation of the subject access provisions. The government has also stated that s. 2(5) they intend to use powers given to the Secretary of State to restrict the disclosure of personal health data. The third category relates to any s. 34(2) existing enactment which prohibits or restricts the disclosure of personal data. The Secretary of State must, however, be satisfied that the information is of such a nature that its confidentiality ought to prevail over the subject access provisions in the Act in the interests of the data subject or any other individual. In general, the subject access provisions of the Act override all existing legal restrictions on the disclosure of information. However, where there is an existing statutory prohibition or restriction on the disclosure of a certain type of personal data and the Secretary is convinced that the confidentiality given by that statute ought to take precedence over the subject access provisions of the DPA, he may grant an exemption. For example, there are currently restrictions on the right of an adopted person to obtain access to information which would allow him to obtain a copy of his original birth certificate. Whilst the adopted person is below a certain age there is no right of access. Thereafter, access is conditional upon the offer of counselling to the person concerned or, in some cases, his acceptance of counselling. In such a case the Secretary of State may clearly feel that the interests of adopted persons are best served by retaining the procedures of adoption legislation and exempting such procedures from the data subject access provisions of the DPA.

This provision may extend to a variety of data users, including personnel managers, insurance companies and colleges.

5.8   Other exemptions

The following categories of data are completely outside the ambit of the DPA:

(a)   Domestic data — personal data held by an individual and s. 33(1) concerned exclusively with the management of the individual's personal, family or household affairs, or held by him only for recreational purposes. This exemption is intended to take outside the legislation certain uses of personal data that pose no threat to the privacy of data subjects. It largely concerns the home computer user who may hold certain personal data, such as cricket scores, exclusively in pursuit of a hobby. Thus, batting averages held by a.

schoolboy for recreational purposes are exempt, whereas the same averages held by the Test and County Cricket Board would be covered by the legislation.

It is worth noting that the home computer is not exempt if used for a business purpose. For example, the sales representative maintaining records of customers on his own personal computer.

s. 27(1)   (b)   National security — all data that a Minister of the Crown certifies as being exempt from the Act for the purpose of safeguarding

s.27(3), (4)   national security. If a Minister considers that such a complete exemption is not necessary, he may certify an exemption in respect of the non-disclosure provisions only.

The following two categories of personal data are exempt from the subject access provisions:

s. 31(1)   (a)   Data consisting of information received from a third party and held as information relevant to the making of a judicial appointment.

s. 31(2)   (b)   Data consisting of information in respect of which a claim to legal professional privilege could be maintained in legal proceedings.

s. 34(3)   The Consumer Credit Act 1974, s. 158, already gives data subjects wider rights of access than the DPA. Data to which a consumer is given access under the Consumer Credit Act are therefore exempt from the DPA and any request for access under its provisions will be treated automatically as a request under the Consumer Credit Act.

s. 34(4)   Personal data are exempt from the subject access provisions if the data are kept only for the purpose of replacing other data in the event of the latter being lost, destroyed or impaired. This exemption relates to the situation where data are copied from data in use and are held solely for the purpose of replacing the original data in use if they are lost or otherwise rendered unfit for use. The subject access right applies to the data in use but the exemption removes the need for subject access to be given to the copy. Many data users seek to protect their investment in data against the failure of the equipment or the programs which process the data, by regularly taking copies which are stored in a safe place and used only after a failure has damaged the original data. Copies may be taken at regular intervals according to the nature of the processing and the likelihood of failure. Such copies may become out of date as changes are made to the current data but the back-ups will not be processed without first having been brought up to date. It was considered that to grant access to such back-up data might cause confusion in that data subjects may well receive two apparently conflicting sets of information if the back-up data have not been updated recently. In addition, such back-up data are not always stored in a form that makes access easy. To grant access would therefore have required data users to invest in new software or to interrupt processing activities in order to update the data to a form that enabled access to be granted. If the back-up data are kept for any other purpose then the exemption will be lost. Data users must always therefore be able to convince the Registrar that the data are only held for back-up purposes.

It would be pointless applying the provisions of the Act to personal data held by a data user who is already under a statutory duty to make data publicly available. Thus, the Act does not apply to personal data   s. 34(1) which consists of information which a data user is required by legislation to make available to the public. For example, personal data contained in the various files and registers that limited companies are required to maintain under the Companies Act 1985 are exempt from the DPA.

Personal data are exempt from the non-disclosure provisions in any case in which the disclosure is:

   (a)   Required by or under any enactment.   s. 34(5)
   (b)   Required by any rule of law.
   (c)   Ordered by a court.
   (d)   Made for the purpose of obtaining legal advice.
   (e)   Made for the purposes of, or in the course of, legal proceedings in which the person making the disclosure is a party or a witness.

For example, there exists a common law rule that trustees are required to disclose certain information to beneficiaries. Such disclosures would be covered by exemption (b) above and would not be in breach of the non-disclosure provisions.

The exemptions will be of particular assistance to data users who may be exempt from registration under, for example, the payroll and accounting provisions. It will be recalled that these provisions permit only very limited disclosure of payroll or accounting data. If a data user with an exempt accounting system wishes to take legal action against a customer to recover amounts owed to him, it will be necessary to disclose personal data in order to seek legal advice. Such a disclosure would mean that the data user automatically forgoes the accounting exemption, since there is nothing in that exemption allowing for disclosure to a legal adviser, hence the exemptions in (d) and (e) above.

s. 34(8) Personal data are also exempt from the non-disclosure provisions where the disclosure is required as a matter of urgency in order to prevent injury or other damage to the health of any person or persons. For example, the emergency services might need access to personal data such as a list of residents in a given area when dealing with a natural disaster. In such circumstances, a disclosure would be permitted without fear of incurring any of the penalties under the Act for disclosure of data to persons not described in a registration entry. Indeed, should proceedings be brought against a data user for such a disclosure it is specifically a defence to prove that the user had reasonable ground for believing that the disclosure was urgently required, even when it transpires that such a situation did not in fact exist.

Personal data may also be disclosed in the following circumstances without fear of the Act's provisions:

s. 34(6) (a)   Where the disclosure is to the data subject or a person acting on his behalf.

(b)   Where the data subject, or any such person, has requested or consented to the particular disclosure in question.

(c)   Where the disclosure is by a data user or a person carrying on a computer bureau to an employee or agent in order to enable them to carry out their contractual functions.

(d)   Where the person making the disclosure has reasonable grounds for believing that the disclosure falls within circumstances (a) to (c) above. This provision would cover organisations that operate a telephone inquiry system in respect of customer accounts. Although accounting data are exempt from the provisions of the Act, they may not be disclosed except in very limited circumstances. This exemption would, however, permit disclosure of such accounting data by a data user over the telephone to a person who turns out not to be the data subject, provided that the data user had reasonable grounds for believing that the inquirer was the data subject. Such reasonable grounds may be that the inquirer is able to quote an accounting reference number or some other information identifying the subject with the data.

Also note that the following categories of data do not come within the scope of the Act:

44

(a) Text processed data — personal data held on a word   s. 1(8)
processor and used only for the purpose of preparing the text of
documents (see Chapter 4).

(b) Non-personal data — data from which a living individual   s. 1(3)
cannot be identified, or expressions of intention by a data user in
respect of a living individual.

(c) Corporate data — any data of which a corporate body or   s. 1(3)
similar artificial legal entity, is the subject.

(d) Manual data — all data not processed by equipment   s. 1(2)
operating automatically.

PART 3

What procedures and rights are introduced by the Act?

Chapter 6

What is the registration procedure?

6.1 What is the purpose of the register?

A central feature of the DPA is the creation of a register of data users   s. 4(1)
and computer bureaux. The register will essentially satisfy two
purposes.

First, it will serve as a starting-point for data subjects in the process
of tracking down personal data. A right of access to data or a right to
rectify inaccurate data is clearly of little use if the data subject is
unaware of the existence of the data. The register may therefore alert
the data subject to the fact that a person is involved in the processing
of personal data and it will provide sufficient information to enable
the data subject to proceed further with enquiries. In essence, the
information in the register provides an audit trail for data subjects.

Second, the existence of a register will greatly assist the Registrar in
performing his general duty to promote observance of the data
protection principles. The requirement to register clearly puts the
onus on data users and computer bureaux to identify themselves and
specify their processing activities.

In his first Annual Report (HMSO, June 1985), the Data
Protection Registrar identifies three objectives to be achieved in
setting up the registration procedures:

(a)   The register should be readily understandable by individuals
who refer to it. It should offer the opportunity for an individual to
make a broad comparison of the activities of one data user against
another.

(b)   The registration process should be simple for data users to
complete.

(c)   Registration applications should be in a form which allows
them to be checked for acceptability easily and quickly.

Given these objectives, it is no surprise that the registration application form is based on standard descriptions and, for the most part, it involves applicants selecting the appropriate item.

6.2   Who is responsible for maintaining the register?

s. 4(1)
s. 6(3)

The responsibility for maintaining the register is the Registrar's. He is charged by the DPA to process all applications for registration and deal with any alterations to a registration entry.

s. 9(1)

The Registrar is also under a duty to provide facilities for making the information contained in the register available for public inspection.

The information must be in a visible and legible form and any member of the public may consult registered particulars free of charge.

s. 9(2)

Should any member of the public require a copy of the particulars contained in an entry, the Registrar must supply one in writing. He may, however, charge a fee for such a hard copy service.

When the register has been initially created it is anticipated that enquiries by members of the public will be dealt with by a postal and telephone enquiry service at the Registry Office in Wilmslow. In addition, copies of the register may be made available on microfilm at main reference libraries. It has been suggested, however, that because of the volume of data it may be necessary to give access via terminals linked to a computer system. Telephone enquiries may be made to the Registry where the information is relatively straightforward. A member of the public may simply be asking whether a particular organisation is registered, or they may want to know the number of entries that an organisation has on the register. More complex telephone enquiries would, however, be required to be dealt with by post.

6.3   Who must register and how is it carried out?

From 11 November 1985 data users and computer bureaux are required to apply for registration with the Registrar. In some cases a data user may also carry on business as a computer bureau. For example, a data user may hire out computer capacity to other users. In such circumstances the original data users become a computer bureau and the Act provides that rather than make a separate application for their bureau activities, they may indicate in their application that they are seeking registration as a data user and a computer bureau combined.

Applications for registration will only be accepted on the forms published by the Registry and available from the Registry or Post Offices.

In order to facilitate the registration process and fulfil the objectives outlined in para. 6.1 above, data users are strongly encouraged to adopt the standard terms set out on the form, rather than attempt to describe their processing activities by using their own free text description.

Every application for registration must be accompanied by the appropriate fee, which is likely to be around £20. Applicants will be notified when their application has been received and when it has been accepted or rejected. If successful, all the details given in the application form except any contact name and address to be used by the Registrar in any correspondence arising out of the application (see DPR.1 part A3 in Appendix 2), will appear in the public register.

6.4   How is the registration application form structured?

Application forms are divided into two separate parts: A and B.

Part A must be completed by all applicants, data users and computer bureaux. It is designed to elicit basic details about applicants such as name and address (A1 to A7) and certain other information in the case of data users, covering the whole application (A8).

Part B is required to be completed by data users only and is designed to elicit sufficient information to obtain a broad picture of the nature and scope of an applicant's processing activities. The form follows the pattern laid down in the DPA which requires, in addition to the name and address, the following particulars to be provided:

(a)   A description of the personal data to be held and of the purpose or purposes for which the data are to be held or used.   s. 4(3)(b)

(b)   A description of the sources from which the data user intends or may wish to obtain the data.   s. 4(3)(c)

(c)   A description of any person or persons to whom the data user intends or may wish to disclose the data.   s. 4(3)(d)

(d)   The names or a description of any countries or territories outside the UK to which the data user intends or may wish to transfer the data.   s. 4(3)(c)

s. 4(3)(f)   (e)   One or more addresses for the receipt of requests from data subjects for access to the data. (This information is included on the registration form in part A8.)

The key information to be provided in part B is the purpose for which the data is held. A great many data users will hold personal data for several different purposes and in that event, a part B must be completed for each separate purpose, describing the data, the sources from which it was obtained, persons to whom it may be disclosed and any overseas transfers.

6.5   How many register entries can a data user have?

A registration entry consists of a single part A and some number of part Bs.

s. 6(2)   Where a data user holds data for a number of distinct purposes,   s. 6(2)
rather than have one single multipurpose registration entry, the DPA permits separate registration entries for each purpose. Thus a part A and part B would be completed for each separate purpose. Where a data user opts for separate registration entries, a fee is payable for each application.

For example, it has been suggested that the Home Office, a very large-scale data user, which holds information for many different purposes, will make separate registration entries for each of its data bases. Thus, rather than make one comprehensive registration, it will register separately the National Police Computer, the Parole Board's indexes and the Immigration Department's data bases.

One consideration which may persuade data users to have numerous registration entries is the subject access rights. Any user registering under one entry is required to give access to all the subject's data embraced by that entry. Where data are divided between different systems, the user may not want to go to the trouble and expense of accessing each separate system for data about the subject. In such circumstances, multiple registration entries would seem to be appropriate, as only the registration entry and hence the system specified by the subject need be accessed. Of course, a data subject could make access requests on all registration entries for a data user, but this increases the expense considerably. On the other hand, where purposes are logically linked, and it would be impractical or artificial to separate them, a single multipurpose registration would appear to be more appropriate.

The individual register entries in respect of a data user will not give any indication of other entries under the name of that data user. However, it will be possible for a data subject to interrogate the register on user name to locate all separate entries for a particular data user.

Whilst there is no statutory limit to the number of separate registration entries, it is likely that the Registrar would question data users who make an excessive number of separate registrations, thus frustrating subject access rights.

6.6 What information must be provided by data users and computer bureaux — DPR.1 part A?

The first page of part A consists of a declaration which applicants must sign once having completed the rest of the form. Data users must additionally indicate the number of part B forms that comprise the application (see para. 6.7 below). Part A of the application form consists of the following:

A1 Type of application
Applicants must indicate whether they are applying for registration as a data user, a bureau or both.   s. 4(2)

A2 Name and address of the applicant
In the case of an individual the address should be their home address.   s. 4(3)(a) For individuals applying in connection with their business activities, the address should be their principal place of business. In the case of a partnership the name of the firm should be provided and the address of the principal place of business.

Where the applicant is a legal association of persons operating as a corporate body, such as a company registered under companies   CA 1985 legislation, the name provided should be the name that appears on   s. 287 the Register of Companies and the registered address. In the case of organisations incorporated by charter or statute, for example, British Gas, the full name of the organisation must be provided and the principal place of business.

For unincoprorated organisations such as clubs, the name provided should be the name by which the organisation is normally known and the address of the principal place of business.

A3 Contact name and address
Applicants have the option of giving a name or job title and address

for correspondence in respect of the application. This address will however only be used for such correspondence and confirmation of a successful application, other official notices will be sent to the registered address.

A4 Company registration number

For companies registered under the Companies Act 1985, the appropriate number in the Register of Companies must be provided.

A5 Other names

Applicants have the option to associate names other than a registered name with the application. This provision is primarily for the convenience of data subjects, in that it allows trading names or abbreviated names to be included in the form and, hence, simplify register access. For example, John Waddington plc is often referred to as Waddingtons: they may therefore choose to insert that name in this section on the application form. Suitable cross-references will then appear on the register.

A6 Organisation sub-division

Certain organisations are split into one or more major divisions for the convenience of their operations. An organisation may therefore wish to make it clear that the personal data covered by a particular application relates only to a particular part of the organisation. For example, a fictitious company, XYZ Ltd, is organised on a regional basis having four divisions. Each division has a degree of autonomy and it may therefore be appropriate for XYZ Ltd to register on a divisional basis. The division title or description will appear in this section.

A distinction must, however, be drawn between organisations operating on a divisional basis, from organisations operating on a group basis where each sub-division or subsidiary is a separate legal entity. In the latter case each subsidiary will register separately (see para. 6.8).

A7 Period of registration

s. 8(2)   The initial period of registration will be three years. This period commences on the date the entry was made in the register. A person making an application for registration may, however, specify in the
s. 8(3)   application that he requires a shorter period of registration, but such a period can only consist of one or two complete years.

No entry will be retained in the register after the initial period of registration unless a specific renewal application has been made to the Registrar.

A8   Subject access address

All data users must give at least one address for the receipt of requests s. 4(3)(f) from data subjects for access to the data covered in the application. The address may be the address given in A2 or A3 or some other address or addresses.

It is also permissible for large-scale organisations to state generally that subject access requests may be made 'to any branch office', provided that at least one specific address has been provided.

6.7   What information must be provided by data users — DPR.1 part B?

There are four sections in part B and in each section data users are given the option of using standard description codes to provide the information required. This approach is consistent with the Registry's stated objective of ensuring that entries in the register have a clear structure, are expressed in simple terms and exhibit some commonality as between data users. A guidance booklet issued with the application forms lists over 50 standard purposes, each of which is given a code number and a textual description (see Appendix 2).

6.7.1   Section B1 — Purpose for which data are held or used

Applicants are given the choice of two methods of completing this section of the form. The preferred method is selecting one of the standard purposes, if necessary, qualifying a purpose in relation to a specific application or part of the organisation.

Data users may, however, describe a purpose in their ówn words. This method is not favoured by the Registry and should only be used where method one is totally inappropriate. By using the standard purposes data users can ensure that the registration process is simpler and quicker; free text applications will be subjected to much closer scrutiny by the Registry and are likely to need further elaboration, possibly delaying registration. The Registrar does have the power to accept registration particulars expressed in very general terms in cases where it is appropriate; that is, in cases where he is satisfied that s. 7(3) more specific terms would be likely to prejudice the purpose or purposes for which the data are held. However, this power is likely to be exercised very sparingly in the context of a free text registration.

The intention of the standard descriptions outlined in the guidance notes is to provide a common framework for register entries. Whilst the descriptions and examples associated with each purpose will be included in the public register entry, they are not intended to be all embracing: data users must opt for a purpose code that most closely represents their own particular applications and systems.

Some of the standard purposes describe basic processing functions and activities that are common to most organisations. Others are more specific and describe purposes relating to particular sectoral or industry-wide purposes.

Within the range of activities for each purpose is included 'analysis for management purposes and statutory returns'. This is merely to allow data users to analyse statistics for purposes incidental to the standard purpose and for statutory disclosure of personal data to public authorities, without the need for a separate purpose registration for such analyses.

6.7.2 Standard purposes

The purposes as outlined in the guidance notes are listed below. The text of what follows is a combination of the authors' notes and observations and some material paraphrased or reproduced from the official guidance notes. Readers should of course carefully consult the full text of the Registrar's guidance notes (reproduced in Appendix 2) before completing any application form.

P001 Personnel/employee administration

This includes the administration of prospective, current and past employees, including, where applicable, self-employed or contract personnel, secondees, temporary staff or voluntary workers.

Whilst payroll data may be exempt (see para. 5.2), the activities covered by this purpose include more sophisticated payroll data, including payment of other benefits, recruitment, recording of working time, assessment and training, negotiation or communication with workforce, manpower and career planning, compliance with corporate and legislative policy in respect of health, safety and other employment issues.

P002 Work planning and management

This includes the planning and management of the data user's workload or business activity.

Whilst certain of these data may not be personal data in that the data indicate the intentions of the data user in respect of an individual data subject (see para. 4.3), the activities covered by P002 include job scheduling, roster administration, progress or piecework monitoring, identification of relevant resources, monitoring the allocation, use or performance of plant, equipment or services.

P003 Marketing and selling (excluding direct marketing to individuals)
This includes the identification of potential customers and administration of promotional campaigns.

This purpose includes the classification, rating or checking of individuals or organisations' advertising and other promotion; dealing with complaints or enquiries; and analysis for management purposes. It includes the marketing of further business to present or former customers.

Where an organisation is seeking to promote a corporate identity or image, purpose P006 would be the appropriate code to select.

It will be recalled that personal data consisting only of names and addresses are exempt from registration (see para. 5.3). However, given the narrow scope of that exemption, most name and address files used for marketing and selling purposes will require to be registered under this purpose.

P004 Marketing and selling (including direct marketing to individuals)
This involves identifying potential customers and the administration of marketing campaigns which may include selling or promotion to individuals via direct marketing methods.

The range of activities within this purpose would include the classification, rating or checking of individuals; distributing promotional material by mail, door-to-door delivery or other means; telephone or face-to-face canvassing; dealing with complaints or enquiries.

It should be noted that this purpose is wider than the marketing and selling of goods and services. It includes marketing and selling ideas, concepts and membership via direct marketing such as might be carried on by political organisations. However, the fund raising activities of charitable and other voluntary organisations should be registered under P005.

Like P003, this purpose encompasses marketing further business to existing or past customers.

Traditional market research survey work would be more accurately described by P016.

P005   Fund raising

This purpose is intended to cover fund raising by charitable or other voluntary bodies and it therefore includes such activities as the administration of appeals and continuing fund raising, including the use of direct marketing techniques.

This purpose only covers the fund raising activities of charities and other voluntary organisations, any processing of personal data in respect of their main objects, other than fund raising, should be registered under P019 or where appropriate under one or more of the other standard purposes.

P006   Public relations and external affairs

This includes promoting mutual understanding between the data user and representatives of the public, public authorities or other organisations.

The activities within this purpose include identifying individuals or organisations for lobbying or representations on matters of concern to the data user and the maintenance of associated records.

P007   Management of agents and intermediaries

This includes the administration of agents or other intermediaries, either for sales of goods or services or for the provision of after sales support.

This purpose may include the identification, selection and checking of intermediaries, recording and processing payments, monitoring performance.

P008   Purchase/supplier administration

This includes the administration of supplies of goods and services to the data user, by whatever method of contract or payment, including subscriptions and standing orders as well as discrete purchases.

Whilst certain of this data may be covered by the accounting data exemption (see para. 5.2), the purpose extends beyond purchase ledger data to include the identification, checking and selection of suppliers, ordering, and monitoring supplier performance.

P009   Business and technical intelligence

This purpose is aimed at the maintenance of information on the business or technical environment in which the data user operates. It includes all data held in respect of persons specifically identified in advance as being of interest to the data user. It therefore includes such activities as competitor analysis, acquisition and divestment planning, market forecasting, recording and monitoring technical developments. It does not include general data banks maintained as a reference tool, these should be registered under P017.

P010   Membership administration
Organisations based on a membership as opposed to a shareholder/stockholder based constitution will use this purpose for the administration of membership. This purpose will apply to trade unions, professional bodies, trading associations and similar bodies.

The activities include recruitment, registration, maintenance of professional standards, administration of subscriptions, the production of directories or yearbooks, processing of enquiries or complaints, and advice to the membership. A very limited exemption exists for unincorporated members' clubs (see para. 5.3) which may be relevant here.

If an organisation engages in wider activities such as the provision of advice to the public (see P040) or the supply of goods or services to the public, these should be registered under an appropriate purpose. Where, for example, an organisation engages in recruitment by direct marketing, it should be registered under P004.

P011   Share and stockholding registration
This includes the maintenance of registers of share and stockholders, whether in compliance with statutory or other obligations, or as a management resource.

All personal data which a data user is required to make available to the public under the companies legislation is exempt from the DPA (see para. 5.8). However, the processing of additional information such as applications and allotments, recording of transfers, payment of dividends, interest and administration of other benefits, distribution of documents and identification of relevant expertise or experience, would be typical activities within this purpose.

P012   Ancillary and support function
This includes the provision of ancillary services supporting the data user's business.

This purpose is perhaps only appropriate for the large-scale data user that requires to operate ancillary services to support the organisation. It may be used in respect of functions and applications relating to a financial, legal, estates, computing, security or engineering department within an organisation.

Activities may include the maintenance of internal directories, filing including electronic mail, planning and administration of repair and maintenance, access, security and safety arrangements, computer system testing, computer assisted learning, and dealing with enquiries, complaints and claims from the public.

Where an organisation is so large that support departments maintain a considerable volume of personal data, the activities of such support departments should be registered as a separate specific purpose. For example, if an organisation has a large legal services unit P039 (legal services) may be used.

When this purpose is used the whole range of specific purposes or functions that is intended to be covered should be listed. Indeed it is permissible if necessary to use the purpose more than once in order to separate specific functions.

If electronic mail or filing systems are used other than for internal administrative purposes, then the personal data held must be registered under the appropriate purpose. For example, if they are used for marketing and selling, purpose P003 should be selected, or for business intelligence purpose P009.

Although this purpose encompasses data held for testing and demonstrating systems and software, and computer-assisted learning, if live or back-up data are held for some other purpose, such as employee administration, and are used for testing in respect of that purpose, that use will be covered by the standard purpose specification P001 and does not therefore require to be registered under this purpose.

P013 Customer/client administration

This includes the administration of orders and accounts relating to customers or clients.

Whilst basic financial and management accounting data are exempt from registration (see para. 5.2) provided that such data are not needed for any other purpose, this purpose covers a wider range of activities than accounting data. It includes, in addition to recording and processing of sales ledger data, credit checking and rating, control and monitoring of after sales service or maintenance, customer complaints and enquiries.

P014 Lending and hire service administration

This purpose and P015 below are intended as alternative specialised versions of P013 above. It is aimed at data users engaged in any leasing, hiring and lending which involves actually issuing goods. It is intended to extend to the activities of libraries and other organisations that issue books, records and tapes, in addition to the activities of organisations involved in the hiring of plant, vehicles, tools and software.

Activities within this purpose include: reservation and recall systems, processing of payments, credit checking and rating, customer complaints and enquiries.

Companies involved in operating leasing, that is, where equipment is let out on a lease to a number of different users in sequence, the rent being fixed according to the equipment use-value, should register under this purpose; those engaged in finance leasing, which is more akin to conditional sale or hire purchase, should register such activities under P023.

P015   Administration of reservations, bookings and ticket issue
The leisure industry is covered by this purpose: in particular, the administrative and logistics operations of travel, hotel and catering and entertainment organisations and agencies operating in this sector. Data users in this sector operate systems for: reservations and recording customer requirements and preferences, processing of payments, credit checking and rating, dealing with customer complaints.

P016   Research and statistical analysis
This includes research or statistical analysis in all fields, including scientific, technical, medical, social, economic or market research.

Personal data held only for statistical or research purposes are exempt from the subject access provisions of the DPA (see para. 5.4): such data must, however, be registered. In addition, applicants using this standard purpose must indicate the nature of the research or analysis that they undertake by using one of the following terms: scientific research, technical research, medical research, social research, economic or market research, or an appropriate alternative. Health research is taken to include such things as epidemiological research, clinical trials, biomedical research, as well as research into the prevention, prognosis and treatment of disease.

Activities within this purpose include: the identification of subjects for survey or analysis, collection or abstraction of data, including distribution of questionnaires and telephone or face-to-face

s. 33(6)

interviews. Schedules, analysis, modelling or simulation, evaluation of behaviour, attitudes or characteristics, and the output/ presentation of results or findings.

Certain research data or anlaysis carried out in connection with data held for another purpose may be covered by another purpose code. For example, the analysis of personnel/employee data would be covered by P001, and the analysis of purchase records by P008 and, hence, a registration under P016 would not be necessary. Indeed, all the purpose descriptions include within them analysis of the data for management purposes.

P017   Information and data bank administration

This includes the maintenance of information or data banks as a reference tool or general resource. Examples would be catalogues, lists, directories, bibliographic and free text data bases.

This purpose is intended to cover the information storage activities of libraries, museums, commercial information services and news media organisations in broadcasting and publishing. Typical activities include the gathering or updating of data banks, monitoring of access or use.

Organisations that actually sell or otherwise deal in information from data banks consisting primarily of personal data, should use purpose P018.

It is worth noting that this purpose only extends to the storage functions of data users; other data processing functions, notably customer administration, should be registered in the appropriate purpose (P014).

P018   Trading in personal information

This purpose involves commercial dealing in personal data whether by sale, exchange or hire. It covers, for example, selling mailing lists.

P019   Charity and voluntary organisation objectives

This purpose is intended to encompass the main objectives of charities or voluntary organisations. Fund raising should be registered under P005 and, if appropriate, services to the public by way of advice, under P040.

P020   Property management and rent administration

This is aimed at organisations involved in the management and administration of land and property; in particular, the activities of estate agents and companies involved in property management. It may also be appropriate for larger organisations that have a division involved in estate management. Organisations involved in the management of residential property should register under P021 below.

P021   Housing management

This is aimed at organisations involved in the administration and management of residential property. It extends to cover activities such as dealing with applications, allocation of accommodation and related legal and accounting matters.

It is intended to cover the activities of both the public and private sector. In the case of local authority housing departments ancillary functions such as licensing and loan administration should be registered under a further appropriate purpose.

P022   Education and training administration

This purpose covers organisations such as universities, polytechnics, local education authorities and any other institution providing education or training as a business activity. It extends to cover activities such as registration and monitoring of students, accounting matters, planning and control of curricula and examinations, commissioning and validating educational materials, processing examination results and providing references.

The research activities of institutions covered by this purpose should be registered under P016; and staff administration, development and training under P001.

It should be noted that where any organisation provides training courses for its own staff and sells spare places to other organisations, it should register such activities under this purpose even though the provision of training is not its principal business activity.

P023   Borrower account/credit facilities administration

This purpose is aimed particularly at building societies that operate systems to administer and service the accounts of customers borrowing from them. It includes such specific activities as administering surveys, insurance and legal matters related to mortgage advances.

It also covers the activities of finance houses engaged in finance leasing (for operating leasing see P014) and finance houses and retailers running hire purchase and conditional and credit sale agreements.

P024   Investment/deposit account administration
This purpose is intended to cover a range of financial institutions such as banks, building societies and other related organisations that operate systems for the adminstration and servicing of accounts of customers depositing, saving or investing with them.

P025   Combined borrower/saver account administration
This purpose combines P023 and P024 by permitting the registration under one purpose of saving and borrowing account administration.

P026   Personal banking
The personal banking services, both domestic and international, provided by high street banks and building societies should be registered under this purpose. Institutions may wish to register their international banking services separately. In that event, this purpose may be used with an appropriate qualification in the text relating the purpose to international activities.

Banks and financial institutions provide an increasing range of other services in addition to personal banking: for example, investment management, broking, legal services. Such activities should be separately identified using an appropriate standard purpose.

P027   Credit and charge card administration
The administration of credit and charge card accounts operated by banks, financial institutions and retailing organisations would be caught under this purpose.

P028   Corporate banking
This purpose covers the administration of accounts for corporate clients, including the checking of financial status, recording transactions, trade financing and corporate advisory services. Since much of these data relate to companies and not individuals, they will fall outside the scope of the legislation. However, where data subjects are referenced in corporate banking activities this is the appropriate purpose code.

P029   Corporate financing
This includes the provision of services connected with capital issues, sale of securities, takeovers and mergers.

P030   Investment management
The management of investments, in securities, options, futures, commodities, currencies, etc, on behalf of personal or corporate customers would be covered by this purpose.

P031   Life and health insurance administration
This purpose covers the administration of life, health and pensions insurance business.

P032   General insurance administration
This purpose covers property, motor and other general insurance business.

The investment management activities of insurance companies should be registered under P030.

P033   Pensions administration
Pension fund and superannuation scheme administration are covered by this purpose. It includes the processing of contributions, maintenance of accounts, payment of benefits, actuarial advice, processing of persons leaving the scheme and making returns to relevant authorities.

It should be stressed that organisations which administer pension funds on behalf of trustees of the fund, act as agent and are not data users themselves, they are therefore not responsible for registering the pension fund administration.

P034   Factoring and discounting of trade debts
This purpose encompasses the purchasing of trade debts from businesses on a continuing basis as an administrative service, for the provision of funds, or as protection against bad debts.

P035   Credit reference
Organisations involved in the evaluation of the financial status of individuals or organisations on behalf of other organisations should register under this purpose.

P036   Accounting and related services
The activities of professional accountants and financial consultants are caught by this purpose. It includes the administration of client accounts in connection with services such as payroll, bookkeeping,

accounts preparation, audit other than statutory audit (see P037), tax and insolvency matters.

Applicants that use this purpose will invariably be a computer bureau in respect of data that they process for client data users.

P037   Statutory auditing

This covers the activities of accountants in carrying out audits required by statute. Unlike the activities of accountants covered by P036 above, the auditor may hold and utilise a client's data as part of the audit function and not as agent for the client; thus the auditor would in such circumstances be the data user and not simply a computer bureau.

P038   Other financial services including broking and dealing

The activities of intermediary service organisations are encompassed by this purpose. It is intended to cover any financial transaction and financial advisory service not caught by any other standard purpose. For example, stockbrokers, insurance brokers and intermediaries dealing in commodities and bullion will register under this purpose. Applicants must separately state the nature of the service that they provide, and in the case of insurance broking, should indicate whether the business relates to life, health or pension cover.

P039   Legal services

Any organisation providing legal services, including advising and acting on behalf of clients, will register under this purpose. In addition to solicitors and barristers it may be used by organisations such as banks and companies that operate a legal services division.

P040   Other consultancy and advisory services

This purpose is intended to cover a wide range of personal or business services of an advisory, consultancy or intermediary nature. It would apply to surveyors, architects, consulting engineers, marketing and management consultants and similar professions/occupations. It also covers the activities of professional or charitable bodies where they offer advice, irrespective of whether a charge is made.

Applicants are required to specify the type of service or advice that they give the client.

6.7.3   Public sector standard purposes

Standard purposes P041-P070 are designed to encompass the

operational activities of local and central government and other public agencies. In addition to the operational functions within these standard purposes, authorities should, where appropriate, use the general purposes, for example, P001 Employee administration, P006 Public relations, P008 Purchase/supplier administration, P039 Legal services. In some cases a public authority may operate services equivalent to those provided in the private sector and for which there is an appropriate standard general purpose, in that case the general purpose should be used. For example, P021 Housing management for local authority housing departments; P017 Information and data bank administration and P014 Lending and hire service for the activities of public libraries.

The standard purposes are listed below (see Appendix 2 for details of the activities caught by each purpose). Where data users select P041, P042, P045, P054, P057, P058, P061, P062, P068, P069 and P070 some additional information should be provided to elaborate on the type of activities that the authority engages in.

P041   Government benefits administration
P042   Assessment and collection of taxes and other revenue
P043   Collection of rates
P044   Valuation of real property (in Scotland, valuation of lands and heritages)
P045   Licensing and registration
P046   Grant and loan administration
P047   Consumer protection and trading standards
P048   Environmental health
P049   Electoral registration
P050   Fire prevention and control
P051   Highways and transport planning
P052   Passenger transport operations
P053   Planning and development control
P054   Social services/social work
P055   Waste collection and disposal
P056   Water and drainage services
P057   Policing
P058   Crime prevention and prosecution of offenders
P059   Courts administration
P060   Discharge of court business
P061   Other administration of justice
P062   Provision of health care

P063 Ambulance services
P064 Blood transfusion services
P065 Occupational health services
P066 Public health
P067 Health care administration
P068 Other central government
P069 Other local government
P070 Other public sector

6.7.4 Section B2 — Description of personal data

In order to assist individuals in identifying organisations that may hold personal data relating to them, the Registry have divided data subjects and personal data into numerous different categories. Thus, applicants must indicate by selecting the appropriate category the various type of person for whom personal data are to be held. Further, the types of data which are to be held for the purpose described in section B1 of the form requires to be indicated.

6.7.5 Data subject

In essence this part of the form refers to the relationship between the data user and the data subject. This relationship may be as employees, customer/clients, claimants, members, donors, tenants, patients, students, vehicle keepers and simply members of public. One data subject may have several relationships with a data user. He may be, for example, both an employee and a customer. The application form identifies 40 different types of data subject and in most cases data users must indicate for each type of data subject whether the relationship is a current one, a past one or a potential one.

A complete list of data subject types appears in Appendix 2. Applicants may add additional descriptions of data subjects where they consider that the standard types are inappropriate but only where it is absolutely necessary.

Where applicants indicate that they hold personal data on members of the public, they can expect that their application will be subjected to additional scrutiny by the Registry.

6.7.6 Personal data classes

The objective of this section of the form is to describe the class of personal data to be held for the purpose identified in B1. Data class codes are listed on the application form, with additional explanatory information in the guidance notes and example data items for each code. These are reproduced in Appendix 2.

The standard description of each data type ticked will appear in the register but not the example data items. There are over 100 standard data type descriptions. The descriptions are divided into 11 groups:

IDENTIFICATION DATA
PERSONAL CHARACTERISTICS
FAMILY CIRCUMSTANCES
SOCIAL CIRCUMSTANCES
EDUCATION, SKILLS, PROFESSION
EMPLOYMENT DETAILS
FINANCIAL DETAILS
DETAILS OF TRANSACTIONS
BUSINESS INFORMATION
HEALTH CLASSES AND OTHER
MISCELLANEOUS INFORMATION

Each group contains a number of standard descriptions: for example, in the group headed EMPLOYMENT DETAILS, the following standard descriptions appear:

C061   Current occupation
C062   Recruitment details
C063   Termination details
C064   Career history
C065   Work record
C066   Health and safety record
C067   Trade union or staff association membership
C068   Payments and deductions
C069   Property held by employee
C070   Work management details
C071   Work assessment details
C072   Training record
C073   Security details

Example data items for each description are given in the guidance notes. Thus, under C062 recruitment details, items include, date recruited, method of recruitment, source of recruitment, references, details of probationary period. The items listed are not intended to be all embracing. The fact that an applicant has ticked a data class will not automatically denote that he is holding the entire range of data items listed against that type.

Free text may be used instead of, or in addition to, the standard description. This may be necessary where the applicant holds particularly sensitive data types and the standard descriptions require refinement or modifications. Additional standard descriptions may be added in text if the applicant holds data not described by any of the standard codes.

6.7.7 Section B3 — Sources and disclosures

For convenience, the source from which data users intend or may wish to obtain the data and the persons to whom they intend to or may disclose the data, are combined on the same section of the form. There are two columns against each standard description, column A for the sources from which data was obtained and column B for disclosures.

The standard descriptions for source and disclosures are divided into three groups. The first contains individuals and organisations that have a direct association or relationship with the data subjects described in section B2. The second lists those individuals and organisations directly associated with the data user, for example, claimants or tenants. The third group contains general descriptions of organisations and individuals, for example, Inland Revenue, housing department or Customs and Excise.

It is important that all sources and disclosures are identified. The motivation behind a particular disclosure is irrelevant, if it is not registered the disclosure could result in criminal penalties.

Applicants should select as many codes as they require to present a complete picture of their activities, obvious duplications should be avoided. For example, if D109 (the data subject's doctor) is selected, it should not be necessary to tick D353 (medical practitioners) unless the source or disclosure is in respect of a practitioner other than the data subject's own doctor or medical adviser, in which case both should be selected.

It will be recalled that certain disclosures of personal data are permissible under the Act even though such disclosures are not registered (see Chapter 5). For example, disclosure to the data subject or a person acting on his behalf is permitted without fear of the DPA's provisions.

6.7.8 Section B4 — Overseas transfers

Applicants must indicate on the form the names or a description of any countries or territories outside the UK to which they intend or may wish to transfer data (see Chapter 13 for a full discussion of transborder data flows).

The expression transfer of data is not defined in the Act. In essence a transfer takes place if the information transferred is in machine readable form whereas a disclosure does not have this constraint (see Chapter 4 for further details). It should be stressed, therefore, that overseas transfers and disclosures of data are not mutually exclusive. If an overseas transfer box is selected it will often imply a disclosure which must also be indicated in section B3.

Applicants should select the appropriate standard code overseas transfer box to signify which country or countries they transfer data to. Where the nature of an applicant's business requires personal data to be transferred to any country worldwide, such as in the provision of international travel services, they should select the worldwide transfer box. Such applications will however be subjected to additional scrutiny by the Registrar.

6.8 Where there are a number of companies in a group how should they register?

The central feature of the definition of a data user is the ability to control the contents and use of the data. Since a subsidiary company is, in law, a separate and distinct legal person, even though it may be actually owned by another company, it is capable of controlling data and thus being a data user in its own right and should register accordingly.

It is common within groups for data to be transferred freely from one subsidiary to another, thus companies within a group should indicate on the registration application form that data is obtained from and disclosed to other companies in the group.

Where processing is carried out for the entire group by the holding company, that company must register as a computer bureau and the subsidiaries as data users.

6.9 Can the registration be altered at any time?

Once registered a data user may apply at any time for the alteration or removal of any particulars included in their entry. In particular, the Registrar must be informed immediately if a data user changes the address contained in the entry a form DPR.2 will require to be

s. 6(5)

completed for such changes. A failure to notify the Registrar of a change of address could result in a prosecution.

Registration particulars must be altered to reflect any changes in the processing operations of the data user: If, for example, data are held or used for a new purpose then an amendment form must be completed. If a charge is made for amendments it will be less than the full registration fee. However in the Registrar's Annual Report he states that it is 'hoped to process amendments to entries within the standard charge' (page 9).

6.10   In what circumstances can the Registrar refuse registration?

s. 7(2)(a)

Registration can be refused where the Registrar considers that the particulars proposed for registration would not give sufficient information about the matters to which they relate. Given the structure of the application form where an applicant uses the standard description codes, a refusal to register by the Registrar is unlikely.

Where an applicant completes the form improperly the Registry will doubtless endeavour to return it for completion and resubmission. Such return of the application form will not usually constitute a formal refusal.

From November 1987 registration or renewal of registration may additionally be refused on the following grounds:

s. 7(2)(b)

(a)   The Registrar is satisfied that the applicant is likely to contravene any of the data protection principles.

s. 7(2)(c)

(b)   The Registrar considers that the information available to him is insufficient to satisfy him that the applicant is unlikely to contravene any of the principles.

Where the Registrar does refuse an application he is required to state his reasons and inform the applicant of the right to appeal to the Data Protection Tribunal.

6.11   Can the applicant process data pending the outcome of an application?

s. 7(6)(a)

Persons applying for registration, or the alteration of particulars already registered, are permitted to engage in the activities covered by

s. 7(6)(b)

the application whilst it is being considered.

72

Even if the Registrar refuses the application the applicant may still continue to operate his data processing activities. They may continue until the outcome of the appeal is known, or if no appeal is lodged, the end of the period within which an appeal can be lodged. The appeal period is to be fixed by the Secretary of State. `Sch. 3 para. 4(2)(a)`

The right to continue to process up to the outcome of an appeal is curtailed in two situations. First, if the Registrar considers that there are special circumstances that necessitate a refusal of registration taking effect as a matter of urgency, he may include such a statement in the refusal notice. In such circumstances the applicant has seven days from the date when he receives the notification in which to terminate processing activities. Second, where the applicant has in the previous two years already had an application refused, or all or any of the particulars removed under a de-registration notice (see para. 7.10), the applicant may not process the data during the period of the application. In such circumstances, however, the Registrar must respond to the application within two months rather than the usual six months. Should he require longer than two months he must give the applicant written notification and, from the date of such notification, the applicant is permitted to act as if his application had been successful. Provided, therefore, the Registrar deals with the application within two months, the applicant cannot carry out the activities covered by the application unless the Registrar accepts the application or a Tribunal later overturns the Registrar's refusal. If the Registrar takes longer than two months to deal with the application, the applicant may carry on the activities once notified of the delay, up to the decision of the Registrar and, if appropriate, the outcome of an appeal. `s. 7(7)` `s. 7(8)`

To avoid confusion about the precise date upon which a notice of application may be treated as having been made or withdrawn, if the notice is sent by registered post or recorded delivery the relevant date will be the date on which it is received by the Post Office. In any other case it is the date on which it is received by the Registrar. `s. 7(9)`

6.12 How will renewal applications be dealt with?

An application for the renewal of registration follows the same procedure as an original application. Registered persons may only lodge a renewal application in the period of six months ending with the expiration of the initial period of registration or, if there have been previous renewals, six months before the end of the current renewal period. `s. 8(5)`

Before an entry expires, registered persons will receive a reminder from the Registrar and be invited to renew their registration entry. It is intended that a simple procedure for renewal will be established where no change in the entry is needed.

s. 8(2)   Like the initial period of registration the renewal period may be for three years, or a shorter period if the applicant requests it in the renewal application.

6.13   What are the implications of non-registration for data users?

s. 5(5)   A person who is not registered, and not exempt from registration, is absolutely prohibited from holding personal data and if such a person processed personal data an offence would be committed, irrespective of motivation or intent. Proof that personal data have been processed will be sufficient to establish guilt.

6.14   What are the implications of non-registration for a computer bureau?

s. 5(4)   Similarly, a person shall not, in carrying on a computer bureau, provide services in respect of personal data unless there is an entry in respect of that person in the register as a computer bureau or a data
s. 5(5)   user who also carries on a bureau. This prohibition, unlike the one in para. 6.13 above, is not an offence of strict liability. To be found guilty the prosecution must prove that the person knowingly or recklessly contravened the provision.

6.15   What are the implications of undertaking activities not covered by a registration?

A registered person must not:

s. 5(2)(a)   (a) Hold personal data of any description other than that specified in his registration entry.
s. 5(2)(b)   (b) Hold any such data, or use any such data held by him, for any purpose other than the purpose or purposes described in the entry.
s. 5(2)(c)   (c) Obtain such data, or information to be contained in such data to be held by him, from any source which is not described in the entry.
s. 5(2)(d)   (d) Disclose such data held by him to any person who is not described in the entry. A disclosure in relation to data includes
s. 1(9)   disclosing information taken from the data. Where identification of

74

the data subject is dependent partly on information constituting the data and partly on other information in the possession of the data user (see para. 4.3) there will be no disclosure within the meaning of the Act unless both the data and the other information are disclosed.

A disclosure may therefore take place where a disk, printout or photocopy of a printout is delivered; or where data is electronically transmitted from one person to another, or where access is granted to the data or information extracted from the data or a written or verbal communication of information taken from the data is made. In all of these instances if a data user is not registered in respect of that disclosure and it is not within an exemption, he may be guilty of an offence.

(e)   Directly or indirectly transfer such data to any country or territory outside the UK other than the ones named or described in the entry.   s. 5(2)(e)

A servant or agent of a registered person is subject to the same restrictions on the use, disclosure or transfer of data ((b), (d) and (e) above) as his employer or principal. Similarly, in respect of data to be held, a servant or agent is subject to the same restrictions on the sources from which it may be obtained ((c) above).   s. 5(3)

A data user, or an employee or agent of a user, who knowingly or recklessly contravenes this prohibition will be guilty of an offence.   s. 5(5)

For example, if an employee of a data user knowingly transferred data to a country not specified in the registration document the employee would be guilty of a criminal offence. If the data user knew of the intended transfer, or manifestly ought to have known, then the data user would also be guilty of a criminal offence.

Chapter 7

What are the powers of the Registrar?

7.1 What is the principal function of the Registrar?

s. 2(1)
(2)

The foundation of the DPA is the eight data protection principles set out in sch. 1 to the Act. The first seven principles apply to personal data held by data users, and the eighth applies both to data users and to persons carrying on computer bureaux. Both data users and bureaux must seek to ensure that their operations are carried out in compliance with the principles, and any modifications to the principles that the Secretary of State may make in respect of sensitive data. If they engage in activities which involve a breach of the

s. 36(1)

principles the Registrar may take action against them. Indeed, the Registrar is primarily charged with the duty of promoting observance of the principles.

7.2 What powers does the Registrar have?

s. 16

sch. 4
paras.
1–7

If the Registrar's suspicions are aroused by a complaint in respect of the activites of any person then the Registrar may give notice to that person seeking access to the data user's premises at a reasonable hour. If such access is refused then the Registrar may apply to a circuit judge for the issue of a warrant for the inspection of the premises. To obtain the warrant he must supply the judge with sufficient information on oath to satisfy the judge that there are reasonable grounds for suspecting either that an offence has been, or is being, committed under the Act, or that the principles have been, or are being, contravened and that evidence of the offence or contravention is to be found on the relevant premises. Before a warrant is issued the judge must be satisfied in respect of the following matters:

What are the powers of the Registrar?

(a)   That the Registrar has given seven days' notice in writing to the occupier of the premises, demanding access.

(b)   Such access was demanded at a reasonable hour and was unreasonably refused.

(c)   After the refusal, the Registrar notified the occupier of the application for the warrant and the occupier has had an opportunity of being heard by the judge on the question of whether or not it should be granted.

In cases of urgency, or where prior notification would be likely to defeat the object of entry, the judge may dispense with the above notice requirements. If the warrant is granted it will authorise the Registrar, or his officers or servants, at any time within seven days of the date of the warrant:

(a)   To enter the relevant premises.

(b)   To search the relevant premises.

(c)   To inspect, examine, operate and test any data equipment found there.

(d)   To inspect and seize any documents and other material found there which may be evidence of the commission of an offence, or of the contravention of the principles. It is noteworthy that this power extends to documents that are not computer processed.

The Registrar, or his representatives, must make the inspection at a reasonable hour unless there are grounds for suspecting that the evidence would not be found if the inspection were executed at a reasonable hour.

The person who occupies the premises is entitled to be shown the warrant and supplied with a copy of it. If they are not present when the warrant is executed, a copy of it must be left in a prominent place on the premises.

If any documents or other material are seized the occupier of the premises is entitled on request to be given a receipt for them. Such documents or materials may be retained by the Registrar for as long as is necessary in the circumstances, but the data user may be given a copy of anything that is seized if the person carrying out the search considers that it can be done without delay.

7.3 Is there anything that the Registrar cannot inspect or seize?

sch. 4
paras.
8-10

The powers of inspection and seizure conferred by a warrant are not exercisable in respect of three categories of documents or material. These are: first, personal data which are exempt from the registration requirements of the DPA, for example, accounting data. Second, communications between a professional legal adviser and his client (or person representing such a client) in the context of advice to the client with respect to his obligations, liabilities or rights under the Act. Third, any communication between a professional legal adviser, or between the adviser and his client and any other person, made in connection with, or in contemplation of, any proceedings under, or arising out of, the Act. The exemptions relating to communications between a legal adviser and client extend to any copy and other record of the communications. They also extend to documents or articles enclosed with, or referred to, in the communications, provided they are made in connection with giving advice or in connection with, or contemplation of, proceedings under the Act.

It must be stressed, however, that the exemptions in respect of such communications only extend to things in the possession of the legal adviser or the client and not to anything in the possession of any other person. Nor do the exemptions relating to legal communications apply to anything held with the intention of furthering a criminal purpose.

It may be that the person in occupation of the premises has material, some of which is outside the powers conferred by the warrant, and some of which is caught by the inspection and seizure provisions. In that event, the person may rightly object to the proposed inspection but the Registrar may request a copy of the part of the material that is covered by the warrant.

The Registrar must return to the court a warrant issued under the Act, once it has been executed, with an endorsement stating what powers have been exercised under the authority of the warrant. If the warrant is not executed it must also be returned to the court within seven days.

7.4 What happens if the data user or bureau
fails to assist the Registrar?

sch. 4
para. 12

Any person who intentionally obstructs the Registrar in the execution of a warrant, or who fails without reasonable excuse to give such assistance as may reasonably be required, will be guilty of an offence.

7.5 What action may the Registrar take after an inspection

If, as a result of the inspection, the Registrar finds the necessary evidence of an offence he may institute proceedings against the alleged offender. If such proceedings are successful the offender may be liable to a fine and, in certain circumstances, computer-related material connected with the commission of the offence may be forfeited, destroyed or erased.   s. 19

If, on the other hand, the Registrar finds a breach of the principles he may consider using the powers described in 7.8 below.

7.6 What penalties may be imposed by the courts?

A person who is found guilty of an offence under any of the provisions of the DPA, apart from s. 6 (change of address not notified to the Registrar and false or misleading particulars supplied to the Registrar) and para. 12 of sch. 4 (offences in connection with the execution of a warrant), will be liable on conviction on indictment (trial before a judge and jury in the Crown Court) to a fine of unlimited amount or on summary conviction (before a magistrates' court) to a fine not exceeding the statutory maximum (currently £2,000). A person who is found guilty under s. 6 or sch. 4 may be liable to a fine not exceeding the fifth level on the standard scale under s. 37 of the Criminal Justice Act 1982 (currently £2,000).   s. 19(2)   s. 19(3)

The court may also order computer-related material to be forfeited, destroyed or erased if it appears to be connected with the commission of any of the following offences of which the court has found an offender guilty: s. 19(4)

(a) Holding data without being registered.
(b) Failing to comply with an enforcement notice.
(c) Contravening a transfer prohibition notice.
(d) Unauthorised disclosure by a computer bureau.

Where, however, someone other than the offender claims to be the owner of the material, or a person otherwise interested in it, the court must, on an application by them, give them the opportunity to make a case against the order.

7.7 Can individual directors be liable to a fine?

s. 20

If an offence is committed by a corporate body, then any director, manager, secretary or similar officer, or any person who purports to act in such capacity, may also be guilty of an offence and be similarly liable to fines. The prosecution must, however, prove that the offence by the company was committed with the individual's consent or connivance or is attributable to their neglect. Members of a company may also incur liability where they are engaged in the management of the company in respect of acts or defaults in connection with their management functions, in the same way as if they were directors.

7.8 How can the Registrar ensure compliance with the principles?

If, perhaps after an inspection, the Registrar's suspicions are confirmed that a breach of the principles has occurred, he may issue one of three types of notice in order to ensure compliance. These are enforcement notices, de-registration notices and transfer prohibition notices.

s. 18

Such notices may be served, in the case of an individual, by delivering it to the individual personally, by sending it by post addressed to the individual's usual or last known place of residence or business, or by leaving it at the individual's residence or business. In the case of corporate or unincorporated bodies, the notice may be served by sending it by post to the secretary or other executive officer at the principal office, or by leaving it at the office. In the case of a company its principal office will be its registered office.

7.9 What are enforcement notices?

s. 10(1)

If the Registrar is satisfied that a registered person has contravened, or is contravening, any of the data protection principles he may serve the person with an enforcement notice. The notice will require the person to take steps to comply with the principles within a specified time period.

The notice must contain the following:

s. 10 (5)
(a)

(a) A statement of the principle or principles which it is alleged have been, or are being, contravened.

s. 10 (5)
(a)

(b) The reasons why the Registrar is satisfied that the principles have been contravened.

80

(c) Particulars of the rights of appeal to the Data Protection Tribunal.

s. 10 (5) (b)

(d) The time period within which the person must comply with the principle(s).

s. 10(1)

The decision to serve an enforcement notice is entirely at the discretion of the Registrar. In the majority of cases the Registrar may encourage compliance with the principles through informal persuasion and negotiation. He will presumably only resort to serving an enforcement notice where such techniques of persuasion break down or where the contravention of a principle is causing immediate injury to a data subject. In fact, the Registrar, when deciding whether to serve an enforcement notice is specifically charged with the duty of considering whether a contravention has caused, or is likely to cause, any person damage or distress.

s. 10(2)

Much will depend on the nature of the infringement. There may be circumstances where a contravention does not cause damage or distress but the Registrar may nevertheless decide to serve a notice. For example, if a data user's security system is lax the Registrar may not be aware of any actual or potential damage or distress but may still wish to serve a notice in order to maintain the sanctity of the principles and discourage other data users from ignoring them. A failure to issue an enforcement notice in such circumstances may encourage the data user to believe that the principles can be disregarded.

On the other hand, even if a contravention has caused damage or distress, the Registrar may decide that an enforcement notice is inappropriate. It may be that the contravention was the result of a genuine error or accident which could not have been foreseen and is unlikely to recur.

If the enforcement notice is in respect of the fifth principle, that personal data must be accurate and up to date, the notice may require the rectification or erasure of the data and any data held by the data user which contain an expression of opinion which appears to be based on the inaccurate data.

s. 10(3)

In the case of data which a data user receives or obtains from the data subject or a third party, the accuracy of which is challenged, the Registrar may require data users in any enforcement notice:

(a) to rectify or erase the data; or
(b) to insert indications of the source of the data and that they are

considered inaccurate or misleading by the data subject; or

(c)   if he thinks fit, to insert a supplementary statement of the true facts relating to the matters dealt with by the data.

The seventh principle entitles data subjects to be informed by any data user whether that user holds any personal data on that individual and, if so, gives him a right of access to such data. The data user is required to provide the data without undue delay or expense for the subject. The ultimate enforcement right is to seek the assistance of the courts if the data user refuses to comply with the request for access. To serve an enforcement notice requiring compliance with this principle the Registrar must be satisfied that the information has been duly requested in the prescribed manner and the data user has failed to respond.

s. 10(4)

s. 21

s. 10(6)   Data users will be allowed at least the length of time prescribed for an appeal in which to comply with an enforcement notice. In the event of an appeal against the enforcement notice the data user is not required to comply with the notice until the appeal process has been determined or the appeal withdrawn.

s. 10(7)   If there are, however, special circumstances and the Registrar considers that compliance should be undertaken as a matter of urgency, then he may include a statement to that effect in the notice. In that event, the person has seven days from the date on which the notice was served to comply.

s. 10(8)   The Registrar has, at any time, the option to cancel an enforcement notice by written notification if he so decides.

s. 10(9)   If a person fails to comply with an enforcement notice it is an offence. In the event of a prosecution it is a defence if the person can prove that he exercised all due diligence to comply with the notice.

7.10   What are de-registration notices?

The most powerful weapon in the hands of the Registrar to ensure compliance with the data protection principles is a de-registration notice. This may be served either as a follow-up to an enforcement notice or an alternative if the principles have been contravened so grossly and persistently that no amount of detailed improvement would make the system acceptable.

s. 11(1)   If the Registrar is satisfied that a registered person has contravened, or is contravening, the principles he may serve a de-registration notice. The notice will state that he proposes, at the end of a specific period, to remove from the register, or modify on the register, all or any of the particulars constituting the entry. At the end of the period the Registrar may proceed to amend or remove the registered entry with the result that the processing activities of data users or the services provided by computer bureaux may be seriously curtailed or completely stopped.

Before the Registrar can serve a de-registration notice he must be satisfied that compliance with the principles cannot adequately be secured by an enforcement notice. He must also consider whether the contravention has caused or is likely to cause any person damage or distress, although the existence of such damage is not a precondition of issue.   s. 11(2)

The de-registration notice must contain the following information:

(a) A statement of the principle or principles which the Registrar is satisfied have been or are being contravened.   s. 11(3) (a)

(b) The reasons why the Registrar has reached the conclusion that the principle or principles have been breached and decided that compliance cannot be adequately secured by an enforcement notice.   s. 11(3) (b)

(c) Particulars of the existence of the right of appeal to the Data Protection Tribunal.   s. 11(4) (b)

(d) The specified time period after which the Registrar will remove the entry in question.   s. 11(1) (a)

Data users will be allowed at least the length of time prescibed for an appeal for them to comply with a de-registration notice.   s. 11(4)

If an appeal is made the particulars must not be removed from the register until the Tribunal confirms the Registrar's decision or the appeal is formally withdrawn by the registered person.

If the Registrar considers that there are special circumstances that warrant the particulars being removed as a matter of urgency he may include a statement to that effect in the notice. In such a situation the particulars may then be removed seven days from the date on which the notice is served.   s. 11(5)

The Registrar may at any time cancel a de-registration notice by written notification to the person on whom it was served. But once a de-registration notice has been put into effect, if the persons concerned continue to hold data or carry on as a computer bureau, they may be subject to the penalties outlined in Chapter 6.   s. 11(6)

7.11   What are transfer prohibition notices?

s. 12(1)   If it appears to the Registrar that a registered person or an applicant for registration proposes to transfer personal data to a place outside the UK, he may serve them with a transfer prohibition notice. Such a notice will prohibit them from transferring the data either absolutely or until certain steps specified in the notice have been taken, in order to protect the interests of data subjects. The whole question of transfer prohibition notices is part of the problem of transborder data flows considered in Chapter 13.

Chapter 8

What duties does the Registrar have?

8.1   What are the Registrar's duties?

The Registrar has a central role to play in the scheme of the Act. It will be his specific duty to maintain the register of data users and persons carrying on computer bureaux, and to consider all applications for registration. He must also provide facilities for making the register available for inspection by members of the public and supplying them with copies of particulars in a registration entry.

s. 4(1)

s. 9

In addition to carrying out the above specific duties, the Registrar is also under a general duty to perform his functions under the Act so as to promote observance of the data protection principles by data users and persons carrying on computer bureaux. He is required to interpret and enforce the principles, subject to the direction of the Data Protection Tribunal. In the words of the Minister of State:

s. 36(1)

> the Registrar is in effect the guardian of the data subject's rights or, perhaps, a data protection ombudsman. It is to him that data subjects will turn if they believe that data users are breaching any of the principles and it would be for him to uphold their rights by taking whatever action is appropriate, bearing in mind always his duty to promote the observance of the principles. (Standing Committee H, Data Protection Bill, 15 March 1984, col. 391.)

As well as receiving complaints from data subjects, the Registrar may offer advice and guidance to any person likely to be affected by the Act. He must arrange for the dissemination of information about the Act and his functions under it. A series of guides are planned; the first of which is available. Initially, data users will be eager for guidance on registration and on how to arrange their processing activities in order to comply with the principles. In this respect, codes of practice may be a useful means by which the registrar could foster

s. 36(2)

s. 36(4)

s. 36(4)   compliance with the principles, and at the same time avoid developing an adversary relationship with data users.

The Lindop Committee proposed that statutory codes of practice be drawn up by an independent Data Protection Authority in order to provide the 'flexibility needed to cope with the wide differences between the many users of personal data'. Such an approach was not favoured by the government. The DPA simply imposes a general duty on the Registrar, where he considers it appropriate to encourage trade associations, or other bodies representing data users, to prepare and to disseminate to their members codes of practice for guidance in complying with the data protection principles. Such a duty is similar to that of the Director General of Fair Trading, who has a duty under the Fair Trading Act 1973 to encourage trade associations to draw up codes of practice. In the context of data protection, such codes, drawn up after consultation with the Registrar, would simply act as a yardstick for data users in a particular trade or association against which to measure their processing activities in order to comply with the principles.

8.2   How is the Registrar accountable?

sch. 2
Part I
para. 7

The Registrar is under a duty to keep proper accounts and other records in relation to the accounts, and to prepare a statement of account in respect of each financial year. Such accounts must be examined and certified by the Comptroller and Auditor General, and laid before each House of Parliament.

s. 36(5)

The Registrar is also under a duty to lay before each House of Parliament a general report on the performance of his functions under the Act. He may also, from time to time, lay before each House any other reports on his functions which he thinks fit.

8.3   Does the Registrar fulfil any obligation in respect of the Convention?

s. 37

By art. 13 of the Convention the parties to it are under a duty to render mutual assistance to other signatories in order to implement the convention. Each party is therefore required to designate an authority for the purposes of the Convention and in the UK the Registrar will be the designated authority. In fulfilling such a role, the Registrar will therefore be required to respond to any request from the designated authority of another party to the Convention for information on the UK's law and administrative practice in the field of data protection. He may also be required to take appropriate measures for furnishing factual information relating to specific data users' automatic processing carried out in the UK.

Chapter 9

Can data users appeal against the Registrar's decision and actions?

9.1 Introduction

Chapters 7 and 8 illustrated the wide powers that the Registrar can exercise. He can deprive people of their livelihoods by refusing to accept their registration applications; he can issue an enforcement notice which may impose additional expenditure and inconvenience on data users; and in the last resort he can impose the ultimate sanction of the issue of a de-registration notice. It is therefore necessary that data users and persons carrying on a computer bureau should have a right of appeal against any decision or action that the Registrar may take.

s. 3(1)(b)
    For the purpose of dealing with such appeals the Act creates a Data Protection Tribunal, to which all data users and persons who carry on computer bureaux may appeal: data subjects have no access to the Tribunal.

9.2 Who comprises the Tribunal?

s. 3(3)
The Tribunal consists of a chairman and a number of deputy chairmen. These officials are appointed by the Lord Chancellor after consultation with the Lord Advocate. The number of deputy chairmen appointed is at the discretion of the Lord Chancellor. Persons appointed chairman or deputy chairmen must have been barristers, advocates or solicitors of not less than seven years' standing.

s. 3(5)
    The Secretary of State appoints the other members of the Tribunal, who must include persons to represent the interests of data users and data subjects.

9.3   What rights of appeal do persons have to the Tribunal?

Persons may appeal to the Data Protection Tribunal against a decision of the Registrar:

(a)   To refuse an application for registration.   s. 13(1)(a)
(b)   To refuse an application for the alteration of registration particulars.
(c)   To serve an enforcement notice, de-registration notice or   s. 13(1) transfer prohibition notice.   (b)
(d)   To accompany a notification of refusal or registration or   s. 13(2), service of a notice with a statement that it should take effect as a   (3) matter of urgency. See Chapter 7 for an explanation of statements of urgency.

For the purpose of hearing and deciding appeals, or any   sch. 3 preliminary or incidental matter to an appeal, the chairman or, if   para. 1 appropriate, the deputy chairman, has complete discretion to allow the Tribunal to sit at such times and in such places as he may direct. Since the Tribunal may sit in two or more groups it is quite likely that it will sit in regional centres.

When hearing appeals against any decision of the Registrar, other   sch. 3 than a statement that a notification should have immediate effect, the   para. 2 Tribunal must consist of:

(a)   the chairman or a deputy chairman; and
(b)   an equal number of representatives of data users and data subjects.

The chairman or deputy chairman must always preside. The membership of the Tribunal will be nominated in advance by the chairman or, if he is for any reason unable to act, by a deputy chairman. If the chairman is not presiding over the Tribunal, the senior deputy chairman will preside: such seniority being decided in accordance with the dates of appointment.

Questions to be determined by the Tribunal will be arrived at according to the opinion of the majority of the members hearing the appeal.

Where an appeal is made against the Registrar's decision to include   sch. 3 a statement that a notification of refusal or service of a notice is to   para. 3 take effect as a matter of urgency, the jurisdiction of the Tribunal will be exercised by the chairman or deputy chairman sitting alone.

9.4   How are appeals heard?

sch. 3
para. 4
(1), (2)

The Secretary of State has the power to make rules regulating the exercise of the rights of appeal conferred by the Act, and in particular the practice and procedure of the Tribunal. Particular issues to which the Secretary of State's attention must be directed are:

(a)   The period within which an appeal can be brought and the burden of proof on an appeal.

(b)   The summoning of witnesses and the administration of oaths.

(c)   The production of documents and data material.

(d)   The inspection, examination, operation and testing of data equipment and the testing of data material.

(e)   The hearing of an appeal wholly or partly in private.

(f)   Hearing an appeal in the absence of the appellant or determining an appeal without a hearing.

(g)   Enabling any matter preliminary or incidental to an appeal to be dealt with by the chairman or a deputy chairman.

(h)   The awarding of costs.

(i)   The publication of reports of the Tribunal's decisions.

(j)   Conferring on the Tribunal such ancillary powers as the Secretary of State thinks necessary for the proper discharge of its functions.

9.5   What powers does the Tribunal have to deal with obstructive persons?

sch. 3
para. 5
(1), (2)

If a person appearing before the Tribunal is guilty of any act or omission in respect of the proceedings which, if the proceedings were before a court with power to commit for contempt, would constitute contempt, then the Tribunal may report the offence to the High Court in England, or the Court of Session in Scotland. The court to which the offence is reported may then deal with the matter in the same way as any other contempt proceedings.

9.6   What are the possible decisions of the Tribunal?

s. 14(1)

Where the appeal is against the refusal to register or alter registered particulars, or against the service of a notice, the Tribunal may allow the appeal or substitute such other decision or notice as the Registrar could have made or served, if:

(a)   the Registrar's action was not in accordance with the law; or

(b)   the Registrar ought to have exercised his direction differently.

The Tribunal are not therefore simply confined to issues of law. They may review any determination of fact on which the refusal or notice was based. For example, the Tribunal may decide that registration is permissible with the addition of some further information, or they may substitute an enforcement notice for a de-registration notice if they consider that it is more appropriate in that particular case. Where, however, the Tribunal can find no fault with the exercise of the Registrar's discretion and the refusal or notice was made entirely in accordance with the law, they must dismiss the appeal.

Where the appeal is against the Registrar's decision to include a statement in the refusal of registration that his decision should take effect as a matter of urgency, the Tribunal may decide that the notification of refusal shall be treated as if the statement of urgency were not included in the refusal. This will mean that the person can carry out the particular activities covered by the application until an appeal against refusal to register is determined or withdrawn or the period during which an appeal may be made has expired.   s. 14(3)

Similarly, where the appeal is against a statement in a notice that it should take effect as a matter or urgency, the Tribunal may either direct that the notice shall have effect as if it did not contain the statement or that the inclusion of the statement shall not have effect in respect of any part of the notice. In the latter case the Tribunal may make such modifications in the notice as may be required.   s. 14(4)

9.7   Is there an appeal from the Tribunal?

Any party to an appeal to the Tribunal may make a further appeal to the courts, but only on a point of law. If the address of the person who was the appellant before the Tribunal was in England or Wales, the appeal will be to the High Court. If the address of the appellant was in Scotland the appeal will be to the Court of Session, and in Northern Ireland it will be to the High Court of Northern Ireland.   s. 14(5)

Chapter 10

What rights are introduced for data subjects? — the Courts

10.1 Introduction

The DPA creates a number of basic rights for data subjects. These are:

s. 21   (a)   The right of access to personal data.
s. 22   (b)   The right to seek compensation for damage suffered where the data held are inaccurate.
s. 23   (c)   The right to claim compensation where personal data are lost or where there is unauthorised access.
s. 24   (d)   A limited right to have inaccurate data rectified or erased.

10.2 Access rights

s. 21(1)
The DPA gives individuals two basic rights enforceable against data users. First, a right to be informed by any data user, subject to exemptions mentioned later, whether that user holds personal data on him. Second, the right to be supplied with a copy of that information. This may take an alphabetic form or a pictorial form. For example, a set of finger-prints or pictures of the data subject would need to be included if they were on file in image form, in addition to the more usual details held in alphabetic form.

A data user cannot frustrate the object of these access provisions by supplying information to the data subject in an encoded form. If the information supplied is not intelligible without an explanation the information must be accompanied by an explanation of the terms and codes used. For example, an entry on a customer file of 'W' would need to be accompanied by an explanation that 'W' stands for 'wholesaler'.

s. 21(2)
The Act makes it clear that if a data subject asks a data user

92

whether he holds information on him, the data user will treat that request also as a request to provide a copy of any such information.

As pointed out in Chapter 5, data users may choose to make a number of separate registrations for different purposes. One reason for following such a practice is to facilitate the granting of subject access and avoid having to search all their data bases for data relating to a particular individual. Where separate registration entries have been made, data subjects must make a separate request and pay a fee in respect of the data to which each entry relates.   s. 6(2)

A data user is not obliged to respond to a request for information unless:

(a)   The data user is satisfied that the person making the request is the data subject.   s. 21(4)

(b)   The request is made in writing.   s.21(2)

(c)   Revealing the information would not disclose information relating to another individual who can be identified from the information.   s.21(4)

(d)   The request is accompanied by the appropriate fee which is not to exceed a statutory maximum to be fixed under the Act.   s. 21(2)

In view of the prohibition on the disclosure of personal data to third parties, it is important that data users take steps to check the identity of the individual making a request before data are released. The Act allows the data user to impose reasonable requirements in respect of the individual making a request to supply information to establish his identity. If the individual fails to satisfy such requirements the data should not be revealed.   s. 5(2)(d)

s. 23

s. 23(4)
(a)

Reasonableness is an inherently flexible notion and hence the standard that might be expected may well vary in accordance with the sensitivity of the data to be disclosed. However, all data users must exercise a minimum standard. This might be a matching of data given in the request with data held on file. An address or reference number may well suffice. Higher standards of identification may include having requests notarised by a legally qualified individual, or even requiring fingerprint checks for the most sensitive data.

If data users impose oppressive or unreasonable requirements the Registrar's attention could well be drawn to the matter and he may make informal representations to data users, backed up by the ultimate threat of an enforcement notice (see Chapter 8).

Alternatively, the data subject may apply to the courts, who would then consider the reasonableness of a data user's identity checks.

It should be noted that, although the Act does not impose criminal sanctions on a person who impersonates a data subject in order to obtain information held by a data user, if such a person were to make such a request in writing, criminal sanctions could be imposed under ss. 9(1)(a) and 10(1)(c) of the Forgery and Counterfeiting Act 1981.

s. 21(4)(b)

A data user is not obliged to comply with a request for information if disclosing this would reveal information relating to another individual who can be identified. In such circumstances the data user should only give access to a data subject if he is satisfied that the other identifiable individual has consented to the disclosure. However, simply because there exists information relating to another person within the data does not mean that the data user is completely free to withhold the data. The Act requires the data user to supply as much of the information sought by the data subject as can be supplied without actually disclosing the identity of the other individual concerned.

s. 21(5)

For example, if a data user has on his computer records personal data stating that Mr X has reported certain facts in respect of data subject Y, the data user may disclose the information providing he omits any reference to Mr X, or is satisfied Mr X has agreed to disclosure.

At the time of writing there is no indication of the level of fee that is likely to be fixed as the statutory maximum. Indeed, some companies may, as a means of fostering good public relations, elect to charge no fee for supplying the data. In debate, the Minister of State at the Home Office indicated that he expected the fee to be somewhere between £3 and £8, a figure calculated by governmental data users as the fee necessary to recoup their expected costs. It is worth pointing out that the equivalent fee chargeable for access to a credit reference agency file under the Consumer Credit Act 1974 is £1. However, credit files tend to be relatively easy to trace and extract, usually containing a list of any county court judgments against the individual and his history of previous credit transactions. Access under the DPA may be a rather more complex matter for the data user, especially if personal data are held about a data subject in various parts of a system which perhaps incorporates a number of microcomputers possibly linked to a mainframe. The data also have to be checked in order to see whether any part is exempt from subject access, and that no information is revealed about another identifiable individual. Thus, subject access for most data users is likely to involve greater expense than for a credit reference agency giving access to a consumer file.

Data users are required to comply with a request within 40 days, once having satisfied the identity requirements. In practice, most data users could delay processing requests but because of the need, to be discussed later, for providing the information as at the time of the request it is likely that speedy attention will be thought desirable. Experience in other European countries suggests that the number of requests in proportion to the number of records held will be relatively small. **s. 21(6)** **s. 21(7)**

The information to be supplied to the data subject is the data existing at the time the request is received. The information may, however, take account of any amendments or deletions made to the data between the request being received and the time when the information is supplied, though such changes may only be taken into account where they would have been made regardless of the receipt of the request. Thus it is not permissible once the request for access has been received to amend or delete data in order to be able to supply a less embarrassing version to the subject. **s. 21(7)**

In the case of personal data consisting of examination marks or other information held for the purpose of determining the results of an examination, the Act makes special provision to alleviate any administrative problems that might arise for data users when faced with requests for access before results are officially announced. In such cases the 40-day period within which the request for access must be dealt with does not commence until the date the results are announced. Such date may be the date they are first published or, if not published, when they are first made available or communicated to the candidate in question. The request must, however, be dealt with within five months of its receipt. The intention is that examining bodies should be able to put requests for access to one side until they have completed the marking process and announced the results. Because, however, the Convention requires access to be granted 'without excessive delay', a five-month maximum is laid down, within which data users must respond to a request. The data may be held by the body which actually conducts the examination or by any other body which contributes to the assessment process. For example, if examination scripts are marked by a school before being moderated by an examining board the data held by the school will also be covered by this section. For the purpose of this provision, 'examination' includes work which is the subject of continuous **s. 35(1)** **s. 35(4)** **s. 35(5)** assessment, and not only marks are covered by the provision but any associated information. Examination marks include not only those used in traditional educational establishments, but also any skill or aptitude tests conducted by any organisation. For example, typist proficiency testing upon application for employment is included.

Examining bodies may prefer not to make use of the special provisions since the information to be supplied is more exhaustive than that required under the general provision. For example, if a student requests access to his examination marks that may have been subject to revisions during the course of the examining procedure, the information supplied without taking advantage of special provisions is that existing at the time of the request. However, if the special provisions are used, the full set of marks as they have been adjusted between the request date and compliance must be disclosed.

In the event of a data user failing to comply with a request for information, a data subject has the right to invite a court to order compliance with the request. The court, however, has the discretion to refuse to make an order if it considers that, in all the circumstances, the data user's refusal was reasonable. The court may consider the seventh data protection principle and the interpretation of that principle given in sch. 1 to the Act, which refers to the data subject rights of access 'at reasonable intervals'. The Registrar in interpreting that principle shall have regard to: 'the nature of the data, the purpose for which the data are held and the frequency with which the data are altered'.

The Act elaborates on this theme by reminding the court to consider the 'frequency with which the applicant has made requests to the data user'. If it appears that the applicant's motives in making the request are frivolous, abusive or vexatious, the court would be more inclined to refuse to make an order.

It is worth reiterating at this stage that data subjects do not need to be of full age in order to exercise the rights under the Act. Provided that a person is of an age where the common law would consider them capable of acting on their own behalf, they may exercise the rights under the Act.

The Secretary of State may, by order, provide a procedure for requests for access made on behalf of individuals incapable of managing their own affairs by reason of mental disorder.

A data subject's right of access is limited in certain specified situations. This right may be completely eliminated as, for example, in the case of a data user processing statistical and research

s. 21(8)

sch. 1
Part II
para. 5(2)
s. 21(8)

s. 21(9)

s. 33(6)

data. In some cases, as, for example, health data, the Secretary of State will have delegated powers to remove or modify a subject's access rights. This ministerial action also exists for social work records but the extent of power is limited to circumstances in which the Secretary of State considers that the access provisions would be likely to prejudice effective social work. A third possibility exists, that is where other legislation confers greater rights of access upon the data subject. In such a case the other legislation takes precedence. For example, the Consumer Credit Act 1974 confers greater rights of access upon data subjects and hence access should be obtained via that Act.

It should also be noted that the right of access provisions are not available to data subjects until a period of two years has elapsed from the 'appointed day': that is, 11 November 1987. See Chapter 14 for a discussion of the timetable for implementing the Act.

s. 29(1)

s. 29(2)

s. 41(4)

10.3   Compensation for inaccuracy

The DPA is in essence a preventative statute rather than a remedial one: it seeks to ensure that things do not go wrong in the first place by the application of sound principles of data management. However, if such principles are ignored and a data subject suffers injury in the form of financial loss the Act provides the remedy of compensation. In awarding compensation for damage, the courts may also take into account any distress that the data subject may have suffered as a result of inaccurate data.

s. 22(1)

The Act provides that a data subject who suffers damage by reason of the inaccuracy of the data is entitled to claim compensation from the data user. Such a right to claim compensation is in addition to any other rights he might have under, for example, the law of defamation. The term 'inaccuracy' means that the data are either incorrect or misleading on any matter of fact. Matters of opinion, however erroneous, cannot be categorised as 'inaccurate', however misleading they may be.

s. 22(1)

s. 22(4)

A data user may, however, avoid having to pay compensation in the following circumstances. First, where the damage was suffered before 11 May 1986. Second, if the data user can prove that he had taken such care as in all the circumstances he was reasonably required to take to ensure the accuracy of the data at the time the damage was caused. Third, where the data were received either from the data subject himself or from a third party and the user has marked the data

s. 22(2)

as having been so received. Thus, if the data user receives inaccurate information from the data subject himself or any other person and proceeds to process that data, he cannot be liable to pay compensation as long as the data or information extracted from the data indicate that the data came from someone other than the data user.

In the event of a data subject requesting access and subsequently finding the data stored by the data user were obtained from an outside source and are inaccurate or misleading, he is entitled to insist that the data user indicates in the data or in any information subsequently extracted that the data subject regards the data as inaccurate or misleading. If the data user does not include such an indication then he cannot avoid having to pay compensation in the event that such inaccuracy causes damage to the subject. Thus, there is nothing but the powers of the courts to prevent a data user maintaining a collection of erroneous data on data subjects provided that:

s. 22(2)

(a) the data were obtained from a third party; and, if applicable,

(b) he indicates on the data, or on any information extracted from the data, whenever a data subject has questioned the accuracy of the data.

In the debates on this part of the Act, the Minister of State at the Home Office justified the section on third-party information in the following terms:

Where a data user records inaccurate information supplied by someone else, the data are accurate. They are an accurate record of what someone else said, which is why this complies with the Convention.

It should be stressed, however, that although the subject would be unable to claim compensation under the DPA, he may be able to claim damages under the law of defamation if inaccurate and defamatory information has been published about him.

In terms of the law and legal remedies, s. 22 represents a somewhat radical reform. In effect, it amounts to the creation of a novel statutory civil liability, that of processing inaccurate information. It is a liability from which the data user can only escape by proving:

(a)   that he obtained the data from a third party and he gives an indication that the data subject considers the data to be inaccurate; or   s. 22(2)

(b)   that he took all reasonable care to ensure the data were accurate; or   s. 22(2)

(c)   no loss arises to the data subject as a result of the inaccuracy.   s. 22(1)

10.4   Compensation for loss or unauthorised access

The DPA allows a data subject to claim compensation from a data user or computer bureau for damage suffered in three situations:

(a)   Where data are lost.   s. 23(1)(a)

(b)   Where data are destroyed without the authority of the data user or bureau.   s. 23(1)(b)

(c)   Where data are disclosed without authority or access to data is obtained by a third party without the authority of the data user or bureau.   s. 23(1)(c)

It should be noted that this right to compensation only exists where the data are disclosed without the authority of the user or where, as a result of his negligence, an outsider gains access to the data.

In awarding compensation for damage the courts may also take into account any distress that the data subject has suffered by reason of the loss, destruction, disclosure or access.

This right does not apply to damage suffered before the end of two months from the date the Act is passed. This section became operative on the 12 September 1984.

It is a defence to any of the above three claims if the user or bureau can establish that they have taken such care as in all the circumstances was reasonably required to prevent the loss, destruction, disclosure or access in question.

In essence, s. 23 provides a course of action where there is damage as a result of breach of the eighth data protection principle. That principle requires data users and computer bureaux to take appropriate security measures against unauthorised access to, or alteration, disclosure or destruction of, personal data and against accidental loss or destruction of personal data. The section covers not only deliberate action resulting in loss to the data subject but also negligent disclosure whereby a third party is able to gain direct access to equipment and operate that equipment illicitly himself.

It should be stressed that the provision only provides the data subject with a right to compensation where the destruction or disclosure of the data was unauthorised by the data user or computer bureau. For example, if a data user deliberately discloses data to an outsider, then such a disclosure would be an 'authorised disclosure' and a data subject could not claim compensation under the DPA. If the disclosure was to a person specified in the registration particulars as someone to whom disclosure might be made, then no action could be taken against the data user. If, however, the disclosure was to some other person, then the Registrar could take action and criminal proceedings could be commenced against the data user. The individual data subject would not, however, be able to claim compensation under the Act because the disclosure was authorised.

In a debate on the Act the government spokesman justified confining the compensation rights to unauthorised destruction or disclosure on the basis that the 'concept of paying compensation for damages which result from the dissemination of true information, regardless of any breach of confidence, is a novel one which ought not to be considered solely in the context of automatic processing, at which the Bill is aimed'.

As the above quote indicates, where accurate data are deliberately disclosed to outsiders and the data subject is damaged, legal redress may be available in an action for breach of confidence, although the law in this area is in a somewhat unsatisfactory state (see Chapter 1).

10.5   Rectification and erasure

CCA
1974
s. 153
s. 24

Unlike the Consumer Credit Act 1974, under which individuals are given a right to have an inaccurate entry corrected, the DPA only gives data subjects the right of correction by taking proceedings in -the courts.

s. 24(1)

s. 22(3)
s. 22

s. 24(1)

Provided that the court is satisfied that personal data held by a data user are inaccurate, the court may, on application from the data subject, order the rectification or erasure of the data. The term 'inaccurate data' carries the meaning of information which is incorrect or misleading about any matter of fact. Furthermore, in contrast to the provisions on compensation for inaccuracy, rectification or erasure is permitted where data contain an expression of opinion which appears to the court to be based on inaccurate data.

Even where the data accurately record information received from third parties, the courts may make the normal order for the full rectification or erasure of the data, or one of the following orders:

100

(a)   If the information came from the subject or a third party and,   s. 22(2)
if appropriate, the subject considers it inaccurate or misleading, the
requirements have been complied with, and thereafter the court may,
instead of making an order for full rectification, make an order
requiring the data to be supplemented by a statement of the true facts.

(b)   If all or any of the requirements mentioned in para(a) above
have not been complied with the court may order insertion of the
missing indications and also have the option to make further orders
requiring the data to be supplemented with a statement of the true
facts.

In most instances it must be assumed, in the absence of cogent
arguments from the parties, that the court will simply order the
rectification or erasure of the data in question.

Where a data subject can satisfy a court that he has suffered   s. 24(3)
damage because of the unauthorised disclosure of personal data, or
of access to the data having been obtained without the authority of
the data user or bureau, the court may order the complete erasure of
the data. The court must, however, be satisfied that there is a
substantial risk of further unauthorised disclosure of, or
unauthorised access to, the data. Where, however, the liability for
breach of the security provisions falls on a person carrying on a
computer bureau, the court cannot make an order for erasure unless
steps are taken for notifying the data user and giving him an
opportunity to be heard. The data user may have engaged the services
of a bureau in good faith after having inquired into its security
arrangements. The provision, therefore, enables the data user to be
consulted before the data are erased, and to make representations to
the court. He may, for example, wish to engage the services of another
bureau with better security arrangements, and have the data
transferred to that bureau. The court cannot, in any case, act unless
the damage was suffered after 12 September 1984.

10.6   Who will hear claims by data subjects?

Given the intensely technical nature of the DPA and the flexible   s. 25
manner in which many of the provisions are drafted, it might have
been assumed that special tribunals, similar to industrial tribunals,
would have been created to hear all claims. That is not the case,
however. All claims under these provisions will come before the
ordinary courts, that is, in England the High Court or a county court
and in Scotland the Court of Session or the Sheriff Court.

Chapter 11

What rights are introduced for data subjects? — the Registrar

11.1 Introduction

So far we have examined the rights of data subjects to pursue claims before the courts. Not all data subjects will, however, wish to go to the trouble and expense of legal action. Indeed, many may not even be aware of their rights. In a great many cases a letter from the Registrar asking data users why they have ignored a request for access from a data subject may be far more effective and efficient than the sometimes laborious processes of the law.

11.2 How does the Registrar deal with complaints?

s. 36(2)
The Registrar may consider any complaint that the data protection principles, or any provision of the DPA, has been or is being contravened. Indeed, if the complaint appears to him to raise a matter of substance and it has been made without delay by a person directly affected, usually a data subject, the Registrar must consider it. In the event that the Registrar decides to pursue a complaint he must notify the complainant of the result of his deliberations and of any action which he proposes to take.

The Registrar is not therefore bound to investigate every direct complaint made to him by a data subject; he simply has a discretion to take up those complaints which are not matters of substance which allege that one of the principles, or any of the provisions of the Act, have been contravened. If the new statutory rights given to data subjects have been infringed, that is essentially a matter for the courts to determine, not the Registrar. However, in so far as the infringement involves a breach of the principles, such as a denial of access, the Registrar may consider exercising any of the powers outlined in Chapter 7. It may be, for example, that a data subject is concerned about the accuracy of data to which he has no right of access because the particular data are exempt from the subject access provisions. In such circumstances a data subject may make representations to the Registrar to the effect that he is concerned about the accuracy of data held by a data user and the Registrar may then investigate the matter. The Registrar cannot, however, raise an action on behalf of a data subject in respect of the subject's statutory rights; he can only seek to influence a data user by informal discussions, formal representations or recourse to his supervisory powers to issue notices or institute criminal proceedings.

Complaints received from data subjects will be an important part of the Registrar's work. Given the relatively small number of staff at his disposal such complaints are indeed likely to form the first stages of most investigations that the Registrar undertakes. It is not, however, the intention that he investigate all complaints. Some he may consider to be ill-founded or frivolous. On the other hand, he may receive several individual complaints against a data user in respect of breach of one of the principles but decide to pursue only one complaint as a test case at less cost and greater speed than a full-scale investigation of them all.

In summary, whilst data subjects have an absolute right to pursue claims through the courts, they cannot insist that the Registrar takes action. They may seek advice from the Registrar on what course of action they may have and they may invite the Registrar to initiate an investigation of a data user. If the complaint raises a matter of substance, the Registrar must consider it.

In extreme cases where data subjects consider that the Registrar is not performing his statutory duties or otherwise acting unreasonably and in abuse of his powers, they may apply for a judicial review of his actions in the same way that any other public official's activities may be subjected to judicial scrutiny. However, such an investigation would not be appropriate merely because an aggrieved data subject disagrees with the Registrar in the exercise of his discretionary powers.

PART 4

How will users need to respond?

Chapter 12

What are the administrative implications of the Act?

12.1 Introduction

Managers reading this book who have responsibility for implementing the DPA will have noted implications for their companies at many points in this book. This chapter brings together these points and outlines procedures for dealing with them. The actions will vary from organisation to organisation but essentially the same tasks and decisions will need to be considered by all: this chapter is a discussion of those tasks and decisions and of the factors influencing them.

The decisions can be grouped into six categories which reflect the stage in the registration and use process that they need to be considered. These are:

(a) Policy matters.
(b) Preparation for registration.
(c) Maintaining a current registration.
(d) Processing requests for access.
(e) Updating records to reflect changes required by a data subject.
(f) Anticipating problems.

12.2 Policy matters

Each organisation will need to appoint a senior officer to coordinate the efforts of the organisation with regard to data protection. The tasks that require to be undertaken suggests that if a director is to be selected then he should be the director responsible for the information systems function. In reality the officer selected will delegate a great deal of the effort to his subordinates. These operating personnel will require detailed knowledge of the systems operating on the organisation's mainframe computer and the ability to interact with many individuals in the organisation who operate micro-computer systems. Individuals such as 'systems analysts' strongly suggest themselves for selection as operating personnel. This would suggest that the director responsible for the computer department should be appointed as the responsible officer.

The organisation will need to consider the posture it intends to adopt in responding to the Act. A negative posture would involve removing personal data from the computer; delaying responses to requests for access to the maximum of 40 days usually allowed by the Act; demanding extreme proof of identity prior to responding to a request and generally using the Act to minimise its obligations to data subjects. A positive posture would involve offering copies of the information held at no charge; dealing with such requests promptly; providing suitable forms to correct any inaccurate data held and generally acting in the spirit of the Act. The decision on the posture to adopt is a board matter. In reality different postures may be selected for different systems depending upon the sensitivity of the data held. It is not inconceivable that some universities will adopt a negative posture rather than release examination marks to students promptly.

A major consideration that requires to be decided at the outset is the responsibility that will be retained by the responsible officer and that which will be delegated. Some organisations, particularly those that utilise an organisational philosophy of decentralisation, may decide to delegate virtually all responsibility for registration to the decentralised units and produce multiple registrations. Others of a more centrally organised nature may take any point between these two extremes. Such decisions will be strongly influenced by the practicality of a central group ascertaining organisational information flows. In many organisations this will be highly impractical and hence a decentralised approach will be used.

A further consideration required is to devote sufficient resources to the project. It should be recognised from the outset that considerable effort may be required to satisfy the provisions of the Act. For example, it may be necessary to develop new programs to provide a complete listing of all data on a file relating to a data subject as it is possible this does not presently exist. In general the board should recognise the possible magnitude of changes required and allocate sufficient resources.

12.3 Preparation for registration

As a preparation for registration a file of all relevant data held by the organisation must be compiled. A request to all automatic processors of data within the organisation asking for an overview of all data held should provide sufficient details to decide which systems should be further investigated. Not only should the obvious data processors, such as the accounts department and the personnel department, be questioned but also users of microcomputers whether they be managers or other employees should be involved. In general organisations should err on the side of asking too many employees rather than too few. Larger firms may well decide to organise seminars to familiarise selected employees with the Act to ensure that no relevant data is omitted from the registration.

Having attained an overview of all the systems these details can be examined to select those that appear to be relevant to the Act. For these, further investigations should be conducted to determine eligibility. When a system is deemed to be relevant the following details should be collected:

(a)   A description of the personal data held by the system and the purpose or purposes for which it is held or used. Thought should be given to the purposes as not only the obvious ones should be registered but also purposes for which the data are used only occasionally or have not yet been used but may be in the future.

(b)   A description of the sources from which the data user intends or may wish to obtain the data. Personal data files may well originate from many sources and hence extensive thought should be given to this aspect of the registration. For example, a file of data held on employees could originate with at least the employee, referees, other management employees providing reports, external selection agencies, Inland Revenue, DHSS, and the payroll department. In addition many other individuals and organisations could contribute to this information.

(c)   A description of any person or persons to whom the data user intends or may wish to disclose the data. Thought should be given to this item since if a destination is excluded an amendment may have to be made to the registration particulars.

(d)   The names of or a description of any countries outside the UK to which the organisation may wish to transfer data. A desire to transfer data to other subscribers to the Convention should not present difficulty in registration but transfer to non-signatory countries may be challenged by the Registrar if he feels this may lead to a contravention of the principles.

Having collected the above details relating to each relevant system it is necessary for a knowledgeable individual to ascertain if the details comply with the Act. In case of doubt, reference could be made to any relevant codes of practice that have been approved by the Registrar or in the event of extreme problems the Registrar may be consulted. In general the pertinent question is: Does the system contravene any of the principles?

The remaining aspect of registration involves obtaining the relevant forms from the office of the Registrar or a central post office and duly completing and returning them with the appropriate fee. It then becomes a matter of waiting for the Registrar's reply which will be forthcoming within six months. Processing will be allowed whilst awaiting the Registrar's decision.

Remember that an organisation always has the option of removing any sensitive data from the computer to avoid registration.

12.4   Maintaining a current registration

The matter is by no means completed having obtained a registration: it then becomes necessary to keep the registration up to date. This might be necessary for any of the following reasons:

(a)   The registration period will shortly expire.
(b)   The registered details of an existing system have altered.
(c)   A new system has been added.
(d)   An existing system is no longer in use.

Registrations last for three years. It might be assumed that renewal of a previously satisfactory entry will be automatic subject to the compilation of the paperwork. Organisations will be reminded by the Registrar when to renew their registration.

It may be necessary to amend registered particulars. Organisations will need to monitor all the items in the original application (description of the data held, sources of the data, persons it will be disclosed to, any countries to which the data is to be sent) to report any amendments. This is the item that is likely to cause problems for many organisations as it is a job which will continue after the initial hullabaloo of registration. The major problem is recognising that a change has occurred. It will be necessary to maintain an awareness of the Act both in systems analysts and users as either group can effectively cause a need to amend the registration particulars. Current awareness of something that may appear trivial to operating managers is always difficult to achieve but attempts must be made. This can partly be achieved by adding a 'privacy audit' to the internal audit function. If it appears from this that relevant changes are being made to systems but not notified to the Registrar a repeat of the initial awareness measures may be called for.

Possibly a greater problem exists upon the creation of new systems that require to be registered. If such systems constitute large projects then they are likely to involve systems analysts who should know of the Act as part of their professional training. Such cases are unlikely to lead to difficulty but imagine the problems when a newly appointed manager or even worse a remotely located representative decides to create a very small system on his own personal computer. Just about the only way to control this is to insist that all systems are registered with a responsible official when they are created irrespective of the need to register under the DPA. That official will then decide if the new system requires DPA registration. Some observers of this Act have noted that it will force organisations to tighten their internal controls to comply with the Act: this is an example of just such a necessary control. Information on all applications processed should be known by the organisation to avoid reinventing the wheel but alas it is all too infrequently available today in many organisations.

When a system is no longer in use it should be removed from the register. The internal controls to capture changes should identify such systems so that a request for removal may be sent to the Registrar.

12.5   Processing requests for access

The Act provides that a data subject has a right to access data held concerning himself. A data user therefore needs to create procedures for dealing with such requests. Prior to discussing the form of these procedures it is worth noting that countries with such legislation generally record a very low volume of requests for access. This, of course, might not be the situation in the UK but most pundits suggest that this is likely to be the case.

The first important task is to appoint an officer to coordinate the processing of such requests for access. He will act as the link between requestors and the departments that will supply the data.

The first task on receipt of a request is to check that it is correctly composed:

(a) It must be in writing.

(b) It must be accompanied by the appropriate fee.

(c) It must contain the details of the files to be searched if the organisation has opted for multiple registrations.

If the request passes the first clerical hurdle it is then necessary for the official to satisfy himself that the requestor is in fact the person he purports to be. This is most difficult to achieve with a high degree of certainty without forcing the data subject to undertake a great deal of effort. At the simplest level an organisation could ask the requestor to supply an item of information they already possess to act as a check. An individual's National Insurance number might be a most appropriate item to request if this is available to the organisation. A much more stringent request would be to ask the data subject to have his request notarised by a notary public. This would certainly be most inconvenient to the data subject but may be necessary for very sensitive data. Organisations will need to be careful not to use this requirement as a restriction on the supply of information as data subjects have a right to complain to the courts or the Registrar that access is being unnecessarily denied, and may do so if there are unreasonable requirements for proof of identity.

The officer, having satisfied himself of the identity of the requestor, should then pass the request to the processor for the request to be satisfied. It would be useful for the officer to keep a master record of unsatisfied requests to ensure that processors reply to his request in a suitable time for him to pass the information to the data subject within the 40 days normally allowed. There is no need to stop processing the affected files in the normal course of operations even if this may change the record relating to an outstanding request.

All information on the data subject relating to the registration particulars quoted in the request should be printed from whatever sources have to be used. If an organisation has only a single entry in the register this may mean interrogating many files.

As the information arrives from each source it should be retained until all the information is available. At that stage the information should be considered in total to identify if any individual, other than the data subject, can be identified. If such other references do exist they should be deleted. Any of the data that could be described as disclosing organisational intentions can be deleted from the data if so required although they may be disclosed if desired. In addition consideration should be given to whether the data fall into one of the exempt categories, for example health data, to which individuals may be denied access. Any codes that may be in the data should be explained in an accompanying note. Having edited the data as described it would be wise to retain a copy of the data as dispatched in case of subsequent litigation. All that remains now is to dispatch the data to the data subject. Recorded delivery would be a useful method of dispatch to act as a proof of responding to the request.

12.6 Updating records to reflect changes required by a data subject

When a data subject receives a copy of the personal data on him held by a data user he may well check it and if it is erroneous may inform the data user of any corrections required. In fact the data user does not, by law, have to amend the data unless directed to do so by a court or the Registrar. However, as it is likely to be in a data user's interests to retain accurate and up-to-date information, the usual course of action will be to amend the data. Hence a procedure should be established to amend offending files when inaccuracies are reported by a data subject. The computer procedures to do this will probably exist already as there is a capability to amend records in most systems. The only changes required, therefore, in most organisations, are to provide the authority and the necessary forms to the coordinating officer to effect amendments to files. It would be courteous to provide the data subject with a record of the file subsequent to the change although this is not required by the DPA.

12.7 Anticipating problems

There are a small number of tasks that can be undertaken by a data user to avoid problems that do not fit in the classification used to date. These are considered at this point.

First, a data user may care to insure against possible liability in connection with the DPA. A number of insurance companies will quote rates to assume liability in the event of damages being awarded against an organisation.

113

Second, the coming into force of the relevant provision can be used as a defence to avoid liability in the case of claims for compensation for inaccurate data: it would therefore appear sensible to retain copies of all files held prior to 11 May 1986. These should be retained for a period of time, considerably longer than the usual retention period, for use in the event of litigation.

Third, to maintain a constant awareness of the Act it may be worthwhile including a message each time a user logs onto a relevant database. The message would include the uses to which that data can be put within the registration. No doubt this would not be read by users but it may be some sort of defence to a lawsuit specifying use for an unregistered purpose.

Lastly the Act imposes a requirement upon data users to maintain adequate security arrangements. Most users will have examined their security arrangements and be constantly monitoring factors that might affect them in the normal course of business. For users that do no adequately consider security this Act could be used to force organisational management to devote resources to security. This legislation can be seen very positively by data processing managers as a means of securing increased resources for a very important but often neglected task: that of monitoring security arrangements.

Chapter 13

Does the Act have international implications?

13.1 What is the objective of the Convention and which countries does it extend to?

As indicated in Chapter 2, one of the principal motives behind the DPA is the desire to comply with the Council of Europe Convention for the Protection of Individuals with Regard to Automatic Processing of Personal Data (the Convention). At the heart of the Convention lie two principal concerns. First, that data users in countries with privacy and data protection controls might seek to relocate their operations to countries with no protective legislation, so called 'data havens', thus frustrating the legislative policy of their home state. The second and related concern was that in order to deter data users from transferring their operations to other areas, countries would impose controls, such as export licences, on the transfer of data outside their territory, jeopardising the free flow of information. Hence the Convention, which states in the preamble that it recognises the necessity of reconciling 'the fundamental values of the respect for privacy and the free flow of information between peoples'.

It is worth stressing that the Convention emanates from the Council of Europe in Strasbourg, not the European Community in Brussels, although the Council keeps in close contact with the Commission of the European Communities. The Council was created in 1949 with the aim of achieving 'a greater unity between its members for the purpose of safeguarding and realising the ideals and principles which are their common heritage and facilitating their economic and social progress'. It consists of the following twenty-one states: Austria, Belgium, Cyprus, Denmark, France, Federal Republic of Germany, Greece, Iceland, Italy, Liechtenstein, Luxembourg, Malta, the Netherlands, Norway, Portugal, Republic of Ireland, Spain, Sweden, Switzerland, Turkey and the United Kingdom. However, art. 23 of the Convention does provide that non-member states of the Council may be invited by the Committee of Ministers to accede to the Convention. This could include, amongst others, Australia, Canada, New Zealand and the United States of America.

13.2 Does the Act comply with the Convention?

It has been suggested that the Act does not in fact comply with the Convention. In its original form, clause 28 of the Bill exempted personal data held for the control of immigration and a strong case was made to the effect that such an exemption was not permitted within the terms of the Convention. The government then agreed to drop that particular exemption.

It has also been argued forcefully that the limited definition of personal data in the Act is inconsistent with the definition in the Convention which describes personal data as 'any information relating to an identified or identifiable individual' (art. 2). Similarly, it has been argued that the exemption from subject access covering physical or mental health is contrary to the Convention.

Nevertheless, it must be assumed that the government is justified in asserting that the Act is consistent with the Convention and the UK will be permitted to ratify it. The fact that the UK has chosen to enact data protection laws which adopt a narrow interpretation of the terms of the Convention is hardly sufficient grounds for asserting that the UK has not, in good faith, complied with the letter and spirit of the Convention.

13.3 What does the Convention say about transborder data flows?

Article 12 of the Convention defines transborder data flows, in wide terms, as the transfer across borders, by whatever medium, of personal data. The article then goes on to state that a party to the Convention shall not for the sole purpose of the protection of privacy, prohibit or subject to special authorisation, transborder flows of personal data going to the territory of another party. It is implicit in that provision that where data is transferred to a non-party state, such prohibitions or special authorisation may be imposed.

The article does, however, permit restrictions on the free flow of information between states that are parties to the Convention in two situations. First, it allows a party to restrict the flow of information where it has legislation which includes specific regulations for certain categories of personal data because of the nature of that data, and the other party does not provide an equivalent protection. Second, when the transfer is made from a signatory's territory to the territory of a non-signatory state, via the territory of another signatory the sender may depart from the Convention in order to avoid the transfers resulting in circumvention of its legislation.

13.4 What powers does the Registrar have to regulate transborder data flows under the Act?

It will be recalled that when a data user applies for registration he must lodge with the Registrar 'the names or a description of any countries or territories outside the United Kingdom to which he intends or may wish directly or indirectly to transfer the data'.   s. 4(3)(e)

If a data user, knowingly or recklessly, transfers data to any country or territory outside the UK, other than those mentioned in the registration entry, the user commits an offence.   s. 5(2)(d)

The Registrar is thus able to monitor transborder data flows and, if necessary, impose conditions and limitations on such transfers. The ultimate sanction that the Registrar possesses in such circumstances is a transfer prohibition notice. If it appears to the Registrar that an applicant for registration or a registered person proposes to transfer personal data to a place outside the UK, he may serve such a notice. Obviously, such a notice cannot be issued in respect of the transfer of data which are already outside the UK. The notice may prohibit the transference of the data either absolutely or until specified steps have been taken in order to protect the interests of data subjects.   s. 12

The power of the Registrar to issue a transfer prohibition notice is modelled on art. 12 of the Convention discussed earlier. In essence, it depends upon whether the destination of the data is a state that is party to the Convention or not.

In a case where the state to which the personal data are to be sent is not bound by the Council of Europe Convention, the Registrar may issue the notice where he is satisfied that the transfer will contravene, or lead to contravention of, any of the principles.   s. 12(2)

Where the destination state is bound by the Convention, the Registrar's discretion to serve a transfer prohibition notice is more limited. In such circumstances, the Registrar must be satisfied that one of the following circumstances exist. First, the receiving data user intends to give instructions for the further transfer of the data to a state not bound by the Convention: the Registrar must be satisfied that such further transfer is likely to contravene, or lead to a   s. 12(3) (a)

117

contravention of, any of the principles.

s. 12(3)
(b)

Second, if the data come within the category of sensitive personal data (race, political or religious beliefs, health, sexual life or criminal convictions), whereby the Secretary of State can modify or supplement the data protection principles for the purpose of

s. 2(3)

providing additional safeguards, the Registrar must be satisfied that the transfer is likely to contravene, or lead to a contravention of, the supplemented principles.

s. 12(4)

When the Registrar is deciding whether to serve a transfer prohibition notice, he must consider whether the notice is necessary to prevent damage or distress to any person. In addition, he must have regard to the general desirability of facilitating the free transfer of data between the UK and other states and territories, as enshrined in the preamble to the Convention.

s. 12(5)
(a)

A transfer prohibition notice must contain the following information:

(a)   A statement of the principle or principles which the Registrar is satisfied are likely to be contravened.

(b)   The reasons why the Registrar has reached the conclusion that the principles are being breached.

s. 12(5)
(b)

(c)   Particulars of the right of appeal to the Data Protection Tribunal.

(d)   The time when the notice is to take effect.

s. 12(6)

The time specified in the notice, when it is to take effect, must not be before the expiry of the appeal period which is yet to be specified. If an appeal is made, the notice shall not take effect until the Tribunal confirms the Registrar's decision or the appeal is formally withdrawn.

The Registrar may, however, consider that there are special circumstances that necessitate the notice taking effect as a matter of

s. 12(7)

urgency. In such circumstances, the Registrar must include a statement to that effect in the notice, and the data user will be required to take the appropriate action within seven days of the date when the notice is served. There is, however, a specific right of appeal

s. 13(3)

against the Registrar's decision to include the urgency statement in the notice, irrespective of whether the data user appeals against service of the notice.

s. 12(9)

A transfer prohibition notice cannot prohibit a transfer of data which is authorised or required by any enactment, or required by any convention or other instrument imposing an international obligation on the UK.

If a data user contravenes a transfer prohibition notice, it is an offence. If, however, the user can prove that he exercised all due diligence to avoid contravention of the notice, he may escape liability.   s. 12(10)

13.5   What does the Act say about data held and services provided outside the UK?

The basic rule is that the Act does not apply to a data user in respect of data held outside the UK. Similarly, the Act does not apply to a person carrying on a computer bureau in respect of services provided outside the UK. However, the terms, 'data held and services provided', are used in a very narrow and closely defined sense. Data are treated as held where the data user exercises control over the contents and use of the data comprising the collection, irrespective of where the processing takes place. Services are treated as provided where the person carrying on the bureau either (a) causes data held by other persons to be processed, or (b) where he allows other persons the use of equipment in his possession for processing data held by them, irrespective of location in both cases.   s. 39(1)

s. 39(2)

In essence, therefore, the Act will apply where the persons controlling the data are within the UK. It is not the whereabouts of the processing of personal data that determines the territorial effect of the legislation but that of the persons in charge. To this rule there are, however, two basic exceptions. First, the Act provides that where a person outside the UK exercises the control, or provides the services through a servant or agent within the UK, the servant or agent is treated as doing those things on his own behalf. This means that where a person such as a branch manager is effectively in charge of operations within the UK, the legislation cannot be avoided by arguing that ultimate control is exercised outside the UK, no matter where the data are processed. Where such a servant or agent is treated as a data user or person carrying on a computer bureau, he may be described for registration purposes by the position or office which he holds. This means that the actual identity of the servant or agent at any one time is irrelevant. The description in the registration entry will be treated as applying to the person who, for the time being, holds the position or office.   s. 39(3)

Second, the Act does not apply to data processed wholly outside the UK, unless the data are used, or are intended to be used, in the   s. 39(5)

UK. This means that the Act would not apply where the person in charge of operations happens to be in the UK directing operations, but the data are processed and used wholly outside the UK.

Controller resident (and hence data are deemed to be held)	Data processed in UK — Data used: in UK	Abroad	Data processed abroad — Data used: in UK	Abroad
In UK	✓	✓	✓	✗
Abroad but with servant or agent in the UK	✓	✓	✓	✗
Abroad and without servant or agent in the UK	○	○	✗	✗

✓ = Act applies
✗ = Act does not apply
○ = Can logically only be a bureau

Table 1 Are international data users subject to the Act?

The territorial effect of the legislation is summarised in Tables 1 and 2. Table 1 summarises the effect for data users in terms of where the data are held and controlled. Table 2 summarises the effect of the

120

legislation for computer bureaux in terms of where the data are caused to be processed and used.

Where are they caused to be processed? (Where are services provided?)	Data processed in UK — Data used: in UK	Abroad	Data processed abroad — Data used: in UK	Abroad
In UK	✓	✓	✓	✗
Abroad but with servant or agent in the UK	✓	✓	✓	✗
Abroad and without servant or agent in the UK	✓	✓	✗	✗

✓ = Act applies
✗ = Act does not apply

Table 2 Are international bureaux covered by the Act?

Chapter 14

What is the timescale for action?

Like many statutes the DPA did not become fully operational as soon as it received the royal assent. Its provisions are being gradually phased in over a period of years. The relevant provisions and duties are summarised in Figure 5.

The 11 November 1985 is the important date, that is the appointed day on which applications may be made for registration as a data user or a computer bureau. The other provisions of the Act will come into force at various intervals after 11 November 1985 and the Act will be completely operational on 11 November 1987 (see Figure 5).

Figure 5 Commencement of the Data Protection Act 1984 and transitional arrangements

	Date the Act was passed	Two months from the date the Act was passed	Appointed day for first applications for registration	Six months from the appointed day	Two years from the appointed day
Statutory provision	12.7.84	12.9.84	11.11.85	11.5.86	11.11.87
Applications for registration begin:					
Prohibition on unregistered obtaining, holding, disclosing and transferring of personal data begins:					

What is the timescale for action?

Statutory provision	Date the Act was passed 12.7.84	Two months from the date the Act was passed 12.9.84	Appointed day for first applications for registration 11.11.85	Six months from the appointed day 11.5.86	Two years from the appointed day 11.11.87
Prohibition on unauthorised disclosure by a computer bureau begins:				▓▓▓	▓▓▓
Registrar has power to refuse applications for registration, in addition to grounds of insufficient data:					▓▓▓
Registrar's powers to serve effective notices begin:					▓▓▓
Access rights for data subjects begin:					▓▓▓
Power to issue warrants where breach of the principles occurs begins:					▓▓▓
Compensation provisions for inaccurate data begin:				▓▓▓	▓▓▓
Fifth principle (accuracy) applies to data held from:				▓▓▓	▓▓▓
Compensation for loss or unauthorised disclosure in respect of damage suffered applies after:		▓▓▓	▓▓▓	▓▓▓	▓▓▓
Power of the court to order erasure where damage suffered starts:		▓▓▓	▓▓▓	▓▓▓	▓▓▓
General power of the Court to order rectification or erasure begins:				▓▓▓	▓▓▓

Appendix 1

Text of the Data Protection Act 1984

1984, c. 35. An Act to regulate the use of automatically processed information relating to individuals and the provision of services in respect of such information. Royal assent 12 July 1984.

BE IT ENACTED by the Queen's most Excellent Majesty, by and with the advice and consent of the Lords Spiritual and Temporal, and Commons, in this present Parliament assembled, and by the authority of the same, as follows:—

Part I Preliminary

Definition of 'data' and related expressions

1. (1) The following provisions shall have effect for the interpretation of this Act.

(2) 'Data' means information recorded in a form in which it can be processed by equipment operating automatically in response to instructions given for that purpose.

(3) 'Personal data' means data consisting of information which relates to a living individual who can be identified from the information (or from that and other information in the possession of the data user), including any expression of opinion about the individual but not any indication of the intentions of the data user in respect of that individual.

(4) 'Data subject' means an individual who is the subject of personal data.

(5) 'Data user' means a person who holds data, and a person 'holds' data if—

(a) the data form part of a collection of data processed or intended to be processed by or on behalf of that person as mentioned in subsection (2) above; and

(b)   that person (either alone or jointly or in common with other persons) controls the contents and use of the data comprised in the collection; and

(c)   the data are in the form in which they have been or are intended to be processed as mentioned in paragraph (a) above or (though not for the time being in that form) in a form into which they have been converted after being so processed and with a view to being further so processed on a subsequent occasion.

(6)   A person carries on a 'computer bureau' if he provides other persons with services in respect of data, and a person provides such sevices if—

(a)   as agent for other persons he causes data held by them to be processed as mentioned in subsection (2) above; or

(b)   he allows other persons the use of equipment in his possession for the processing as mentioned in that subsection of data held by them.

(7)   'Processing', in relation to data, means amending, augmenting, deleting or re-arranging the data or extracting the information constituting the data and, in the case of personal data, means performing any of those operations by reference to the data subject.

(8)   Subsection (7) above shall not be construed as applying to any operation performed only for the purpose of preparing the text of documents.

(9)   'Disclosing', in relation to data, includes disclosing information extracted from the data; and where the identification of the individual who is the subject of personal data depends partly on the information constituting the data and partly on other information in the possession of the data user, the data shall not be regarded as disclosed or transferred unless the other information is also disclosed or transferred.

The data protection principles

2.   (1)   Subject to subsection (3) below, references in this Act to the data protection principles are to the principles set out in Part I of Schedule 1 to this Act; and those principles shall be interpreted in accordance with Part II of that Schedule.

(2)   The first seven principles apply to personal data held by data

users and the eighth applies both to such data and to personal data in respect of which services are provided by persons carrying on computer bureaux.

(3) The Secretary of State may by order modify or supplement those principles for the purpose of providing additional safeguards in relation to personal data consisting of information as to—

(a) the racial origin of the data subject;
(b) his political opinions or religious or other beliefs;
(c) his physical or mental health or his sexual life; or
(d) his criminal convictions;

and references in this Act to the data protection principles include, except where the context otherwise requires, references to any modified or additional principle having effect by virtue of an order under this subsection.

(4) An order under subsection (3) above may modify a principle either by modifying the principle itself or by modifying its interpretation; and where an order under that subsection modifies a principle or provides for an additional principle it may contain provisions for the interpretation of the modified or additional principle.

(5) An order under subsection (3) above modifying the third data protection principle may, to such extent as the Secretary of State thinks appropriate, exclude or modify in relation to that principle any exemption from the non-disclosure provisions which is contained in Part IV of this Act; and the exemptions from those provisions contained in that Part shall accordingly have effect subject to any order made by virtue of this subsection.

(6) An order under subsection (3) above may make different provision in relation to data consisting of information of different descriptions.

The Registrar and the Tribunal

3. (1) For the purposes of this Act there shall be—

(a) an officer known as the Data Protection Registrar (in this Act referred to as 'the Registrar'); and
(b) a tribunal known as the Data Protection Tribunal (in this Act referred to as 'the Tribunal').

(2)   The Tribunal shall consist of—

(a)   a chairman appointed by the Lord Chancellor after consultation with the Lord Advocate;
(b)   such number of deputy chairmen appointed as aforesaid as the Lord Chancellor may determine; and
(c)   such number of other members appointed by the Secretary of State as he may determine.

(4)   The members of the Tribunal appointed under subsection (3)(a) and (b) above shall be barristers, advocates or solicitors, in each case of not less than seven years' standing.
(5)   The members of the Tribunal appointed under subsection (3)(c) above shall be—

(a)   persons to represent the interests of data users; and
(b)   persons to represent the interests of data subjects.

(6)   Schedule 2 to this Act shall have effect in relation to the Registrar and the Tribunal.

Part II   Registration and supervision of data users and computer bureaux

Registration

Registration of data users and computer bureaux
4.   (1)   The Registrar shall maintain a register of data users who hold, and of persons carrying on computer bureaux who provide services in respect of, personal data and shall make an entry in the register in pursuance of each application for registration accepted by him under this Part of this Act.
(2)   Each entry shall state whether it is in respect of a data user, of a person carrying on a computer bureau or of a data user who also carries on such a bureau.
(3)   Subject to the provisions of this section, an entry in respect of a data user shall consist of the following particulars—

(a)   the name and address of the data user;
(b)   a description of the personal data to be held by him and of

the purpose or purposes for which the data are to be held or used;

    (c)   a description of the source or sources from which he intends or may wish to obtain the data or the information to be contained in the data;

    (d)   a description of any person or persons to whom he intends or may wish to disclose the data;

    (e)   the names or a description of any countries or territories outside the United Kingdom to which he intends or may wish directly or indirectly to transfer the data; and

    (f)   one or more addresses for the receipt of requests from data subjects for access to the data.

(4)   Subject to the provisions of this section, an entry in respect of a person carrying on a computer bureau shall consist of that person's name and address.

(5)   Subject to the provisions of this section, an entry in respect of a data user who also carries on a computer bureau shall consist of his name and address and, as respects the personal data to be held by him, the particulars specified in subsection (3)(b) to (f) above.

(6)   In the case of a registered company the address referred to in subsections (3)(a), (4) and (5) above is that of its registered office, and the particulars to be included in the entry shall include the company's number in the register of companies.

(7)   In the case of a person (other than a registered company) carrying on a business the address referred to in subsections (3)(a), (4) and (5) above is that of his principal place of business.

(8)   The Secretary of State may by order vary the particulars to be included in entries made in the register.

Prohibition of unregistered holding etc. of personal data

5.   (1)   A person shall not hold personal data unless an entry in respect of that person as a data user, or as a data user who also carries on a computer bureau, is for the time being contained in the register.

(2)   A person in respect of whom such an entry is contained in the register shall not—

    (a)   hold personal data of any description other than that specified in the entry;

    (b)   hold any such data, or use any such data held by him, for any purpose other than the purpose or purposes described in the entry;

(c) obtain such data, or information to be contained in such data, to be held by him from any source which is not described in the entry;

(d) disclose such data held by him to any person who is not described in the entry; or

(e) directly or indirectly transfer such data held by him to any country or territory outside the United Kingdom other than one named or described in the entry.

(3) A servant or agent of a person to whom subsection (2) above applies shall, as respects personal data held by that person, be subject to the same restrictions on the use, disclosure or transfer of the data as those to which that person is subject under paragraphs (b), (d) and (e) of that subsection and, as respects personal data to be held by that person, to the same restrictions as those to which he is subject under paragraph (c) of that subsection.

(4) A person shall not, in carrying on a computer bureau, provide services in respect of personal data unless an entry in respect of that person as a person carrying on such a bureau, or as a data user who also carries on such a bureau, is for the time being contained in the register.

(5) Any person who contravenes subsection (1) above or knowingly or recklessly contravenes any of the other provisions of this section shall be guilty of an offence.

Applications for registration and for amendment of registered particulars

6. (1) A person applying for registration shall state whether he wishes to be registered as a data user, as a person carrying on a computer bureau or as a data user who also carries on such a bureau, and shall furnish the Registrar, in such form as he may require, with the particulars required to be included in the entry to be made in pursuance of the application.

(2) Where a person intends to hold personal data for two or more purposes he may make separate applications for registration in respect of any of those purposes.

(3) A registered person may at any time apply to the Registrar for the alteration of any particulars included in the entry or entries relating to that person.

(4) Where the alteration would consist of the addition of a purpose for which personal data are to be held, the person may,

instead of making an application under subsection (3) above, make a fresh application for registration in respect of the additional purpose.

(5) A registered person shall make an application under subsection (3) above whenever necessary for ensuring that the entry or entries relating to that person contain his current address; and any person who fails to comply with this subsection shall be guilty of an offence.

(6) Any person who, in connection with an application for registration or for the alteration of registered particulars, knowingly or recklessly furnishes the Registrar with information which is false or misleading in a material respect shall be guilty of an offence.

(7) Every application for registration shall be accompanied by the prescribed fee, and every application for the alteration of registered particulars shall be accompanied by such fee, if any, as may be prescribed.

(8) Any application for registration or for the alteration of registered particulars may be withdrawn by notice in writing to the Registrar at any time before the applicant receives a notification in respect of the application under section 7(1) below.

Acceptance and refusal of applications
7. (1) Subject to the provisions of this section, the Registrar shall as soon as practicable and in any case within the period of six months after receiving an application for registration or for the alteration of registered particulars notify the applicant in writing whether his application has been accepted or refused; and where the Registrar notifies an applicant that his application has been accepted the notification shall contain a statement of—

(a) the particulars entered in the register, or the alteration made, in pursuance of the application; and

(b) the date on which the particulars were entered or the alteration was made.

(2) The Registrar shall not refuse an application made in accordance with section 6 above unless—

(a) he considers that the particulars proposed for registration or, as the case may be, the particulars that would result from the proposed alteration, will not give sufficient information as to the matters to which they relate; or

(b)   he is satisfied that the applicant is likely to contravene any of the data protection principles; or

(c)   he considers that the information available to him is insufficient to satisfy him that the applicant is unlikely to contravene any of those principles.

(3)   Subsection (2)(a) above shall not be construed as precluding the acceptance by the Registrar of particulars expressed in general terms in cases where that is appropriate, and the Registrar shall accept particulars expressed in such terms in any case in which he is satisfied that more specific particulars would be likely to prejudice the purpose or purposes for which the data are to be held.

(4)   Where the Registrar refuses an application under this section he shall give his reasons and inform the applicant of the rights of appeal conferred by section 13 below.

(5)   If in any case it appears to the Registrar that an application needs more consideration than can be given to it in the period mentioned in subsection (1) above he shall as soon as practicable and in any case before the end of that period notify the applicant in writing to that effect; and in that event no notification need be given under that subsection until after the end of that period.

(6)   Subject to subsection (8) below, a person who has made an application in accordance with section 6 above shall—

(a)   until he receives a notification in respect of it under subsection (1) above or the application is withdrawn; and

(b)   if he receives a notification under that subsection of the refusal of his application, until the end of the period within which an appeal can be brought against the refusal and, if an appeal is brought, until the determination or withdrawal of the appeal,

be treated for the purposes of section 5 above as if his application had been accepted and the particulars contained in it had been entered in the register or, as the case may be, the alteration requested in the application had been made on the date on which the application was made.

(7)   If by reason of special circumstances the Registrar considers that a refusal notified by him to an applicant under subsection (1) above should take effect as a matter of urgency he may include a statement to that effect in the notification of the refusal; and in that event subsection (6)(b) above shall have effect as if for the words from

'the period' onwards there were substituted the words 'the period of seven days beginning with the date on which that notification is received'.

(8) Subsection (6) above shall not apply to an application made by any person if in the previous two years—

(a) an application by that person has been refused under this section; or

(b) all or any of the particulars constituting an entry contained in the register in respect of that person have been removed in pursuance of a de-registration notice;

but in the case of any such application subsection (1) above shall apply as if for the reference to six months there were substituted a reference to two months and, where the Registrar gives a notification under subsection (5) above in respect of any such application, subsection (6) above shall apply to it as if for the reference to the date on which the application was made there were substituted a reference to the date on which that notification is received.

(9) For the purposes of subsection (6) above an application shall be treated as made or withdrawn—

(a) if the application or notice of withdrawal is sent by registered post or the recorded delivery service, on the date on which it is received for dispatch by the Post Office;

(b) in any other case, on the date on which it is received by the Registrar;

and for the purposes of subsection (8)(a) above an application shall not be treated as having been refused so long as an appeal against the refusal can be brought, while such an appeal is pending or if such an appeal has been allowed.

Duration and renewal of registration
8. (1) No entry shall be retained in the register after the expiration of the initial period of registration except in pursuance of a renewal application made to the Registrar in accordance with this section.

(2) Subject to subsection (3) below, the initial period of registration and the period for which an entry is to be retained in pursuance of a renewal application ('the renewal period') shall be

such period (not being less than three years) as may be prescribed beginning with the date on which the entry in question was made or, as the case may be, the date on which that entry would fall to be removed if the renewal application had not been made.

(3) The person making an application for registration or a renewal application may in his application specify as the initial period of registration or, as the case may be, as the renewal period, a period shorter than that prescribed, being a period consisting of one or more complete years.

(4) Where the Registrar notifies an applicant for registration that his application has been accepted the notification shall include a statement of the date when the initial period of registration will expire.

(5) Every renewal application shall be accompanied by the prescribed fee, and no such application shall be made except in the period of six months ending with the expiration of—

(a) the initial period of registration; or
(b) if there have been one or more previous renewal applications, the current renewal period.

(6) Any renewal application may be sent by post, and the Registrar shall acknowledge its receipt and notify the applicant in writing of the date until which the entry in question will be retained in the register in pursuance of the application.

(7) Without prejudice to the foregoing provisions of this section, the Registrar may at any time remove an entry from the register at the request of the person to whom the entry relates.

Inspection etc. of registered particulars
9. (1) The Registrar shall provide facilities for making the information contained in the entries in the register available for inspection (in visible and legible form) by members of the public at all reasonable hours and free of charge.

(2) The Registrar shall, on payment of such fee, if any, as may be prescribed, supply any member of the public with a duly certified copy in writing of the particulars contained in the entry made in the register in pursuance of any application for registration.

Enforcement notices

10. (1) If the Registrar is satisfied that a registered person has contravened or is contravening any of the data protection principles he may serve him with a notice ('an enforcement notice') requiring him to take, within such time as is specified in the notice, such steps as are so specified for complying with the principle or principles in question.

(2) In deciding whether to serve an enforcement notice the Registrar shall consider whether the contravention has caused or is likely to cause any person damage or distress.

(3) An enforcement notice in respect of a contravention of the fifth data protection principle may require the data user—

(a) to rectify or erase the data and any other data held by him and containing an expression of opinion which appears to the Registrar to be based on the inaccurate data; or

(b) in the case of such data as are mentioned in subsection (2) of section 22 below, either to take the steps mentioned in paragraph (a) above or to take such steps as are specified in the notice for securing compliance with the requirements specified in that subsection and, if the Registrar thinks fit, for supplementing the data with such statement of the true facts relating to the matters dealt with by the data as the Registrar may approve.

(4) The Registrar shall not serve an enforcement notice requiring the person served with the notice to take steps for complying with paragraph (a) of the seventh data protection principle in respect of any data subject unless satisfied that the person has contravened section 21 below by failing to supply information to which the data subject is entitled and which has been duly requested in accordance with that section.

(5) An enforcement notice shall contain—

(a) a statement of the principle or principles which the Registrar is satisfied have been or are being contravened and his reasons for reaching that conclusion; and

(b) particulars of the rights of appeal conferred by section 13 below.

(6) Subject to subsection (7) below, the time specified in an enforcement notice for taking the steps which it requires shall not expire before the end of the period within which an appeal can be brought against the notice and, if such an appeal is brought, those steps need not be taken pending the determination or withdrawal of the appeal.

(7) If by reason of special circumstances the Registrar considers that the steps required by an enforcement notice should be taken as a matter of urgency he may include a statement to that effect in the notice; and in that event subsection (6) above shall not apply but the notice shall not require the steps to be taken before the end of the period of seven days beginning with the date on which the notice is served.

(8) The Registrar may cancel an enforcement notice by written notification to the person on whom it was served.

(9) Any person who fails to comply with an enforcement notice shall be guilty of an offence; but it shall be a defence for a person charged with an offence under this subsection to prove that he exercised all due diligence to comply with the notice in question.

De-registration notices

11. (1) If the Registrar is satisfied that a registered person has contravened or is contravening any of the data protection principles he may—

(a) serve him with a notice ('de-registration notice') stating that he proposes, at the expiration of such period as is specified in the notice, to remove from the register all or any of the particulars constituting the entry or any of the entries contained in the register in respect of that person; and

(b) subject to the provisions of this section, remove those particulars from the register at the expiration of that period.

(2) In deciding whether to serve a de-registration notice the Registrar shall consider whether the contravention has caused or is likely to cause any person damage or distress, and the Registrar shall not serve such a notice unless he is satisfied that compliance with the principle or principles in question cannot be adequately secured by the service of an enforcement notice.

(3) A de-registration notice shall contain—

(a) a statement of the principle or principles which the Registrar is satisfied have been or are being contravened and his reasons for reaching that conclusion and deciding that compliance cannot be adequately secured by the service of an enforcement notice; and

(b) particulars of the rights of appeal conferred by section 13 below.

(4) Subject to subsection (5) below, the period specified in a de-registration notice pursuant to subsection (1)(a) above shall not expire before the end of the period within which an appeal can be brought against the notice and, if such an appeal is brought, the particulars shall not be removed pending the determination or withdrawal of the appeal.

(5) If by reason of special circumstances the Registrar considers that any particulars should be removed from the register as a matter of urgency he may include a statement to that effect in the de-registration notice; and in that event subsection (4) above shall not apply but the particulars shall not be removed before the end of the period of seven days beginning with the date on which the notice is served.

(6) The Registrar may cancel a de-registration notice by written notification to the person on whom it was served.

(7) References in this section to removing any particulars include references to restricting any description which forms part of any particulars.

Transfer prohibition notices
12. (1) If it appears to the Registrar that—

(a) a person registered as a data user or as a data user who also carries on a computer bureau; or

(b) a person treated as so registered by virtue of section 7(6) above,

proposes to transfer personal data held by him to a place outside the United Kingdom, the Registrar may, if satisfied as to the matters mentioned in subsection (2) or (3) below, serve that person with a notice ('a transfer prohibition notice') prohibiting him from transferring the data either absolutely or until he has taken such steps as are specified in the notice for protecting the interests of the data subjects in question.

(2)   Where the place to which the data are to be transferred is not in a State bound by the European Convention the Registrar must be satisfied that the transfer is likely to contravene, or lead to a contravention of, any of the data protection principles.

(3)   Where the place to which the data are to be transferred is in a State bound by the European Convention the Registrar must be satisfied either—

(a)   that—

(i)   the person in question intends to give instructions for the further transfer of the data to a place which is not in such a State; and

(ii)   that the further transfer is likely to contravene, or lead to a contravention of, any of the data protection principles; or

(b)   in the case of data to which an order under section 2(3) above applies, that the transfer is likely to contravene, or lead to a contravention of, any of the data protection principles as they have effect in relation to such data.

(4)   In deciding whether to serve a transfer prohibition notice the Registrar shall consider whether the notice is required for preventing damage or distress to any person and shall have regard to the general desirability of facilitating the free transfer of data between the United Kingdom and other states and territories.

(5)   A transfer prohibition notice shall specify the time when it is to take effect and contain—

(a)   a statement of the principle or principles which the Registrar is satisfied are likely to be contravened and his reasons for reaching that conclusion; and

(b)   particulars of the rights of appeal conferred by section 13 below.

(6)   Subject to subsection (7) below, the time specified in a transfer prohibition notice pursuant to subsection (5) above shall not be before the end of the period within which an appeal can be brought against the notice and, if such an appeal is brought, the notice shall not take effect pending the determination or withdrawal of the appeal.

137

(7)   If by reason of special circumstances the Registrar considers that the prohibition should take effect as a matter of urgency he may include a statement to that effect in the transfer prohibition notice; and in that event subsection (6) above shall not apply but the notice shall not take effect before the end of the period of seven days beginning with the date on which the notice is served.

(8)   The Registrar may cancel a transfer prohibition notice by written notification to the person on whom it was served.

(9)   No transfer prohibition notice shall prohibit the transfer of any data where the transfer of the information constituting the data is required or authorised by or under any enactment or required by any convention or other instrument imposing an international obligation on the United Kingdom.

(10)   Any person who contravenes a transfer prohibition notice shall be guilty of an offence; but it shall be a defence for a person charged with an offence under this subsection to prove that he exercised all due diligence to avoid a contravention of the notice in question.

(11)   For the purposes of this section a place shall be treated as in a State bound by the European Convention if it is in any territory in respect of which the State is bound.

Appeals

Rights of appeal
13.   (1)   A person may appeal to the Tribunal against—

(a)   any refusal by the Registrar of an application by that person for registration or for the alteration of registered particulars;

(b)   any enforcement notice, de-registration notice or transfer prohibition notice with which that person has been served.

(2)   Where a notification that an application has been refused contains a statement by the Registrar in accordance with section 7(7) above, then, whether or not the applicant appeals under paragraph (a) of subsection (1) above, he may appeal against the Registrar's decision to include that statement in the notification.

(3)   Where any such notice as is mentioned in paragraph (b) of subsection (1) above contains a statement by the Registrar in accordance with section 10(7), 11(5) or 12(7) above, then, whether or not the person served with the notice appeals under that paragraph,

he may appeal against the Registrar's decision to include that statement in the notice or against the effect of the inclusion of the statement as respects any part of the notice.

(4) Schedule 3 to this Act shall have effect in relation to appeals under this section and to the proceedings of the Tribunal in respect of any such appeal.

Determination of appeals

14. (1) If on an appeal under section 13(1) above the Tribunal considers—

(a) that the refusal or notice against which the appeal is brought is not in accordance with the law; or

(b) to the extent that the refusal or notice involved an exercise of discretion by the Registrar, that he ought to have exercised his discretion differently.

the Tribunal shall allow the appeal or substitute such other decision or notice as could have been made or served by the Registrar; and in any other case the Tribunal shall dismiss the appeal.

(2) The Tribunal may review any determination of fact on which the refusal or notice in question was based.

(3) On an appeal under subsection (2) of section 13 above the Tribunal may direct that the notification of the refusal shall be treated as if it did not contain any such statement as is mentioned in that subsection.

(4) On an appeal under subsection (3) of section 13 above the Tribunal may direct that the notice in question shall have effect as if it did not contain any such statement as is mentioned in that subsection or that the inclusion of the statement shall not have effect in relation to any part of the notice and may make such modifications in the notice as may be required for giving effect to the direction.

(5) Any party to an appeal to the Tribunal may appeal from the decision of the Tribunal on a point of law to the appropriate court; and that court shall be—

(a) the High Court of Justice in England if the address of the person who was the appellant before the Tribunal is in England or Wales;

(b) the Court of Session if that address is in Scotland; and

(c) the High Court of Justice in Northern Ireland if that address is in Northern Ireland.

(6)   In subsection (5) above references to the address of the appellant before the Tribunal are to his address as included or proposed for inclusion in the register.

Miscellaneous and supplementary

Unauthorised disclosure by computer bureau

15.   (1)   Personal data in respect of which services are provided by a person carrying on a computer bureau shall not be disclosed by him without the prior authority of the person for whom those services are provided.

(2)   Subsection (1) above applies also to any servant or agent of a person carrying on a computer bureau.

(3)   Any person who knowingly or recklessly contravenes this section shall be guilty of an offence.

Powers of entry and inspection

16.   Schedule 4 to this Act shall have effect for the detection of offences under this Act and contraventions of the data protection principles.

Disclosure of information

17.   (1)   No enactment or rule of law prohibiting or restricting the disclosure of information shall preclude a person from furnishing the Registrar or the Tribunal with any information necessary for the discharge of their functions under this Act.

(2)   For the purposes of section 2 of the Official Secrets Act 1911 (wrongful communication of information)—

(a)   the Registrar and his officers and servants;

(b)   the members of the Tribunal; and

(c)   any officers or servants of the Tribunal who are not in the service of the Crown,

shall be deemed to hold office under Her Majesty.

(3)   The said section 2 shall not be construed as precluding the disclosure of information by any person mentioned in subsection (2)(a) or (b) above or by any officer or servant of the Tribunal where the disclosure is made for the purpose of proceedings under or arising out of this Act, including proceedings before the Tribunal.

Service of notices

18. (1) Any notice or notification authorised or required by this Act to be served on or given to any person by the Registrar may—

(a) if that person is an individual, be served on him—

(i) by delivering it to him; or
(ii) by sending it to him by post addressed to him at his usual or last-known place of residence or business; or
(iii) by leaving it for him at that place;

(b) if that person is a body corporate or unincorporate, be served on that body—

(i) by sending it by post to the proper officer of the body at its principal office; or
(ii) by addressing it to the proper officer of the body and leaving it at that office.

(2) In subsection (1)(b) above 'principal office', in relation to a registered company, means its registered office and 'proper officer', in relation to any body, means the secretary or other executive officer charged with the conduct of its general affairs.

(3) This section is without prejudice to any other lawful method of serving or giving a notice or notification.

Prosecutions and penalties

19. (1) No proceedings for an offence under this Act shall be instituted—

(a) in England or Wales except by the Registrar or by or with the consent of the Director of Public Prosecutions;
(b) in Northern Ireland except by the Registrar or by or with the consent of the Director of Public Prosecutions for Northern Ireland.

(2) A person guilty of an offence under any provision of this Act other than section 6 or paragraph 12 of Schedule 4 shall be liable—

(a) on conviction on indictment, to a fine; or
(b) on summary conviction, to a fine not exceeding the

statutory maximum (as defined in section 74 of the Criminal Justice Act 1982).

(3)   A person guilty of an offence under section 6 above or the said paragraph 12 shall be liable on summary conviction to a fine not exceeding the fifth level on the standard scale (as defined in section 75 of the said Act of 1982).

(4)   Subject to subsection (5) below, the court by or before which a person is convicted of an offence under section 5, 10, 12 or 15 above may order any data material appearing to the court to be connected with the commission of the offence to be forfeited, destroyed or erased.

(5)   The court shall not make an order under subsection (4) above in relation to any material where a person (other than the offender) claiming to be the owner or otherwise interested in it applies to be heard by the court unless an opportunity is given to him to show cause why the order should not be made.

Liability of directors etc.
    20.   (1)   Where an offence under this Act has been committed by a body corporate and is proved to have been committed with the consent or connivance of or to be attributable to any neglect on the part of any director, manager, secretary or similar officer of the body corporate or any person who was purporting to act in any such capacity, he as well as the body corporate shall be guilty of that offence and be liable to be proceeded against and punished accordingly.

(2)   Where the affairs of a body corporate are managed by its members subsection (1) above shall apply in relation to the acts and defaults of a member in connection with his functions of management as if he were a director of the body corporate.

Part III   Rights of data subjects

Right of access to personal data
    21.   (1)   Subject to the provisions of this section, an individual shall be entitled—

(a)   to be informed by any data user whether the data held by him include personal data of which that individual is the data subject; and

(b) to be supplied by any data user with a copy of the information constituting any such personal data held by him;

and where any of the information referred to in paragraph (b) above is expressed in terms which are not intelligible without explanation the information shall be accompanied by an explanation of those terms.

(2) A data user shall not be obliged to supply any information under subsection (1) above except in response to a request in writing and on payment of such fee (not exceeding the prescribed maximum) as he may require; but a request for information under both paragraphs of that subsection shall be treated as a single request and a request for information under paragraph (a) shall, in the absence of any indication to the contrary, be treated as extending also to information under paragraph (b).

(3) In the case of a data user having separate entries in the register in respect of data held for different purposes a separate request must be made and a separate fee paid under this section in respect of the data to which each entry relates.

(4) A data user shall not be obliged to comply with a request under this section—

(a) unless he is supplied with such information as he may reasonably require in order to satisfy himself as to the identity of the person making the request and to locate the information which he seeks; and

(b) if he cannot comply with the request without disclosing information relating to another individual who can be identified from that information, unless he is satisfied that the other individual has consented to the disclosure of the information to the person making the request.

(5) In paragraph (b) of subsection (4) above the reference to information relating to another individual includes a reference to information identifying that individual as the source of the information sought by the request; and that paragraph shall not be construed as excusing a data user from supplying so much of the information sought by the request as can be supplied without disclosing the identity of the other individual concerned, whether by the omission of names or other identifying particulars or otherwise.

(6) A data user shall comply with a request under this section

within forty days of receiving the request or, if later, receiving the information referred to in paragraph (a) of subsection (4) above and, in a case where it is required, the consent referred to in paragraph (b) of that subsection.

(7)   The information to be supplied pursuant to a request under this section shall be supplied by reference to the data in question at the time when the request is received except that it may take account of any amendment or deletion made between that time and the time when the information is supplied, being an amendment or deletion that would have been made regardless of the receipt of the request.

(8)   If a court is satisfied on the application of any person who has made a request under the foregoing provisions of this section that the data user in question has failed to comply with the request in contravention of those provisions, the court may order him to comply with the request; but a court shall not make an order under this subsection if it considers that it would in all the circumstance be unreasonable to do so, whether because of the frequency with which the applicant has made requests to the data user under those provisions or for any other reason.

(9)   The Secretary of State may by order provide for enabling a request under this section to be made on behalf of any individual who is incapable by reason of mental disorder of managing his own affairs.

Compensation for inaccuracy

22.   (1)   An individual who is the subject of personal data held by a data user and who suffers damage by reason of the inaccuracy of the data shall be entitled to compensation from the data user for that damage and for any distress which the individual has suffered by reason of the loss, destruction, disclosure or access.

(2)   In the case of data which accurately record information received or obtained by the data user from the data subject or a third party, subsection (1) above does not apply if the following requirements have been complied with—

(a)   the data indicate that the information was received or obtained as aforesaid or the information has not been extracted from the data except in a form which includes an indication to that effect; and

(b)   if the data subject has notified the data user that he regards the information as incorrect or misleading, an indication to that

144

effect has been included in the data or the information has not been extracted from the data except in a form which includes an indication to that effect.

(3) In proceedings brought against any person by virtue of this section it shall be a defence to prove that he had taken such care as in all the circumstances was reasonably required to ensure the accuracy of the data at the material time.

(4) Data are inaccurate for the purposes of this section if incorrect or misleading as to any matter of fact.

Compensation for loss or unauthorised disclosure
23. (1) An individual who is the subject of personal data held by a data user or in respect of which services are provided by a person carrying on a computer bureau and who suffers damage by reason of—

(a) the loss of the data;
(b) the destruction of the data without the authority of the data user or, as the case may be, of the person carrying on the bureau; or
(c) subject to subsection (2) below, the disclosure of the data, or access having been obtained to the data, without such authority as aforesaid,

shall be entitled to compensation from the data user or, as the case may be, the person carrying on the bureau for that damage and for any distress which the individual has suffered by reason of the loss, destruction, disclosure or access.

(2) In the case of a registered data user, subsection (1)(c) above does not apply to disclosure to, or access by, any person falling within a description specified pursuant to section 4(3)(d) above in an entry in the register relating to that data user.

(3) In proceedings brought against any person by virtue of this section it shall be a defence to prove that he had taken such care as in all the circumstances was reasonably required to prevent the loss, destruction, disclosure or access in question.

Rectification and erasure
24. (1) If a court is satisfied on the application of a data subject that personal data held by a data user of which the applicant is the subject are inaccurate within the meaning of section 22 above, the

court may order the rectification or erasure of the data and of any data held by the data user and containing an expression of opinion which appears to the court to be based on the inaccurate data.

(2) Subsection (1) above applies whether or not the data accurately record information received or obtained by the data user from the data subject or a third party but where the data accurately record such information, then—

(a) if the requirements mentioned in section 22(2) above have been complied with, the court may, instead of making an order under subsection (1) above, make an order requiring the data to be supplemented by such statement of the true facts relating to the matters dealt with by the data as the court may approve; and

(b) if all or any of those requirements have not been complied with, the court may, instead of making an order under that subsection, make such order as it thinks fit for securing compliance with those requirements with or without a further order requiring the data to be supplemented by such a statement as is mentioned in paragraph (a) above.

(3) If a court is satisfied on the application of a data subject—

(a) that he has suffered damage by reason of the disclosure of personal data, or of access having been obtained to personal data, in circumstances entitling him to compensation under section 23 above, and

(b) that there is a substantial risk of further disclosure of or access to the data without such authority as is mentioned in that section,

the court may order the erasure of the data; but, in the case of data in respect of which services were being provided by a person carrying on a computer bureau, the court shall not make such an order unless such steps as are reasonably practicable have been taken for notifying the person for whom those services were provided and giving him an opportunity to be heard.

Jurisdiction and procedure

25. (1) The jurisdiction conferred by sections 21 and 24 above shall be exercisable by the High Court or a county court or, in Scotland, by the Court of Session or the sheriff.

(2)   For the purpose of determining any question whether an applicant under subsection (8) of section 21 above is entitled to the information which he seeks (including any question whether any relevant data are exempt from that section by virtue of Part IV of this Act) a court may require the information constituting any data held by the data user to be made available for its own inspection but shall not, pending the determination of that question in the applicant's favour, require the information sought by the applicant to be disclosed to him or his representatives whether by discovery (or, in Scotland, recovery) or otherwise.

Part IV   Exemptions

Preliminary

26.   (1)   References in any provision of Part II or III of this Act to personal data do not include references to data which by virtue of this Part of this Act are exempt from that provision.

(2)   In this Part of this Act 'the subject access provisions' means—

(a)   section 21 above; and

(b)   any provision of Part II of this Act conferring a power on the Registrar to the extent to which it is exercisable by reference to paragraph (a) of the seventh data protection principle.

(3)   In this Part of this Act 'the non-disclosure provisions' means—

(a)   sections 5(2)(d) and 15 above; and

(b)   any provision of Part II of this Act conferring a power on the Registrar to the extent to which it is exercisable by reference to any data protection principle inconsistent with the disclosure in question.

(4)   Except as provided by this Part of this Act the subject access provisions shall apply notwithstanding any enactment or rule of law prohibiting or restricting the disclosure, or authorising the withholding, of information.

National security

27.   (1)   Personal data are exempt from the provisions of Part II of this Act and of sections 21 to 24 above if the exemption is required

147

for the purpose of safeguarding national security.

(2)   Any question whether the exemption mentioned in subsection (1) above is or at any time was required for the purpose there mentioned in respect of any personal data shall be determined by a Minister of the Crown; and a certificate signed by a Minister of the Crown certifying that the exemption is or at any time was so required shall be conclusive evidence of that fact.

(3)   Personal data which are not exempt under subsection (1) above are exempt from the non-disclosure provisions in any case in which the disclosure of the data is for the purpose of safeguarding national security.

(4)   For the purposes of subsection (3) above a certificate signed by a Minister of the Crown certifying that personal data are or have been disclosed for the purpose mentioned in that subsection shall be conclusive evidence of that fact.

(5)   A document purporting to be such a certificate as is mentioned in this section shall be received in evidence and deemed to be such a certificate unless the contrary is proved.

(6)   The powers conferred by this section on a Minister of the Crown shall not be exercisable except by a Minister who is a member of the Cabinet or by the Attorney General or the Lord Advocate.

Crime and taxation

28.   (1)   Personal data held for any of the following purposes—

(a)   the prevention or detection of crime;
(b)   the apprehension or prosecution of offenders; or
(c)   the assessment or collection of any tax or duty,

are exempt from the subject access provisions in any case in which the application of those provisions to the data would be likely to prejudice any of the matters mentioned in this subsection.

(2)   Personal data which—

(a)   are held for the purpose of discharging statutory functions; and

(b)   consist of information obtained for such a purpose from a person who had it in his possession for any of the purposes mentioned in subsection (1) above,

are exempt from the subject access provisions to the same extent as personal data held for any of the purposes mentioned in that subsection.

(3)   Personal data are exempt from the non-disclosure provisions in any case in which—

(a)   the disclosure is for any of the purposes mentioned in subsection (1) above; and

(b)   the application of those provisions in relation to the disclosure would be likely to prejudice any of the matters mentioned in that subsection;

and in proceedings against any person for contravening a provision mentioned in section 26(3)(a) above it shall be a defence to prove that he had reasonable grounds for believing that failure to make the disclosure in question would have been likely to prejudice any of those matters.

(4)   Personal data are exempt from the provisions of Part II of this Act conferring powers on the Registrar, to the extent to which they are exercisable by reference to the first data protection principle, in any case in which the application of those provisions to the data would be likely to prejudice any of the matters mentioned in subsection (1) above.

Health and social work

29.   (1)   The Secretary of State may by order exempt from the subject access provisions, or modify those provisions in relation to, personal data consisting of information as to the physical or mental health of the data subject.

(2)   The Secretary of State may by order exempt from the subject access provisions, or modify those provisions in relation to, personal data of such other descriptions as may be specified in the order, being information—

(a)   held by government departments or local authorities or by voluntary organisations or other bodies designated by or under the order; and

(b)   appearing to him to be held for, or acquired in the course of, carrying out social work in relation to the data subject or other individuals;

but the Secretary of State shall not under this subsection confer any exemption or make any modification except so far as he considers that the application to the data of those provisions (or of those provisions without modification) would be likely to prejudice the carrying out of social work.

(3)　An order under this section may make different provision in relation to data consisting of information of different descriptions.

Regulation of financial services etc.

30. (1) Personal data held for the purpose of discharging statutory functions to which this section applies are exempt from the subject access provisions in any case in which the application of those provisions to the data would be likely to prejudice the proper discharge of those functions.

(2) This section applies to any functions designated for the purposes of this section by an order made by the Secretary of State, being functions conferred by or under any enactment appearing to him to be designed fo protecting members of the public against financial loss due to dishonesty, incompetence or malpractice by persons concerned in the provision of banking, insurance, investment or other financial services or in the management of companies or to the conduct of discharged or undischarged bankrupts.

Judicial appointments and legal professional privilege

31. (1) Personal data held by a government department are exempt from the subject access provisions if the data consist of information which has been received from a third party and is held as information relevant to the making of judicial appointments.

(2) Personal data are exempt from the subject access provisions if the data consist of information in respect of which a claim to legal professional privilege (or, in Scotland, to confidentiality as between client and professional legal adviser) could be maintained in legal proceedings.

Payrolls and accounts

32. (1) Subject to subsection (2) below, personal data held by a data user only for one or more of the following purposes—

　(a)　calculating amounts payable by way of remuneration or pensions in respect of service in any employment or office or making payments of, or of sums deducted from, such remuneration or pensions; or

150

(b)   keeping accounts relating to any business or other activity carried on by the data user or keeping records of purchases, sales or other transactions for the purpose of ensuring that the requisite payments are made by or to him in respect of those transactions or for the purpose of making financial or management forecasts to assist him in the conduct of any such business or activity.

are exempt from the provisions of Part II of this Act and of sections 21 to 24 above.

(2)   It shall be a condition of the exemption of any data under this section that the data are not used for any purpose other than the purpose or purposes for which they are held and are not disclosed except as permitted by subsections (3) and (4) below; but the exemption shall not be lost by any use or disclosure in breach of that condition if the data user shows that he had taken such care to prevent it as in all the circumstances was reasonably required.

(3)   Data held for the purpose mentioned in subsection (1)(a) above may be disclosed—

(a)   to an person, other than the data user, by whom the remuneration c. r nsions in question are payable;

(b)   for the purpose of obtaining actuarial advice;

(c)   for the purpose of giving information as to the persons in any employment or office for use in medical research into the health of, or injuries suffered by, persons engaged in particular occupations or working in particular places or areas;

(d)   if the data subject (or a person acting on his behalf) has requested or consented to the disclosure of the data either generally or in the circumstances in which the disclosure in question is made; or

(e)   if the person making the disclosure has reasonable grounds for believing that the disclosure falls within paragraph (d) above.

(4)   Data held for any of the purposes mentioned in subsection (1) above may be disclosed—

(a)   for the purpose of audit or where the disclosure is for the purpose only of giving information about the data user's financial affairs; or

(b)   in any case in which disclosure would be permitted by any other provision of this Part of this Act if subsection (2) above were included among the nondisclosure provisions.

151

(5)   In this section 'remuneration' includes remuneration in kind and 'pensions' includes gratuities or similar benefits.

Domestic or other limited purposes
33.   (1)   Personal data held by an individual and concerned only with the management of his personal, family or household affairs or held by him only for recreational purposes are exempt from the provisions of Part II of this Act and of sections 21 to 24 above.
(2)   Subject to subsections (3) and (4) below—

(a)   personal data held by an unincorporated members' club and relating only to the members of the club; and
(b)   personal data held by a data user only for the purpose of distributing, or recording the distribution of, articles or information to the data subjects and consisting only of their names, addresses or other particulars necessary for effecting the distribution,

are exempt from the provisions of Part II of this Act and of sections 21 to 24 above.
(3)   Neither paragraph (a) nor paragraph (b) of subsection (2) above applies to personal data relating to any data subject unless he has been asked by the club or data user whether he objects to the data relating to him being held as mentioned in that paragraph and has not objected.
(4)   It shall be a condition of the exemption of any data under paragraph (b) of subsection (2) above that the data are not used for any purpose other than that for which they are held and of the exemption of any data under either paragraph of that subsection that the data are not disclosed except as permitted by subsection (5) below; but the first exemption shall not be lost by any use, and neither exemption shall be lost by any disclosure, in breach of that condition if the data user shows that he had taken such care to prevent it as in all the circumstances was reasonably required.
(5)   Data to which subsection (4) above applies may be disclosed—

(a)   if the data subject (or a person acting on his behalf) has requested or consented to the disclosure of the data either generally or in the circumstances in which the disclosure in question is made;
(b)   if the person making the disclosure has reasonable grounds for believing that the disclosure falls within paragraph (a) above; or

(c) in any case in which disclosure would be permitted by any other provision of this Part of this Act if subsection (4) above were included among the non-disclosure provisions.

(6) Personal data held only for—

(a) preparing statistics; or

(b) carrying out research,

are exempt from the subject access provisions; but it shall be a condition of that exemption that the data are not used or disclosed for any other purpose and that the resulting statistics or the results of the research are not made available in a form which identifies the data subjects or any of them.

Other exemptions

34. (1) Personal data held by any person are exempt from the provisions of Part II of this Act and of sections 21 to 24 above if the data consist of information which that person is required by or under any enactment to make available to the public, whether by publishing it, making it available for inspection or otherwise and whether gratuitously or on payment of a fee.

(2) The Secretary of State may by order exempt from the subject access provisions personal data consisting of information the disclosure of which is prohibited or restricted by or under any enactment if he considers that the prohibition or restriction ought to prevail over those provisions in the interests of the data subject or of any other individual.

(3) Where all the personal data relating to a data subject held by a data user (or all such data in respect of which a data user has a separate entry in the register) consist of information in respect of which the data subject is entitled to make a request to the data user under section 158 of the Consumer Credit Act 1974 (files of credit reference agencies)—

(a) the data are exempt from the subject access provisions; and

(b) any request in respect of the data under section 21 above shall be treated for all purposes as if it were a request under the said section 158.

(4) Personal data are exempt from the subject access provisions if the data are kept only for the purpose of replacing other data in the event of the latter being lost, destroyed or impaired.

(5)   Personal data are exempt from the non-disclosure provisions in any case in which the disclosure is—

(a)   required by or under any enactment, by any rule of law or by the order of a court; or

(b)   made for the purpose of obtaining legal advice or for the purposes of, or in the course of, legal proceedings in which the person making the disclosure is a party or a witness.

(6)   Personal data are exempt from the non-disclosure provisions in any case in which—

(a)   the disclosure is to the data subject or a person acting on his behalf; or

(b)   the data subject or any such person has requested or consented to the particular disclosure in question; or

(c)   the disclosure is by a data user or a person carrying on a computer bureau to his servant or agent for the purpose of enabling the servant or agent to perform his functions as such; or

(d)   the person making the disclosure has reasonable grounds for believing that the disclosure falls within any of the foregoing paragraphs of this subsection.

(7)   Section 4(3)(d) above does not apply to any disclosure falling within paragraph (a), (b) or (c) of subsection (6) above; and that subsection shall apply to the restriction on disclosure in section 33(6) above as it applies to the non-disclosure provisions.

(8)   Personal data are exempt from the non-disclosure provisions in any case in which the disclosure is urgently required for preventing injury or other damage to the health of any person or persons; and in proceedings against any person for contravening a provision mentioned in section 26(3)(a) above it shall be a defence to prove that he had reasonable grounds for believing that the disclosure in question was urgently required for that purpose.

(9)   A person need not comply with a notice, request or order under the subject access provisions if compliance would expose him to proceedings for any offence other than an offence under this Act; and information disclosed by any person in compliance with such a notice, request or order shall not be admissible against him in proceedings for an offence under this Act.

Examination marks

35. (1) Section 21 above shall have effect subject to the provisions of this section in the case of personal data consisting of marks or other information held by a data user—

(a) for the purpose of determining the results of an academic, professional or other examination or of enabling the results of any such examination to be determined; or

(b) in consequence of the determination of any such results.

(2) Where the period mentioned in subsection (6) of section 21 begins before the results of the examination are announced that period shall be extended until—

(a) the end of five months from the beginning of that period; or

(b) the end of forty days after the date of the announcement, whichever is the earlier.

(3) Where by virtue of subsection (2) above a request is complied with more than forty days after the beginning of the period mentioned in subsection (6) of section 21, the information to be supplied pursuant to the request shall be supplied both by reference to the data in question at the time when the request is received and (if different) by reference to the data as from time to time held in the period beginning when the request is received and ending when it is complied with.

(4) For the purposes of this section the results of an examination shall be treated as announced when they are first published or (if not published) when they are first made available or communicated to the candidate in question.

(5) In this section 'examination' includes any process for determining the knowledge, intelligence, skill or ability of a candidate by reference to his performance in any test, work or other activity.

Part V General

General duties of Registrar

36. (1) It shall be the duty of the Registrar so to perform his functions under this Act as to promote the observance of the data protection principles by data users and persons carrying on computer bureaux.

(2)   The Registrar may consider any complaint that any of the data protection principles or any provision of this Act has been or is being contravened and shall do so if the complaint appears to him to raise a matter of substance and to have been made without undue delay by a person directly affected; and where the Registrar considers any such complaint he shall notify the complainant of the result of his consideration and of any action which he proposes to take.

(3)   The Registrar shall arrange for the dissemination in such form and manner as he considers appropriate of such information as it may appear to him expedient to give to the public about the operation of this Act and other matters within the scope of his functions under this Act and may give advice to any person as to any of those matters.

(4)   It shall be the duty of the Registrar, where he considers it appropriate to do so, to encourage trade associations or other bodies representing data users to prepare, and to disseminate to their members, codes of practice for guidance in complying with the data protection principles.

(5)   The Registrar shall annually lay before each House of Parliament a general report on the performance of his functions under this Act and may from time to time lay before each House of Parliament such other reports with respect to those functions as he thinks fit.

Co-operation between parties to Convention
37.   The Registrar shall be the designated authority in the United Kingdom for the purposes of Article 13 of the European Convention; and the Secretary of State may by order make provision as to the functions to be discharged by the Registrar in that capacity.

Application to government departments and police
38.   (1) Except as provided in subsection (2) below, a government department shall be subject to the same obligations and liabilities under this Act as a private person; and for the purpose of this Act each government department shall be treated as a person separate from any other government department and a person in the public service of the Crown shall be treated as a servant of the government department to which his responsibilities or duties relate.

(2)   A government department shall not be liable to prosecution under this Act but—

(a)   sections 5(3) and 15(2) above (and, so far as relating to

156

those provisions, sections 5(5) and 15(3) above) shall apply to any person who by virtue of this section falls to be treated as a servant of the government department in question; and

(b)   section 6(6) above and paragraph 12 of Schedule 4 to this Act shall apply to a person in the public service of the Crown as they apply to any other person.

(3)   For the purposes of this Act—

(a)   the constables under the direction and control of a chief officer of police shall be treated as his servants; and

(b)   the members of any body of constables maintained otherwise than by a police authority shall be treated as the servants—

(i)   of the authority or person by whom that body is maintained, and

(ii)   in the case of any members of such a body who are under the direction and control of a chief officer, of that officer.

(4)   In the application of subsection (3) above to Scotland, for the reference to a chief officer of police there shall be substituted a reference to a chief constable.

(5)   In the application of subsection (3) above to Northern Ireland, for the refernce to a chief officer of police there shall be substituted a reference to the Chief Constable of the Royal Ulster Constabulary and for the reference to a police authority there shall be substituted a reference to the Police Authority for Northern Ireland.

Data held and services provided, outside the United Kingdom
39.   (1)   Subject to the following provisions of this section, this Act does not apply to a data user in respect of data held, or to a person carrying on a computer bureau in respect of services provided, outside the United Kingdom.

(2)   For the purposes of subsection (1) above—

(a)   data shall be treated as held where the data user exercises the control referred to in subsection (5)(b) of section 1 above in relation to the data; and

(b)   services shall be treated as provided where the person carrying on the computer bureau does any of the things referred to in subsection (6)(a) or (b) of that section.

(3)   Where a person who is not resident in the United Kingdom—

(a)   exercises the control mentioned in paragraph (a) of subsection (2) above; or

(b)   does any of the things mentioned in paragraph (b) of that subsection,

through a servant or agent in the United Kingdom, this Act shall apply as if that control were exercised or, as the case may be, those things were done in the United Kingdom by the servant or agent acting on his own account and not on behalf of the person whose servant or agent he is.

(4)   Where by virtue of subsection (3) above a servant or agent is treated as a data user or as a person carrying on a computer bureau he may be described for the purposes of registration by the position or office which he holds; and any such description in an entry in the register shall be treated as applying to the person for the time being holding the position or office in question.

(5)   This Act does not apply to data processed wholly outside the United Kingdom unless the data are used or intended to be used in the United Kingdom.

(6)   Sections 4(3)(e) and 5(2)(e) and subsection (1) of section 12 above do not apply to the transfer of data which are already outside the United Kingdom; but references in the said section 12 to a contravention of the data protection principles include references to anything that would constitute such contravention if it occurred in relation to the data when held in the United Kingdom.

Regulations, rules and orders

40.   (1)   Any power conferred by this Act to make regulations, rules or orders shall be exercisable by statutory instrument.

(2)   Without prejudice to sections 2(5) and 29(3) above, regulations, rules or orders under this Act may make different provision for different cases or circumstances.

(3)   Before making an order under any of the foregoing provisions of this Act the Secretary of State shall consult the Registrar.

(4)   No order shall be made under section 2(3), 4(8), 29, 30 or 34(2) above unless a draft of the order has been laid before and approved by a resolution of each House of Parliament.

(5)   A statutory instrument containing an order under section 21(9) or 37 above or rules under paragraph 4 of Schedule 3 to this Act

shall be subject to annulment in pursuance of a resolution of either House of Parliament.

(6)   Regulations prescribing fees for the purposes of any provision of this Act or the period mentioned in section 8(2) above shall be laid before Parliament after being made.

(7)   Regulations prescribing fees payable to the Registrar under this Act or the period mentioned in section 8(2) above shall be made after consultation with the Registrar and with the approval of the Treasury; and in making any such regulations the Secretary of State shall have regard to the desirability of securing that those fees are sufficient to offset the expenses incurred by the Registrar and the Tribunal in discharging their functions under this Act and any expenses of the Secretary of State in respect of the Tribunal.

General interpretation
41.   In addition to the provisions of sections 1 and 2 above, the following provisions shall have effect for the interpretation of this Act—

'business' includes any trade or profession;

'data equipment' means equipment for the automatic processing of data or for recording information so that it can be automatically processed;

'data material' means any document or other material used in connection with data equipment;

'a de-registration notice' means a notice under section 11 above;

'enactment' includes an enactment passed after this Act;

'an enforcement notice' means a notice under section 10 above;

'the European Convention' means the Convention for the Protection of Individuals with regard to Automatic Processing of Personal Data which was opened for signature on 28th January 1981;

'government department' includes a Northern Ireland department and any body or authority exercising statutory functions on behalf of the Crown;

'prescribed' means prescribed by regulations made by the Secretary of State;

'the Registrar' means the Data Protection Registrar;

'the register', except where the reference is to the register of companies, means the register maintained under section 4 above and (except where the reference is to a registered company, to the registered office of a company or to registered post) references to registration shall be construed accordingly;

159

'registered company' means a company registered under the enactments relating to companies for the time being in force in any part of the United Kingdom;

'a transfer prohibition notice' means a notice under section 12 above;

'the Tribunal' means the Data Protection Tribunal.

Commencement and transitional provisions

42. (1) No application for registration shall be made until such day as the Secretary of State may by order appoint, and sections 5 and 15 above shall not apply until the end of the period of six months beginning with that day.

(2) Until the end of the period of two years beginning with the day appointed under subsection (1) above the Registrar shall not have power—

(a) to refuse an application made in accordance with section 6 above except on the ground mentioned in section 7(2)(a) above; or

(b) to serve an enforcement notice imposing requirements to be complied with, a de-registration notice expiring, or a transfer prohibition notice imposing a prohibition taking effect, before the end of that period.

(3) Where the Registrar proposes to serve any person with an enforcement notice before the end of the period mentioned in subsection (2) above he shall, in determining the time by which the requirements of the notice are to be complied with, have regard to the probable cost to that person of complying with those requirements.

(4) Section 21 above and paragraph 1(b) of Schedule 4 to this Act shall not apply until the end of the period mentioned in subsection (2) above.

(5) Section 22 above shall not apply to damage suffered before the end of the period mentioned in subsection (1) above and in deciding whether to refuse an application or serve a notice under Part II of this Act the Registrar shall treat the provision about accuracy in the fifth data protection principle as inapplicable until the end of that period and as inapplicable thereafter to data shown to have been held by the data user in question since before the end of that period.

(6) Sections 23 and 24(3) above shall not apply to damage suffered before the end of the period of two months beginning with the date on which this Act is passed.

(7) Section 24(1) and (2) above shall not apply before the end of the period mentioned in subsection (1) above.

Short title and extent
43. (1) This Act may be cited as the Data Protection Act 1984.

(2) This Act extends to Northern Ireland.

(3) Her Majesty may by Order in Council direct that this Act shall extend to any of the Channel Islands with such exceptions and modifications as may be specified in the Order.

Schedule 1 The data protection principles

Part I The principles

Personal data held by data users
1. The information to be contained in personal data shall be obtained, and personal data shall be processed, fairly and lawfully.

2. Personal data shall be held only for one or more specified and lawful purposes.

3. Personal data held for any purpose or purposes shall not be used or disclosed in any manner incompatible with that purpose or those purposes.

4. Personal data held for any purpose or purposes shall be adequate, relevant and not excessive in relation to that purpose or those purposes.

5. Personal data shall be accurate and, where necessary, kept up to date.

6. Personal data held for any purpose or purposes shall not be kept for longer than is necessary for that purpose or those purposes.

7. An individual shall be entitled—

(a) at reasonable intervals and without undue delay or expense—

    (i)   to be informed by any data user whether he holds personal data of which that individual is the subject; and

    (ii)   to access to any such data held by a data user; and

    (b)   where appropriate, to have such data corrected or erased.

Personal data held by data users or in respect of which services are provided by persons carrying on computer bureaux
8.   Appropriate security measures shall be taken against unauthorised access to, or alteration, disclosure or destruction of, personal data and against accidental loss or destruction of personal data.

Part II   Interpretation

The first principle
1.   (1)   Subject to sub-paragraph (2) below, in determining whether information was obtained fairly regard shall be had to the method by which it was obtained, including in particular whether any person from whom it was obtained was deceived or misled as to the purpose or purposes for which it is to be held, used or disclosed.

    (2)   Information shall in any event be treated as obtained fairly if it is obtained from a person who—

    (a)   is authorised by or under any enactment to supply it; or

    (b)   is required to supply it by or under any enactment or by any convention or other instrument imposing an international obligation on the United Kingdom;

and in determining whether information was obtained fairly there shall be disregarded any disclosure of the information which is authorised or required by or under any enactment or required by any such convention or other instrument as aforesaid.

The second principle
2.   Personal data shall not be treated as held for a specified purpose unless that purpose is described in particulars registered under this Act in relation to the data.

The third principle
3.   Personal data shall not be treated as used or disclosed in contravention of this principle unless—

(a) used otherwise than for a purpose of a description registered under this Act in relation to the data; or

(b) disclosed otherwise than to a person of a description so registered.

The fifth principle

4. Any question whether or not personal data are accurate shall be determined as for the purposes of section 22 of this Act but, in the case of such data as are mentioned in subsection (2) of that section, this principle shall not be regarded as having been contravened by reason of any inaccuracy in the information there mentioned if the requirements specified in that subsection have been complied with.

The seventh principle

5. (1) Paragraph (a) of this principle shall not be construed as conferring any rights inconsistent with section 21 of this Act.

(2) In determining whether access to personal data is sought at reasonable intervals regard shall be had to the nature of the data, the purpose for which the data are held and the frequency with which the data are altered.

(3) The correction or erasure of personal data is appropriate only where necessary for ensuring compliance with the other data protection principles.

The eighth principle

6. Regard shall be had—

(a) to the nature of the personal data and the harm that would result from such access, alteration, disclosure, loss or destruction as are mentioned in this principle; and

(b) to the place where the personal data are stored, to security measures programmed into the relevant equipment and to measures taken for ensuring the reliability of staff having access to the data.

Use for historical, statistical or research purposes

7. Where personal data are held for historical, statistical or research purposes and not used in such a way that damage or distress is, or is likely to be, caused to any data subject—

(a) the information contained in the data shall not be regarded for the purposes of the first principle as obtained unfairly by reason only that its use for any such purpose was not disclosed when it was obtained; and

    (b) the data may, notwithstanding the sixth principle, be kept indefinitely.

Schedule 2   The Data Protection Registrar and the Data Protection Tribunal

Part I   The Registrar

Status

2. (1) The Registrar shall be a corporation sole by the name of 'The Data Protection Registrar'.

    (2) Except as provided in section 17(2) of this Act, the Registrar and his officers and servants shall not be regarded as servants or agents of the Crown.

Tenure of office

2. (1) Subject to the provisions of this paragraph, the Registrar shall hold office for five years.

    (2) The Registrar may be relieved of his office by Her Majesty at his own request.

    (3) The Registrar may be removed from office by Her Majesty in pursuance of an Address from both Houses of Parliament.

    (4) The Registrar shall in any case vacate his office on completing the year of service in which he attains the age of sixty-five years.

    (5) Subject to sub-paragraph (4) above, a person who ceases to be Registrar on the expiration of his term of office shall be eligible for re-appointment.

Salary etc.

3. (1) There shall be paid—

    (a) to the Registrar such salary, and
    (b) to or in respect of the Registrar such pension,

as may be specified by a resolution of the House of Commons.

    (2) A resolution for the purposes of this paragraph may either specify the salary or pension or provide that it shall be the same as that payable to, or to or in respect of, a person employed in a specified office under, or in a specified capacity in the service of, the Crown.

(3)   A resolution for the purposes of this paragraph may take effect from the date on which it is passed or from any earlier or later date specified in the resolution.

(4)   Any salary or pension payable under this paragraph shall be charged on and issued out of the Consolidated Fund.

(5)   In this paragraph 'pension' includes an allowance or gratuity and any reference to the payment of a pension includes a reference to the making of payments towards the provision of a pension.

Officers and servants

4.   (1)   the Registrar—

(a)   shall appoint a deputy registrar; and
(b)   may appoint such number of other officers and servants as he may determine.

(2)   The remuneration and other conditions of service of the persons appointed under this paragraph shall be determined by the Registrar.

(3)   The Registrar may pay such pensions, allowances or gratuities to or in respect of the persons appointed under this paragraph, or make such payments towards the provision of such pensions, allowances or gratuities, as he may determine.

(4)   The references in sub-paragraph (3) above to pensions, allowances or gratuities to or in respect of the persons appointed under this paragraph include references to pensions, allowances or gratuities by way of compensation to or in respect of any of those persons who suffer loss of office or employment.

(5)   Any determination under sub-paragraph (1)(b), (2) or (3) above shall require the approval of the Secretary of State given with the consent of the Treasury.

5.   (1)   The deputy registrar shall perform the functions conferred by this Act on the Registrar during any vacancy in that office or at any time when the Registrar is for any reason unable to act.

(2)   Without prejudice to sub-paragraph (1) above, any functions of the Registrar under this Act may, to the extent authorised by him, be performed by any of his officers.

Receipts and expenses

6.   (1)   All fees and other sums received by the Registrar in the

exercise of his functions under this Act shall be paid by him into the Consolidated Fund.

(2) The Secretary of State shall out of moneys provided by Parliament pay to the Registrar such sums towards his expenses as the Secretary of State may with the approval of the Treasury determine.

Accounts
7. (1) It shall be the duty of the Registrar—

(a) to keep proper accounts and other records in relation to the accounts;

(b) to prepare in respect of each financial year a statement of account in such form as the Secretary of State may direct with the approval of the Treasury; and

(c) to send copies of that statement to the Comptroller and Auditor General on or before 31st August next following the end of the year to which the statement relates or on or before such earlier date after the end of that year as the Treasury may direct.

(2) The Comptroller and Auditor General shall examine and certify any statement sent to him under this paragraph and lay copies of it together with his report thereon before each House of Parliament.

(3) In this paragraph 'financial year' means a period of twelve months beginning with 1st April.

Part II   The Tribunal

Tenure of office
8. (1) A member of the Tribunal shall hold and vacate his office in accordance with the terms of his appointment and shall, on ceasing to hold office, be eligible for re-appointment.

(2) Any member of the Tribunal may at any time resign his office by notice in writing to the Lord Chancellor (in the case of the chairman or a deputy chairman) or to the Secretary of State (in the case of any other member).

Salary etc.
9. The Secretary of State shall pay to the members of the Tribunal out of moneys provided by Parliament such remuneration and allowances as he may with the approval of the Treasury determine.

Officers and servants
10. The Secretary of State may provide the Tribunal with such officers and servants as he thinks necessary for the proper discharge of its functions.

Expenses
11. Such expenses of the Tribunal as the Secretary of State may with the approval of the Treasury determine shall be defrayed by the Secretary of State out of moneys provided by Parliament.

Part III   General

Parliamentary disqualification
12. (1) In Part II of Schedule 1 to the House of Commons Disqualification Act 1975 (bodies whose members are disqualified) there shall be inserted at the appropriate place 'The Data Protection Tribunal'.

(2) In Part III of that Schedule (disqualifying offices) there shall be inserted at the appropriate place 'the Data Protection Registrar'.

(3) Corresponding amendments shall be made in Parts II and III of Schedule 1 to the Northern Ireland Assembly Disqualification Act 1975.

Supervision by Council on Tribunals
13. The Tribunals and Inquiries Act 1971 shall be amended as follows—

(a) in section 8(2) after 'paragraph' there shall be inserted '5A';
(b) in section 19(4) after '46' there shall be inserted the words 'or the Data Protection Registrar referred to in paragraph 5A';
(c) in Schedule 1, after paragraph 5 there shall be inserted—

'Data protection.   5A. (a) The Data Protection Registrar;
                                (b) The Data Protection Tri-
                                bunal.'

Public records
14. In Part II of the Table in paragraph 3 of Schedule 1 to the Public Records Act 1958 there shall be inserted at the appropriate place 'the Data Protection Registrar'; and after paragraph 4(1)(n) of that Schedule there shall be inserted—

'(nn)   records of the Data Protection Tribunal;'.

Schedule 3   Appeal proceedings

Hearing of appeals

1. For the purpose of hearing and determining appeals or any matter preliminary or incidental to an appeal the Tribunal shall sit at such times and in such places as the chairman or a deputy chairman may direct and may sit in two or more divisions.

2. (1) Subject to any rules made under paragraph 4 below, the Tribunal shall be duly constituted for an appeal under section 13(1) of this Act if it consists of—

(a) the chairman or a deputy chairman (who shall preside); and

(b) an equal number of the members appointed respectively in accordance with paragraphs (a) and (b) of section 3(5) of this Act.

(2) The members who are to constitute the Tribunal in accordance with sub-paragraph (1) above shall be nominated by the chairman or, if he is for any reason unable to act, by a deputy chairman.

(3) The determination of any question before the Tribunal when constituted in accordance with this paragraph shall be according to the opinion of the majority of the members hearing the appeal.

3. Subject to any rules made under paragraph 4 below, the jurisdiction of the Tribunal in respect of an appeal under section 13(2) or (3) of this Act shall be exercised ex parte by the chairman or a deputy chairman sitting alone.

Rules of procedure

4. (1) The Secretary of State may make rules for regulating the exercise of the rights of appeal conferred by section 13 of this Act and the practice and procedure of the Tribunal.

(2) Without prejudice to the generality of sub-paragraph (1) above, rules under this paragraph may in particular make provision—

(a) with respect to the period within which an appeal can be brought and the burden of proof on an appeal;

(b) for the summoning of witnesses and the administration of oaths;

(c) for securing the production of documents and data material;

(d)   for the inspection, examination, operation and testing of data equipment and the testing of data material;

(e)   for the hearing of an appeal wholly or partly in camera;

(f)   for hearing an appeal in the absence of the appellant or for determining an appeal without a hearing;

(g)   for enabling any matter preliminary or incidental to an appeal to be dealt with by the chairman or a deputy chairman;

(h)   for the awarding of costs;

(i)   for the publication of reports of the Tribunal's decisions; and

(j)   for conferring on the Tribunal such ancillary powers as the Secretary of State thinks necessary for the proper discharge of its functions.

Obstruction etc.

5.   (1)   If any person is guilty of any act or omission in relation to proceedings before the Tribunal which, if those proceedings were proceedings before a court having power to commit for contempt, would constitute contempt of court, the Tribunal may certify the offence to the High Court or, in Scotland, the Court of Session.

(2)   Where an offence is so certified, the court may inquire into the matter and, after hearing any witness who may be produced against or on behalf of the person charged with the offence, and after hearing any statement that may be offered in defence, deal with him in any manner in which it could deal with him if he had committed the like offence in relation to the court.

Schedule 4   Powers of entry and inspection

Issue of warrants

1.   If a circuit judge is satisfied by information on oath supplied by the Registrar that there are reasonable grounds for suspecting—

(a)   that an offence under this Act has been or is being committed; or

(b)   that any of the data protection principles have been or are being contravened by a registered person,

and that evidence of the commission of the offence or of the contravention is to be found on any premises specified in the information, he may, subject to paragraph 2 below, grant a warrant authorising the Registrar or any of his offices or servants at any time within seven days of the date of the warrant to enter those premises, to search them, to inspect, examine, operate and test any data equipment found there and to inspect and seize any documents or other material found there which may be such evidence as aforesaid.

2.   A judge shall not issue a warrant under this Schedule unless he is satisfied—

(a)   that the Registrar has given seven days' notice in writing to the occupier of the premises in question demanding access to the premises;
(b)   that access was demanded at a reasonable hour and was unreasonably refused; and
(c)   that the occupier has, after the refusal, been notified by the Registrar of the application for the warrant and has had an opportunity of being heard by the judge on the question whether or not it should be issued;

but the foregoing provisions of this paragraph shall not apply if the judge is satisfied that the case is one of urgency or that compliance with those provisions would defeat the object of the entry.

3.   A judge who issues a warrant under this Schedule shall also issue two copies of it and certify them clearly as copies.

Execution of warrants
4.   A person executing a warrant issued under this Schedule may use such reasonable force as may be necessary.

5.   A warrant issued under this Schedule shall be executed at a reasonable hour unless it appears to the person executing it that there are grounds for suspecting that the evidence in question would not be found if it were so executed.

6.   If the person who occupies the premises in respect of which a warrant is issued under this Schedule is present when the warrant is executed, he shall be shown the warrant and supplied with a copy of it; and if that person is not present a copy of the warrant shall be left in a prominent place on the premises.

7.   (1)   A person seizing anything in pursuance of a warrant under this Schedule shall give a receipt for it if asked to do so.

170

(2)   Anything so seized may be retained for so long as is necessary in all the circumstances but the person in occupation of the premises in question shall be given a copy of anything that is seized if he so requests and the person executing the warrant considers that it can be done without undue delay.

Matters exempt from inspection and seizure
8.   The powers of inspection and seizure conferred by a warrant issued under this Schedule shall not be exercisable in respect of personal data which are exempt from Part II of this Act.

9.   (1)   Subject to the provisions of this paragraph, the powers of inspection and seizure conferred by a warrant issued under this Schedule shall not be exercisable in respect of—

(a)   any communication between a professional legal adviser and his client in connection with the giving of legal advice to the client with respect to his obligations, liabilities or rights under this Act; or
(b)   any communication between a professional legal adviser and his client, or between such an adviser or his client and any other person, made in connection with or in contemplation of proceedings under or arising out of this Act (including proceedings before the Tribunal) and for the purposes of such proceedings.

(2)   Sub-paragraph (1) above applies also to—

(a)   any copy or other record of any such communication as is there mentioned; and
(b)   any document or article enclosed with or referred to in any such communication if made in connection with the giving of any advice or, as the case may be, in connection with or in contemplation of and for the purposes of such proceedings as are there mentioned.

(3)   This paragraph does not apply to anything in the possession of any person other than the professional legal adviser or his client or to anything held with the intention of furthering a criminal purpose.
(4)   In this paragraph references to the client of a professional legal adviser include references to any person representing such a client.

10.   If the person in occupation of any premises in respect of which a warrant is issued under this Schedule objects to the inspection or

seizure under the warrant of any material on the grounds that it consists partly of matters in respect of which those powers are not exercisable, he shall, if the person executing the warrant so requests, furnish that person with a copy of so much of the material as is not exempt from these powers.

Return of warrants
11.   A warrant issued under this Schedule shall be returned to the court from which it was issued—

(a)   after being executed; or
(b)   if not executed within the time authorised for its execution;

and the person by whom any such warrant is executed shall make an endorsement on it stating what powers have been exercised by him under the warrant.

Offences
12.   Any person who—

(a)   intentionally obstructs a person in the execution of a warrant issued under this Schedule; or
(b)   fails without reasonable excuse to give any person executing such a warrant such assistance as he may reasonably require for the execution of the warrant,

shall be guilty of an offence.

Vessels, vehicles etc.
13.   In this Schedule 'premises' includes any vessel, vehicle, aircraft or hovercraft, and references to the occupier of any premises include references to the person in charge of any vessel, vehicle, aircraft or hovercraft.

Scotland and Northern Ireland
14.   In the application of this Schedule to Scotland, for any reference to a circuit judge there shall be substituted a reference to the sheriff, for any reference to information on oath there shall be substituted a reference to evidence on oath and for the reference to the court from which the warrant was issued there shall be substituted a reference to the sheriff clerk.

15.   In the application of this Schedule to Northern Ireland, for any reference to a circuit judge there shall be substituted a reference to a county court judge and for any reference to information on oath there shall be substituted a reference to a complaint on oath.

THE
DATA
PROTECTION
ACT 1984

THE DATA PROTECTION REGISTRAR

NOTES to help
you apply
for Registration

Contents

Preface

Notes:
	page
Purpose of these notes	1
Introduction & Definitions	1
The Registration Process	2
How to use Form DPR-1	4
Introduction to Part A	5
Part A—section by section	5
Introduction to Part B	7
Use of standard descriptions	7
B1 Purpose	8
B2 Description of personal data	8
B3 Sources and Disclosures	9
B4 Overseas Transfers	10
Alteration or Removal of Register Entries	11
Renewals	11
Fee	11
Address Labels	11
Sending Your Application	11

Standard Descriptions:

Purposes
Introduction	12
List of Titles	13
Full descriptions	15

Data Classes with example items	39

Preface

Under the Data Protection Act 1984, certain computer users (Data Users) and Computer Bureaux must register details of their operations with the Data Protection Registrar. The Registrar will then make these details available for inspection by members of the public.

Organisations or individuals who are required to register under the Act must apply for registration on form DPR.1, which can be obtained from Crown Post Offices or from the Office of the Data Protection Registrar.

This booklet contains guidance notes to help you in completing the form. It also contains a list of standard descriptions to which you will need to refer to in completing Part B of the form. The notes include rules which will be applied by the Registrar, and conditions with which you must comply in making your application. **You should therefore read these notes carefully before completing the application form.**

You may apply for registration on or after 11 November 1985. The Registrar will inform you when your application has been accepted and will send you a copy of your Register entry.

After 11 May 1986 it will be an offence to hold personal data without being registered as a Data User (unless you are entitled to an exemption) or to provide bureau services without being registered as a Computer Bureau. It will also be an offence to operate knowingly or recklessly outside the terms of your Register entry.

Please keep this Booklet until you know the result of your application.

Purpose of these notes

These notes are to help Data Users and Computer Bureaux to make an application for registration under the Data Protection Act 1984. They are not intended to explain the Act itself, although a brief explanation of some of the terms used is given in the Introduction. If you need further information you should read **Guideline No 1 — An Introduction to the Act and Guide for Data Users and Computer Bureaux.** The latest version of this Guideline and other supplementary information can be obtained from the Office of the Data Protection Registrar, at the address given on the back cover of this booklet. You may also wish to obtain a copy of the Act itself, which is available through Her Majesty's Stationery Office (HMSO).

Introduction and Definitions

The Data Protection Act is concerned with information about individuals (Personal Data) which is processed automatically (ie. in computer systems); with those who undertake the processing (Data Users or Computer Bureaux); and with the individuals to whom the data relate (Data Subjects).

The Act sets out a number of definitions which interact with each other to determine whether data and their use are covered by the Act or not. These are dealt with more fully in Guideline No 1, but for the purpose of these notes the following broad descriptions are given:

Data means information in a form in which it can be processed automatically

Personal Data consists of information about a living individual, including expressions of opinion about him or her, but excluding any indication of the intentions of the Data User in respect of that individual

A **Data User** is an organisation or individual who controls the contents and use of a collection of personal data processed, or intended to be processed, automatically.

A **Computer Bureau** is an organisation or individual who processes personal data for Data Users, or allows Data Users to process personal data on his equipment. An organisation or individual may thus rank as a Computer Bureau (e.g. by providing back-up facilities for another Data User) without actually being in business as a Computer Bureau as such.

A **Data Subject** is an individual to whom personal data relate.

The Act does not cover the processing of personal data by manual methods, nor does it cover information relating only to corporate bodies. In addition, the scope of the Act is limited by certain exemptions. These may concern the whole of the Act or a part of it. Most of the exemptions are accompanied by provisos or limitations, and they must be examined carefully before a Data User concludes that any of them apply to him. The exemptions are set out fully in Guideline No 1.

The Registration Process

Data Users and Computer Bureaux are required to register with the Registrar certain details defined in the Act. When you apply for registration either as a Data User or as a Computer Bureau it is your responsibility to ensure that your application is complete in all respects and that your requirements with regard to the automatic processing of personal data are covered (within the meaning of the Act).

If you apply for registration as a Computer Bureau only, you are required to give only your name and address and to indicate the period of registration. If you apply for registration as a Data User you must give other details, including a description of the data to be held and the purposes for which the data are to be held or used.

You may describe all the data you hold or use with one Register entry, which may cover one or more purposes, or you may if you wish split your registration into several separate entries, each of which may contain one or more purposes. You should bear in mind that a Data Subject has a right to be given a copy of *all* personal data relating to him described in a single Register entry, regardless of the number of purposes described in that entry. You must decide for yourself how you wish to register your purposes, and consequently how many entries you want in the Register.

Whatever you decide, you must use one *Form DPR-1 Part A* for each application for a single Register entry and one *Form DPR-1 Part B* for each Purpose to be described in that entry. A fee of £22.00 is payable for each application (see page 11)

The Registrar has adopted an approach to registration based on the use of standard descriptions (see page 7) in order to make the forms easier to complete. In the same spirit, you are given the option of subdividing your organisation, either in Part A (for the whole of a Register entry thereby qualifying all purposes described in it) or in Part B (in relation to an individual purpose). The Registrar reserves the right to request further information or to refuse an application if either of these facilities are abused, for instance by subdividing in such a way as to frustrate subject access.

You will be notified by the Registrar when your application has been received and again when it has been accepted or refused. A copy of your Register entry will be sent to you if your application is accepted. You should keep a copy of each form DPR-1 you complete, and use this to make sure your entry has been processed correctly.

You may withdraw your application by notice in writing to the Registrar at any time before you receive the Registrar's decision.

The Act provides that, once you have made your application, you may continue to hold and use personal data as if you were registered, pending the Registrar's decision. This provision does not apply if you have had an application refused or have been de-registered within the previous two years. It only applies if your application contains all the required particulars and is accompanied by the appropriate fee. If you intend to rely on this provision, it is essential that:

the Declaration on page one of Part A is signed

sections A1, A2 and, where appropriate, A4 and A8 of Part A are completed

any necessary Parts B are completed and enclosed

the fee of £22.00 is enclosed with your application

Failure to observe these requirements may result in the commission of one or more criminal offences under section 5 of the Act.

The provisions of the Act relating to refusals, appeals and the implications for continued processing are complex. You will be informed of them in the event of your application being refused.

There may be some delay during the peak registration period in notifying you that your application has been received. If you are concerned about this, you may wish to send your application by recorded delivery or registered post, in which case it will be deemed to have been received when accepted by the Post Office.

If there is likely to be a delay in processing your application, the Registrar will inform you of this. Normally your application will be processed within six months. If you have been de-registered, or had an application refused, within the last two years, different provisions apply. If you are in this position and in any doubt, you should consult the Registrar.

How to use Form DPR-1

The form is in two separate parts.

Part A is for information about the applicant and other details covering the whole application. If you wish to register only as a Computer Bureau you should complete Part A only.

Part B is for the following details, which you are required to provide if you wish to register as a Data User:

a description of the personal **data** to be held by you and of a **purpose** for which the data are to be held or used,

a description of the **source or sources** from which you intend or may wish to obtain the data or the information to be contained in the data,

a description of any person or persons to whom you intend or may wish to **disclose** the data,

the names or a description of any countries or territories outside the United Kingdom to which you intend or may wish directly or indirectly to **transfer** that data.

You must complete a separate Part B in respect of each purpose you wish to register.

If your application is successful, the details you have given in sections A1, A2, A4-A8 and B1 to B4 in any Part B will appear in your Register entry and will be available for public inspection.

4

Introduction to Part A

On the first page of Part A is a Declaration which must be signed before returning the application to the Registrar. Any application without a signed Declaration will be returned to the applicant. The fee for each application is £22.00. See page 11 for details.

Below the Declaration is a box for use by Data Users only. If you are applying as a Data User, you should enter here the number of Parts B which form part of your application.

A1 Type of application

You must say whether your application is for registration as a Data User, a Computer Bureau or both. Before registering as a Data User only, you should think carefully whether there might not be circumstances in which you could be providing Computer Bureau services for others within the meaning of the Act (see the definition of Computer Bureau on page 1). If such circumstances might occur, you should register as both a Data User and a Computer Bureau.

A2 Name and address

You should provide your name and address as shown below:

If you are:	please give:
An Individual or a Sole trader	Your title (Mr. Mrs. Ms etc.) followed by your first names and surname. The address of your principal place of business, or, if you are not in business your home address.
A Partnership	The name of your firm. If your firm does not have a name, give the names of the individual partners. The address of your principal place of business.
A Corporate body	The name that appears on the Register of Companies if you are a registered company or the full name of your organisation if you are incorporated by statute or charter. Your registered address if you are a registered company, or your principal place of business if you are incorporated by statute or charter.
An Unincorporated body	The name by which you are normally known. The address of your principal place of business.

Note that separate legal entities (eg: subsidiary companies) must register separately if they are Data Users or Computer Bureaux.

5

A3 Contact name & address (optional)

You may wish to give a name and address for correspondence concerning this application and any resulting entry in the Register. If you do, you should write it in the space provided. You may also give a job title and telephone number if you wish. Note that any address given here will be used for acknowledgement of your application and for confirmation of a successful application. Notices of refusal, enforcement, de-registration and transfer prohibition, and renewal reminders will be sent to the registered address given in A2.

A4 Company registration number

If the application is on behalf of a registered company, you must supply the company's number in the register of companies. Otherwise, you should leave this section blank.

A5 Other names (optional)

You may find it helpful to associate names other than the registered name of your organisation with this application. For example you may wish to give trading names, abbreviated names or other names by which your organisation is commonly known, for the convenience of both yourself and data subjects. Note that subsidiary companies must register separately if they are Data Users or Computer Bureaux.

A6 Organisation sub-division (optional)

Use this if you want to make it clear that the use of personal data described by your application relates to a specific part or parts of your organisation, where these are of major significance. For example, you may want to shown that this application is on behalf of one or more major divisions of your organisation, which are not in themselves separate legal entities (but see also the note on page 2 concerning this option).

A7 Period of registration

The initial period of registration is normally 3 years, but you may in your application specify a shorter period of either 1 or 2 years. If you do not specify any such period in this section, registration will be for 3 years.

A8 Subject access addresses

You must give at least one address for the receipt of requests from data subjects for access to the data described in your application. If you wish to use the details already given in either A2 or A3, or both, you should indicate by ticking the appropriate box(es). Otherwise, use the space provided here. You may give more than one address if you wish, if necessary using the spaces provided on the back (page 4) of Part A.

You may find it helpful to include a reference or job title in each subject access address, so that requests for subject access can be dealt with more easily. You may also give an address for subject access such as "any branch office" if you wish, provided that you have given at least one specific address. If you use the "any office" option, you should write it on the first line of one of the address spaces.

Introduction to Part B

Part B is the heart of your application for registration. You should read the following notes carefully and examine the list of standard descriptions before trying to complete it. Remember that you need to complete one part B for each purpose you wish to have registered.

You should write on the front of each Part B the application number printed at the top of page 1 of the accompanying Part A. This is necessary to ensure that all the relevant forms are kept together and reach the Register as one entry.

You should aim to be clear and open in Part B. If your Register entry is confusing, firstly the Registrar may not accept it, and secondly you may get more requests for subject access and more general enquiries than you would otherwise.

Use of standard descriptions

In each section of Part B you are given the option of using standard descriptions to provide the detail required. The list of descriptions has been prepared by the Registrar after careful consideration and extensive consultations with many different representative bodies. Although you also have the option of writing your own descriptions in free text, you are strongly encouraged to use the standard description approach. Applications containing text will be closely scrutinised by the Registrar and are more likely to require further clarification. If you must use text, please try and avoid terms that may be unfamiliar to Data Subjects.

You should note that the standard descriptions are offered by the Registrar as acceptable general terms for particulars required under the Act. The Registrar reserves the right to request more precise details in individual cases. The Registrar has the power to refuse an application which he considers does not give sufficient information. The Registrar will also from time to time carry out random checks, for example for statistical purposes or to ensure that the standard descriptions remain adequate and relevant. These checks may request selected Users to give more specific details.

You will find that some standard descriptions overlap. This has been done deliberately to allow some flexibility. You should always use the standard description which is most appropriate to your use of personal data. There is no need to give every one that could apply in your circumstances provided that fewer descriptions still give a complete and accurate picture. A large number of descriptions could be unnecessarily confusing for Data Subjects.

7

B1 Purpose

In this section you are asked to describe the **purpose** for which personal data are to be held or used. You will see that you can choose to use one of two methods: either to select one of the standard purposes listed later in this booklet, or to describe the purpose in your own words. You are strongly encouraged to use the first method. If you do, the standard text description will appear in your register entry. Please note that although each description includes typical activities which may be associated with the purpose, these are example activities only. There is no implication that all of them are carried out, nor that they illustrate all the possible activities involved.

You may find it helpful to relate the purpose to a specific part or parts of your organisation or to a particular business activity, where these are of major significance (but see the note on page 2 concerning this option). For certain of the purposes you are *required* to provide further details of your business activity to clarify the standard purpose description. These cases are indicated in the standard purposes section of this booklet.

B2 Description of personal data

In this section you are asked to describe the types of person for whom personal data are to be held (**Data Subjects**) and the types of data themselves (**Data Classes**).

The standard **Data Subject** descriptions are listed on the form. When selecting data subject types from the list you may find it helpful to consider whether you can best describe the data subject in terms of his primary relationship with you the data user. In other words, is he *your employee* or *your customer?* There is likely to be some overlap between types, for example some of your customers could well be students or self-employed. There is no need to tick boxes other than the primary ones, unless by doing so you add significantly to the description.

You may add extra descriptions in text if you wish, but do not do this unless it is absolutely necessary.

Standard **Data Class** descriptions are also listed on the form, and further explanatory information on these can be found in the standard descriptions section of this booklet in the form of example data items. Please note that *the data items are examples only*. The list is not exhaustive, and the fact that you have ticked a particular Data Class does not necessarily mean that you are holding all or indeed any of the example data items listed against that Class. Also, there is no implication that *all* the Data Classes are held for *all* data subjects.

Nevertheless, you may feel that certain Data Classes are particularly sensitive and that the standard descriptions need some refinement. You can do this in free text if you wish. You can also add extra descriptions in text if you are holding data not covered by any of the standard descriptions.

Please remember in completing this section that you are describing data to be held for the purpose described in section B1.

B3 Sources and Disclosures

In this section you are asked to describe the source or sources from which you intend or may wish to obtain the data or the information to be contained in the data (**Sources**), and any person or persons to whom you intend or may wish to disclose the data (**Disclosures**). Disclosing, in relation to data, includes disclosing information extracted from the data.

The standard descriptions for both Sources and Disclosures are listed on the form. They are in three groups.

The first group contains those directly associated with the Data Subjects described in section B2, eg: the Data Subjects' relatives.

The second group contains those directly associated with the Data User, eg: the Data User's tenants.

The third group contains general descriptions of organisations or individuals.

You should describe all Sources and all registrable Disclosures. Use the third group for any Sources and Disclosures not adequately described in groups 1 or 2, including, for example, Disclosures to other organisations or individuals for their purposes.

Where a category in the third group has an asterisk against it, you should give further details in the space provided at the end of that section.

You should use as many of the descriptions as are applicable, whilst avoiding unnecessary duplication. For instance, if your Source is Data Subjects' Doctors (D109), you need not also tick D353 (Registered Medical Practitioners). Ticking a Source or Disclosure does not imply that all the data held, or data about all subjects, is necessarily received from or disclosed to that category.

Disclosure to some categories may be exempt from registration in certain circumstances — for instance disclosure to the individual data subject to whom the data relates, or to employees or agents of the Data User acting in that capacity. There may however be other circumstances in which disclosure to these categories is registrable, and for this reason they remain an option on the form.

You may add extra descriptions of Sources and Disclosures in text if necessary, indicating clearly whether the new description is a Source, a Disclosure or both.

9

B4 Overseas transfers

In this section you are asked to give the names or a description of any countries or territories outside the United Kingdom to which you intend or may wish to transfer the data. Note that transfers to branch offices overseas must be registered.

Transfer of data is a term not specifically defined in the Act. It is a different term from disclosure, and its meaning is limited by the definition of "data" given in the Act, and summarised on page 1 of this booklet. Data sent overseas on magnetic tape or disk would therefore be covered, as would computer to computer communications.

The standard descriptions for Overseas Transfers are listed on the form in a tick box format. You may add names or extra descriptions in text if necessary. You should note that the United Kingdom includes England, Scotland, Wales and Northern Ireland. For the purposes of the Act, the Channel Islands and the Isle of Man are regarded as Overseas.

If you tick the worldwide box, you must describe the nature of your business in the space provided. You should note that the Registrar will only accept this option if the nature of your business is such that it is necessary for you to transfer data to any country, for example to provide international travel services.

If you need to write in additional descriptions, you should state the particular countries or territories concerned, and avoid the use of imprecise general terms such as Europe or Middle East.

Overseas Transfers and disclosures are not mutually exclusive. Ticking a box in section B4 could imply a disclosure which must also be declared in Section B3.

Note that it may be the case that your data are transferred overseas for processing, for example by a bureau which uses computing facilities in another country. If you are using a bureau to process personal data, you should enquire if there is any likelihood of this happening, and if so make sure that such transfers are covered by your Register entry.

10

Alteration or Removal of Register Entries

The particulars contained in any Register entry may be altered as required to reflect any changes in your operations. You must inform the Registrar immediately if you change your address.

A Register entry may also be removed from the Register in its entirety at any time, by written notice to the Registrar.

Form DPR.2 should be used for notification of alterations and removals. Copies can be obtained from the Office of the Registrar.

Renewals

Your Register entry will be valid for a period of three years, unless you have opted for a shorter period (see note A7). Before your entry expires, you will be sent a reminder by the Registrar.

Fee

A fee of £22.00 is payable for each application for registration, regardless of the number of Parts B forming part of the application. The fee is the same whether you are registering for 1, 2 or 3 years. Cheques or postal/money orders should be made payable to *The Data Protection Registrar*, and crossed *A/C Payee only*. If you are sending more than one application at the same time, you may write one cheque for the total amount due. You are strongly advised not to send cash through the post.

Address Labels

You are asked to complete the two address labels contained in the registration pack. These will be used to acknowledge your application and for any subsequent queries. If you have given a contact address in A3, this should be used on the labels. Otherwise, use the address you have given in A2. You should also copy the application number from Part A on to each label — this will ensure that you are able to match acknowledgements with applications.

Sending Your Application

When you have completed your application and signed the Declaration on page 1 of Part A, send the form together with the appropriate fee and the completed address labels in the envelope provided to the following address:

Office of the Data Protection Registrar
Registration Department
P.O. Box 66
Wilmslow
Cheshire
SK9 5AX

This address should only be used for registration applications. Because of peaks in application receipts, other correspondence sent to the Registrar at this address is likely to be subject to considerable delay. For general enquiries and correspondence, you should use the full address given on the back of this booklet.

Standard Descriptions

This section of the booklet should be used in conjunction with the earlier notes and with Part B of Form DPR-1. It contains a list of Standard **Purpose** descriptions for use under method 1 in Part B.1. These are followed by **example data items** for each Standard **Data Class** description listed in Part B.2.

Standard descriptions for the other particulars — **Data Subjects, Sources & Disclosures,** and **Overseas Transfers,** are listed in Part B itself.

Purposes

Introduction

You are required to complete a separate Part B in respect of each **purpose** for which you hold or use personal data. To make registration easier, the Registrar has devised a number of **Standard Purpose descriptions**, which can be referred to by means of a simple code.

For each Standard Purpose, a general description is given, together with examples of typical activities which would fall within the scope of that code. The typical activities are not intended to be comprehensive or exhaustive. You should select the Purposes that *most closely describe* your use of personal data. *The description and typical activities for the Purposes you have selected will appear in the public Register entry.*

Some of the Purposes are general in that they describe functions and activities common to most organisations. Others are specific to a particular industry, public authority or type of business.

In order to choose the most appropriate Purposes for your circumstances, you will need to look through the entire list of Standard Purpose descriptions.

If you use some Standard Purposes, you are required to give further details. The Purposes for which this is mandatory are marked with an asterisk. You may, if you wish, give further details for any other Purpose, but should only do so if the standard description is misleading in some way.

All Standard Purposes include in the typical activities *analysis for management purposes and statutory returns.* This is to provide for incidental statistical analysis and statutory disclosure of personal data to public authorities without requiring a separate Purpose registration.

Further notes for the benefit of public sector Data Users are included in the Standard Purpose descriptions section after P040, and after P046.

12

Standard Purpose Titles

P001   Personnel/Employee Administration
P002   Work Planning and Management
P003   Marketing and Selling (excluding direct marketing to individuals)
P004   Marketing and Selling (including direct marketing to individuals)
P005   Fund Raising
P006   Public Relations and External Affairs
P007   Management of Agents and Intermediaries
P008   Purchase/Supplier Administration
P009   Business and Technical Intelligence
P010   Membership Administration
P011   Share and Stock-Holding Registration
P012   Ancillary and Support Functions *
P013   Customer/Client Administration

P014   Lending and Hire Services Administration
P015   Reservations, Bookings and Ticket Issue
P016   Research and Statistical Analysis *
P017   Information and Data Bank Administration
P018   Trading in Personal Information
P019   Charity and Voluntary Organisation Objectives *
P020   Property Management
P021   Housing Management
P022   Education or Training Administration

P023   Borrower Account/Credit Facilities Administration
P024   Investment/Deposit Account Administration
P025   Combined Borrower/Saver Account Administration
P026   Personal Banking
P027   Credit Card and Charge Card Administration
P028   Corporate Banking
P029   Corporate Finance
P030   Investment Management
P031   Life and Health Insurance Administration
P032   General Insurance Administration
P033   Pensions Administration
P034   Factoring and Discounting of Trade Debts
P035   Credit Reference
P036   Accounting and Related Services
P037   Statutory Auditing
P038   Other Financial Services Including Broking and Dealing *
P039   Legal Services
P040   Other Consultancy and Advisory Services *

13

189

P041	Government Benefits Administration*
P042	Assessment and Collection of Taxes & Other Revenue*
P043	Collection of Rates
P044	Valuation of Real Property (— in Scotland, Valuation of Lands & Heritages)
P045	Licensing & Registration*
P046	Grant and Loan Administration
P047	Consumer Protection and Trading Standards
P048	Environmental Health
P049	Electoral Registration
P050	Fire Prevention and Control
P051	Highways and Transport Planning
P052	Passenger Transport Operations
P053	Planning and Development Control
P054	Social Services/Social Work*
P055	Waste Collection & Disposal
P056	Water and Drainage Services
P057	Policing*
P058	Crime Prevention & Prosecution of Offenders*
P059	Courts Administration
P060	Discharge of Court Business
P061	Other Administration of Justice*
P062	Provision of Health Care*
P063	Ambulance Services
P064	Blood Transfusion Services
P065	Occupational Health Services
P066	Public Health
P067	Health Care Administration
P068	Other Central Government*
P069	Other Local Government*
P070	Other Public Sector*

* If you use these Standard Purposes, you are required to give some further information. The notes following each full description explain what is required in each case.

14

Standard Purposes—Full descriptions

P001 Personnel/Employee Administration

The administration of prospective, current and past employees, including, where applicable, self employed or contract personnel, secondees, temporary staff or voluntary workers.

Typical activities are: recruitment; recording or working time; administration and payment of wages, salaries, pensions and other benefits with deductions; employee assessment and training; negotiation or communication with employees; manpower and career planning; compliance with company policy and/or legislation in relation to health, safety and other employment matters; analysis for management purposes and statutory returns.

Note 1: When trustees are appointed to administer pensions, they should register separately using purpose P033.

Note 2: There is a separate Standard Purpose for Occupational Health Services, (P065) which should be used where appropriate.

P002 Work Planning and Management

The planning and management of the data user's workload or business activity.

Typical activities are: job or task scheduling; roster administration; progress or piecework monitoring; identification of relevant resources; monitoring the allocation, use or performance of plant, equipment, vehicles or services; analysis for management purposes and statutory returns.

Note 1: For some organisations, particularly in the service sector, work planning and management activities may be inseparable from other activities. In such cases, Data Users need not register this purpose separately.

P003 Marketing & Selling (Excluding Direct Marketing To Individuals)

The identification of potential customers and administration of promotional campaigns other than by direct marketing to individuals.

Typical activities are: the classification, rating or checking of individuals or organisations; advertising and other promotion; dealing with complaints or enquiries; analysis for management purposes and statutory returns.

Note 1: Promotion of corporate or organisational image may be more accurately described by purpose P006.

Note 2: This purpose includes the marketing of further business to existing or past customers.

15

P004 Marketing and Selling (Including Direct Marketing to Individuals)

The identification of potential customers and administration of promotional campaigns including selling or promotion to individuals by direct marketing methods.

Typical activities are: the classification, rating or checking of individuals; distribution of promotional materials by mail, door to door delivery or other means; telephone or face to face marketing or canvassing; dealing with complaints or enquiries; analysis for management purposes and statutory returns.

Note 1: This purpose is not restricted to the selling or promotion of goods and services. It includes the marketing of ideas, concepts and membership by direct marketing methods. The campaigning activities of political parties would for instance by covered if they employed direct marketing techniques.

Note 2: This purpose includes the marketing of further business to existing or past customers.

Note 3: The fundraising activities of charities and other voluntary bodies should be registered under P005.

Note 4: Survey market research is more accurately described by purpose P016.

P005 Fundraising

Fundraising in support of the objectives of charities or other voluntary bodies.

Typical activities are: the administration of appeals or continuing fundraising, whether or not involving the use of direct marketing techniques; analysis for management purposes and statutory returns.

Note 1: The activities of charities and voluntary bodies in connection with their principal objectives should be registered using P019, or one of the other Standard Purposes if more appropriate.

16

P006 **Public Relations and External Affairs**

The promotion of mutual understanding between the data user and representatives of the public, public authorities or other organisations.

Typical activities are: the identification of individuals or organisations for representations or lobbying on matters of concern to the data user, the maintenance of associated records; analysis for management purposes and statutory returns.

P007 **Management of Agents and Intermediaries**

The administration of agents or other intermediaries, either for sales of goods or services or for the provision of after-sales support.

Typical activities are: the identification, checking and selection of intermediaries; recording and processing payments including commission; monitoring performance; analysis for management purposes and statutory returns.

P008 **Purchase/Supplier Administration**

The administration of supplies of goods or services to the data user, by whatever method of contract or payment, including subscriptions and standing orders as well as discrete purchases.

Typical activities are: the identification, checking and selection of suppliers; ordering; recording and processing of goods received and payments (purchase ledger); monitoring supplier performance; analysis for management purposes and statutory returns.

P009 **Business & Technical Intelligence**

The maintenance of information on the business or technical environment in which the organisation operates.

Typical activities are: competitor analysis; acquisition and divestment planning; market forecasting; recording and monitoring technical developments; analysis for management purposes and statutory returns.

Note 1: This purpose covers all record keeping in which data are held about individuals or organisations specifically identified in advance as being of interest to the data user. This contrasts with the holding of information banks as a general resource, which should be registered using purpose P017.

17

P010 Membership Administration

The administration of membership, other than share/stock-holding registration.

Typical activities are: recruitment; maintenance of professional standards; administration of subscriptions; maintenance of lists of consultants; production of directories or yearbooks; processing of enquiries or complaints; provision of advice or assistance to members; analysis for management purposes and statutory returns.

Note 1: This purpose applies to professional institutes, learned societies, trades unions, associations and similar bodies. It, should not be used by commercial organisations which use the term 'member' to describe their customers eg: holiday savings or book clubs.

Note 2: Recruitment by direct marketing to individuals should be registered under P004.

Note 3: This purpose covers only the internal "housekeeping" functions of a membership organisation. The provision of advice or consultancy services to the general public by membership bodies should be registered separately using P040. The provision of goods or services to a wider market or to the general public should also be registered separately using appropriate standard descriptions.

Note 4: Registration by companies of their share or stock holders should be under purpose P011.

P011 Share- & Stock-Holding Registration

The maintenance of registers of share or stockholders, whether in compliance with statutory or other obligations, or as a management resource.

Typical activities are: the processing of applications and allotments; recording of transfers; payment of dividends and interest; administration of other benefits; distribution of documents; and identification of relevant expertise or experience; analysis for management purposes and statutory returns.

Note 1: This purpose is for data held in connection with Share and Stock registers which fall outside the scope of the exemption for data which the User is required by law to make public (section 34 (1) of the Act).

18

194

P012   Ancillary and Support Functions *

The provision of ancillary services in support of the Data User's main business activity. This purpose may be used for a wide range of functions and applications, including those of legal, finance, property and estate management, computing, security and engineering/maintenance departments within an organisation, as well as office administration.

Typical activities are: the maintenance of internal directories; filing (including electronic mail); planning and administration of repair and maintenance, access, security, and safety arrangements; testing or demonstration of computer systems; computer-assisted teaching or instruction; dealing with enquiries, complaints and claims from the general public; analysis for management purposes and statutory returns.

Note 1: If you use this purpose, you *MUST* list the range of specific purposes or functions you intend it to cover. You may, if you wish, use the purpose more than once (on separate Parts B), in order to separate specific functions. Alternatively, if the function justifies it, one of the other "industry specific" Standard Purposes may be used — for instance PO39 (Legal Services) and P020 (Property Management) by legal or estate management departments.

Note 2: Electronic mail or filing systems may be registered under this purpose, provided that they are used solely for internal 'housekeeping' purposes. If they are used for other purposes, such as employee administration, marketing and selling or business intelligence, then the personal data held should also be registered under the appropriate purpose description.

Note 3: This purpose should also be used to register personal data held specifically for the purpose of testing or demonstrating computer systems and software, or for computer-assisted teaching or instruction. Live or back-up personal data held by the Data User for another purpose, eg: personnel administration, and used incidentally for testing, demonstration or instruction in connection with that purpose (eg installing a new version of a payroll system), would be covered by the appropriate standard description and need not be registered separately.

19

PO13 Customer/Client Administration

The administration of orders and accounts relating to customers or clients.

Typical activities are: recording and processing of orders and payments (sales ledger); credit checking or rating; control and monitoring of after sales service or maintenance; dealing with customer complaints or enquiries; analysis for management purposes and statutory returns.

Note 1: This purposes covers the provision of continuing services as well as discrete sales.

Note: The next two purposes PO14 and PO15 are specialised versions of Customer/Client Administration, and should be used where appropriate instead of PO13.

PO14 Lending and Hire Services Administration

The management of lending, leasing and hire services involving the physical issue of items, materials or equipment, long term or short term.

Typical activities are: the maintenance of reservation/booking and recall systems, together with any associated ticket and account administration; processing of payments; credit checking or rating; dealing with customer complaints and enquiries; analysis for management purposes and statutory returns.

Note 1: This purpose applies to libraries and other collections issuing books, tapes and other items; and to companies of organisations involved in the hire of plant, tools, equipment vehicles, software or other items.

Note 2: Operating leasing is covered by this purpose — see PO23 for finance leasing.

PO15 Reservations, Bookings and Ticket Issue

The provision of reservation, booking or ticket issuing services.

Typical activities are: the recording of customer/client requirements and preferences; the control of agencies for this type of service; processing of payments; credit checking and rating; dealing with customer complaints; analysis for management purposes and statutory returns.

Note 1: This purpose applies to industries such as travel, hotel & catering, and leisure and entertainment.

20

P016   Research & Statistical Analysis *

Research or statistical analysis in all fields, including scientific, technical, health, social, economic or market research.

Typical activities are: the identification of subjects for survey or analysis; collection or abstraction of data, including distribution of questionnaires and telephone or face-to-face interviews; analysis, modelling or simulation; evaluation of behaviour, attitudes or characteristics; the output/presentation of results or findings; analysis for management purposes and statutory returns.

Note 1: If you use this purpose, you *MUST* describe the general nature of the research or analysis which you carry out, using one or more of the terms in the definition in the first paragraph above, (eg: scientific) or an appropriate alternative.

Note 2: Health Research includes epidemiological research, clinical trials, biomedical research, research into the prevention, prognosis, treatment of disease etc.

Note 3: Incidental analysis of information already held for another purpose, in direct support of that purpose, will be covered by the appropriate purpose code. All purpose descriptions include the typical activity "analysis for management purposes" to cover this incidental function.

Note 4: There is a limited exemption from the subject access provision of the Act for personal data held only for preparing statistics or carrying out research (section 33 (6)), but a Register entry is still required, and should use this purpose.

P017   Information and Data Bank Administration

Maintenance of information or data banks as a reference tool or general resource. This includes catalogues, lists, directories, bibliographic and free text data bases.

Typical activities are: the compilation or updating of data banks; monitoring of access or use; maintenance for historical purposes; analysis for management purposes and statutory returns.

Note 1: This purpose applies primarily to the information storage functions of libraries, museums and other collecting bodies, to commercial information services and to the news media. The customer/client administration function of such organisations should be registered using one of the other standard purpose codes, such as P014 (Lending and Hire Services Administration).

Note 2: Any organisation dealing commercially in information which primarily consists of personal details should use purpose P018.

21

P018 Trading in Personal Information

The Sale, hire of exchange of personal information.

Typical activities are: the maintenance and distribution, as a business activity, of information or data banks consisting primarily of data about individuals; analysis for management purposes and statutory returns.

Note 1: This purpose applies, for example, to commercial trading in mailing lists (list broking), and also to the incidental sale or exchange of lists collected for another purpose. Credit checking and reporting agencies are covered by a separate purpose (P035).

P019 Charity & Voluntary Organisation Objectives*

The pursuit of the main objectives of charities or voluntary organisations.

Typical activities will vary depending on the objectives of the organisation, which have to be specified, but may include analysis for management purposes and statutory returns.

Note 1: This purpose covers the processing of personal data in connection with the principal objects of a voluntary organisation. It does not cover fundraising (P005), membership administration (P010) or public relations (P006), which should be registered separately.

Note 2: The provision of goods or services to the general public by a voluntary organisation should also be registered separately (eg: advice clinics under P040 (Other Consultancy & Advisory Services)) The activities of associated trading companies, if they are separate legal entities, will require a separate application for registration.

P020 Property Management

The Management and administration of land and property.

Typical activities are: the preparation and maintenance of agreements, leases and rents; buying and selling property; checking the financial status of tenants and purchasers; keeping accounts; and managing construction, installation, improvements, repair and maintenance, analysis for management purposes and statutory returns.

Note 1: This purpose applies to businesses operating specifically in this area, eg: estate agents and property companies. It may also be used for the estate management function of other organisations. Organisations specialising in the management of residential property should use the Housing Management purpose (P021), which applies to the private or voluntary sectors (eg: Housing Associations) as well as to public authorities.

P021 Housing Management

The administration and management of residential property.

Typical activities are: the receipt and processing of applications; allocation of accommodation; rent accounting; keeping of maintenance records; related legal and accounting matters; analysis for management purposes and statutory returns.

Note 1: This purpose applies to Public Housing Authorities and to private and voluntary sector organisations (eg: Housing Associations). Related functions of Public Authority Housing Departments such as grant & loan administration or inspection and licensing should be registered separately using the appropriate standard purposes.

P022 Education & Training Administration

The provision of education or training as a primary function or as a business activity.

Typical activities are: the registration and monitoring of students; accounting for fees and grants; planning and control of curricula and examinations; commissioning and validating educational materials; calculation and publication of examination results; the provision of references; analysis for management purposes and statutory returns.

Note: 1: This purpose should be used by Local Education Authorities, Universities and Colleges as well as by private educational establishments.

Note 2: This purpose should be used either where training/ education are provided as a main business activity, or where training is provided "incidentally" to another party, eg: by selling extra places on an in-company course.

Note 3: This purpose should not be used for academic research (see P016) or for the personnel administration of academic or training staff (see P001).

Note 4: The training of employees is covered within purpose P001, and training of members by membership organisations, as long as it is not a principal activity, can be included in P010.

23

P023 Borrower Account/Credit Facilities Administration

The administration and servicing of accounts of customers or clients borrowing money or obtaining credit from the data user.

Typical activities are: checking the acceptability of applicants, and of security offered; preparing and issuing offers of advance/credit facility; processing repayments of interest and capital; maintaining accounts and issuing statements; analysis for management purposes and statutory returns.

Note 1: This purpose applies particularly to Building Societies, Finance Houses and other providers of credit, including Retailers.

For Building Societies it would include such typical activities as administering surveys, insurance and legal matters related to· mortgage advances.

For Finance Houses it would include such typical activities as finance leasing, hire purchase, conditional or credit sales. (see P014 for operating leasing).

For Retailers it would include such typical activities as credit sales and hire purchase.

It may also be used by other Data Users who find it a more satisfactory description of their activity than any of the alternative Standard Purposes.

P024 Investment/Deposit Account Administration

The administration and servicing of accounts of customers or clients depositing, saving or investing with the data user.

Typical activities are: maintaining details of account holders; processing receipts and withdrawals; payment of interest; providing automatic cash facilities; analysis for management purposes and statutory returns.

Note 1: This purpose may be appropriate for a wide range of financial institutions, including Banks and Building Societies and any other organisation operating a saving scheme.

24

P025 Combined Borrower/Saver Account Administration

The administration and servicing of accounts which are designed to offer both saving and borrowing facilities.

Typical activities are: checking the acceptability of applicants and of security offered; preparing and issuing offers of advance; processing payments or repayments of interest and capital, receipts and withdrawals; maintaining accounts and issuing statements; providing automatic cash facilities; analysis for management purposes and statutory returns.

Note 1: This purpose applies to "budget" type accounts offered by a range of financial and other organisations.

P026 Personal Banking

The provision of personal banking services, both domestic and international.

Typical activities are: the provision of current account, overdraft and other lending facilities and the maintenance of relevant accounts; the provision of automatic cash facilities; the issue and control of cheque guarantee cards; administration of securities, bonds, certificates and items deposited for safekeeping; provision of related financial and other advice to personal account holders; analysis for management purposes and statutory returns.

Note 1: The provision by banks of services such as investment management, broking and dealing, and legal advice should be registered separately using the appropriate standard purpose.

Note 2: If it is wished to register international banking services separately, this may be done using this purpose, but relating it to that specific sector in the qualifying text.

P027 Credit Card and Charge Card Administration

The administration of credit card and charge card accounts.

Typical activities are: checking the financial status of applicants, cardholders and participating suppliers; issuing cards and personal identification numbers; recording and monitoring transactions and keeping accounts; calculation of interest, commission and service charges; preparing and issuing statements; processing payments; analysis for management purposes and statutory returns.

25

201

P028 Corporate Banking

The administration of accounts for corporate customers.

Typical activities are checking the financial status of applicants for new accounts; processing and recording transactions and maintaining accounts; preparing and issuing statements; calculating interest; trade financing and documentation; corporate advisory services; analysis for management purposes and statutory returns.

P029 Corporate Finance

The provision of services connected with capital issues, sale of securities, takeovers and mergers.

Typical activities are: sponsoring and underwriting issues; processing of allotments, refunds and entitlements in respect of capitalisation and rights issues; advice on corporate planning; registration of holders of securities or bonds; the maintenance of related accounts; analysis for management purposes and statutory returns.

P030 Investment Management

The management of investments, in securities, options, futures, commodities, property, currencies etc. on behalf of personal or corporate customers.

Typical activities are: provision of valuations, reports, statements and other information; buying and selling; management of trusts and investor protection services; calculation of fees, commission and service charges; maintenance of related accounts; analysis for management purposes and statutory returns.

Note 1: This purpose applies to the portfolio management activities of all financial institutions, including banks, insurance companies and pension funds, and of other organisations.

P031 Life & Health Insurance Administration

The administration of life, health, and pensions insurance business.

Typical activities are: evaluation of risk; checking the financial status of applicants; issue of policies or contracts; processing premium and loan interest payments; payment of benefits and claims; underwriting, re-insurance; maintenance of related accounts; analysis for management purposes and statutory returns.

Note 1: The investment management side of insurance business should be registered separately using P030.

26

P032 General Insurance Administration

The administration of property, motor, and other general insurance business.

Typical activities are: evaluation of risk; checking the financial status of applicants; issue of policies or contracts; processing premium and loan interest payments; payment of benefits and claims; underwriting, re-insurance or co-insurance; maintenance of related accounts; analysis for management purposes and statutory returns.

Note 1: The investment management side of insurance business should be registered separately using P030.

P033 Pensions Administration

The administration of funded pensions or superannuation schemes.

Typical activities are: processing of contributions; maintenance of accounts; payment of benefits; actuarial advice; processing of persons leaving the scheme; analysis for management purposes and statutory returns.

Note 1: Data Users registering this purpose will usually be the Trustees of pension funds. Organisations whose business is the administration of pensions on behalf of Trustees will be acting as agents, and will not be Data Users in respect of the clients' data.

Note 2: The investment management side of pensions business should be registered separately using P030.

P034 Factoring and Discounting of Trade Debts

The purchasing of trade debts, including rentals and instalment credit payments, from businesses on a continuing basis either as an administrative service, or for the provision of funds, or as protection against bad debts.

Typical activities are: operation of debtor accounts; credit assessment, control and advice; provision of trade or personal references; analysis for management purposes and statutory returns.

P035 Credit Reference

The provision of information relating to the financial status of individuals or organisations on behalf of other organisations.

Typical activities are: investigations into financial status and history; monitoring residential addresses; passing credit reference details to subscribers; analysis for management purposes and statutory returns.

27

P036 Accounting and Related Services

The provision of general financial services related to an individual's or an organisation's accounts or business activities.

Typical activities are: the processing of information in connection with services related to payroll, bookkeeping, accounts preparation, audit other than statutory audit, tax and insolvency matters; analysis for management purposes and statutory returns.

Note 1: This purpose is most clearly applicable to the business of accountants in practice, but may also be used by any other organisation providing this type of financial advice or service to third parties, other than the User's own employees.

Note 2: If you use this purpose, you are likely to need to register as a Computer Bureau as well as a Data User. Where an accountant is processing a client's data, on the client's behalf, then the client will be the Data User, and the accountant a Computer Bureau acting as the client's agent (For statutory audit, see P037).

P037 Statutory Auditing

The provision of an audit where such an audit is required by Statute.

Typical activities included in the audit process are: analysis of information obtained from a client; generation of additional material from data supplied by the client or from such data and other information in the possession of the auditor; selection of samples; circularisation and confirmation of debtors' accounts; derivation of audit plans; processing of audit schedules; analysis for management purposes and statutory returns.

Note 1: In carrying out statutory audits, auditors do not act as agents of their clients, and may hold and use the clients' data as Data Users in their own right.

P038 Other Financial Services, Including Broking and Dealing *

The provision of services as an intermediary in respect of any financial transactions.

Typical activities are: the processing of client applications, orders and portfolios in relation to broking or dealing in insurance, securities, currency, commodities, bullion etc; analysis for management purposes and statutory returns.

Note 1: If you use this purpose, you *MUST* describe in more detail the type of service you provide. If you are involved in Insurance Broking, you should indicate if you deal in Life, Health or Pensions Insurance.

28

P039 Legal Services

The provision of legal services, including advising and acting on behalf of clients.

Typical activities are: the recording and processing of information relating to legal rights, obligations, interests, trusts, estates, litigation or other legal transactions; checking for conflicts of interest; analysis for management purposes and statutory returns.

P040 Other Consultancy and Advisory Services *

The provision of personal or business services of an advisory, consultancy or intermediary nature.

Typical activities are: giving advice or rendering professional services, acting on behalf of clients; analysis for management purposes and statutory returns.

Note 1: If you use this purpose, you *MUST* describe the general type of service or advice which you provide eg: engineering design, welfare rights.

Note 2: This purpose applies to the professional activities of surveyors, consulting engineers, architects, planning and management consultants and similar professions or occupations. Professional institutes or associations, charities and voluntary bodies offering an advice/consultancy service, whether for payment or free of charge, should also use this purpose.

Note 3: This purpose should not be used by those professions whose activities are more accurately described by another purpose:

29

Note for Public Sector Data Users:

Purposes P041-P070 are intended to cover most of the operational functions of Central and Local Government and of other public agencies. All public authorities should, wherever possible, use the general Purposes such as Employee/Personnel Administration (P001) and Purchase/Supplier Administration (P008) as well.

Some Purposes, such as P046 (Licensing & Registration), or P041 (Benefits Administration), are applicable to both Central and Local Government. You may wish to complete separate Parts B in respect of particular applications within the same Standard Purpose. If so you should qualify the purpose in the free text space under Method 1 in section B.1.

Where a Government or Local Authority department holds and uses personal data for a general Purpose such as Benefits Administration, Licensing & Registration, or Prosecution of Offenders, then that Purpose should be registered separately. Purposes such as Highways & Transport Planning, and Consumer Protection, are not designed to cover all the activities of such departments, but only the residual activities.

Where a function of a public authority is clearly parallel to one of the general Purposes already listed above, then that Purpose should be used, eg: Housing Management (PO21) for Housing Departments; Information and Data Bank Administration (P017) and Lending and Hire Services Administration (P014) for Public Libraries, and Education and Training Administration (P022) for Local Education Authorities or Universities.

P041   Government Benefits Administration *

The administration of welfare and other financial or material benefits.

Typical activities are: processing of applications; assessment of eligibility; registration of claims; payment of benefits, either directly or by transfer to another system; analysis for management purposes and statutory returns.

Note 1: If you use this purpose, you *MUST* give further details of the type(s) of benefit you are administering.

Note 2: This purpose applies to social security, unemployment and other government benefits; and to local authority administered benefits such as rent rebates and allowances, housing benefits, student grants, school meals and school clothing.

30

P042 Assessment and Collection of Taxes & Other Revenue*

Assessment and collection of taxes, duties, levies or other charges, and otherwise operating the tax system.

Typical activities are: identification of persons and organisations liable for payment; assessment and calculation of allowances, amounts payable, rebates and refunds, issue of notices and demands; processing of returns and of payments; analysis for management purposes and statutory returns.

Note 1: If you use this purpose, you *MUST* give further details of the type of tax or other revenue concerned.

Note 2: This purpose covers revenue other than local or water authority rates (see P043), and other than fees collected in connection with licensing or registration (P045). It includes those taxes and contributions administered by the Inland Revenue.

P043 Collection of Rates

Collection of local authority or water authority rates.

Typical activities are: the calculation of rates due; processing of precepts on behalf of other authorities; assessment of rate relief, rebates and allowances; issue of rate demands; collection and processing of payments; analysis for management purposes and statutory returns.

Note 1: This purpose applies to local authority and water authority rating departments.

**P044 Valuation of Real Property
(In Scotland, Valuation of Lands and Heritages)**

Property valuation for rating, revenue, compensation and other related statutory purposes.

Typical activities are the maintenance of valuation lists (the Valuation Roll in Scotland); revaluation; holding related information; analysis for management purposes and statutory returns.

P045 Licensing & Registration*

The administration of licensing or maintenance of official registers.

Typical activities are; the receipt and processing of applications; accounting for fees, issuing, renewal and revocation of licences; analysis for management purposes and statutory returns.

Note 1: If you use this purpose, you *MUST* give further details of the licence/register concerned.

31

P046 Grant & Loan Administration

The administration of statutory and discretionary grant or loan schemes.

Typical activities are: the receipt and processing of applications; inspection; payment of grants and loans; accounting for repayment of capital and interest; analysis for management purposes and statutory returns.

Note 1: This purpose applies to a wide range of grant and loan schemes operated by both central government (eg: investment, innovation and export assistance) and local authorities (eg: house improvement and insulation grants).

Note for Local Government and other Public Authority Data Users

Purposes P047 — P070 apply to a wide range of functions carried out mainly by departments of local government and other public authorities. Where they carry out specific activities already covered by another Standard Purpose, such as Licensing & Registration, Grant & Loan Administration etc, then these should be registered separately. The local government Purposes which follow should be used for residual operational activities for which personal data are held.

Some local government functions, such as Housing Management, Libraries and Education, are already covered by general Standard Purposes and are not therefore included in the following list.

P047 Consumer Protection and Trading Standards

The provision of consumer protection, trading standards, and other related services, other than licensing, registration and prosecution.

Typical activities are: investigation of complaints relating to the provision of goods or services or the condition and use of road vehicles; inspection; provision of advice and information; analysis for management purposes and statutory returns.

P048 Environmental Health

The provision of environmental health and related services, other than licensing, registration and prosecution.

Typical activities are: investigation of complaints relating to the environmental health and related matters; inspection; provision of advice and information; analysis for management purposes and statutory returns.

32

P049 Electoral Registration

The preparation and maintenance of lists of current and prospective voters, and of potential jurors.

P050 Fire Prevention and Control

The prevention and detection of fire, protection of life and property, and the provision of fire fighting and emergency services.

Typical activities are: inspection of premises; planning for firefighting; managing response to fires, traffic accidents and other incidents and emergencies; fire prevention and safety advice and education; analysis for management purposes and statutory returns.

P051 Highways and Transport Planning

The provision of road transport infrastructure and related traffic planning and management, and planning for overall transport needs.

Typical activities are: the planning and implementation of highway and bridge works, traffic management, car parking, and traffic accident monitoring; analysis for management purposes and statutory returns.

P052 Passenger Transport Operations

The administration of passenger transport undertakings.

Typical activities are: planning and administration of bus and rail operations, including concessionary fares; analysis for management purposes and statutory returns.

P053 Planning and Development Control

The preparation and monitoring of development plans and the enforcement of development control and building regulations.

Typical activities are: the maintenance of development control or building warrant files on applicants, appellants or relevant third parties including neighbours and objectors; and the maintenance of records concerned with development planning, including registers of property, landowners, occupiers and consultees; analysis for management purposes and statutory returns.

33

P054 Social Services/Social Work*

The provision of social, social work or social welfare services.

Typical activities are: planning and administration in connection with old peoples homes and centres, home help services, school meals and school clothing, children at risk and in care, adoption and fostering services, the disabled, and other clients; the administration of case work; analysis for management purposes and statutory returns.

Note 1: If you hold data for any of the following specific purposes, you *MUST* indicate this in the space provided:

Services connected with:
Child Protection
Adoption
Mental Illness
Sick or handicapped persons (physically or mentally)
The Elderly
Treatment and Rehabilitation of Offenders

P055 Waste Collection and Disposal

Provision of refuse and waste collection, disposal and management services.

Typical activities are: administration in connection with the collection of domestic and industrial refuse and other waste, disposal of waste, and planning and management of waste; analysis for management purposes and statutory returns.

P056 Water and Drainage Services

The provision of water supply, sewerage, drainage and sewage disposal services.

Typical activities are: administration in connection with water supply, cesspit and septic tank emptying; planning and maintenance of water supply and drainage infrastructure; analysis for management purposes and statutory returns.

34

P057 Policing[*]

The prevention and detection of crime; apprehension and prosecution of offenders; protection of life and property; maintenance of law and order, and rendering assistance to the public.

Typical activities are: maintaining details of offenders, suspected offenders, offences, victims, witnesses and other relevant persons; details of police and other resources; analysis for management purposes and statutory returns to relevant authorities.

Note 1: If you use this purpose, you *MUST* give further details in the space provided.

Note 2: This purpose should only be used by recognised police forces. Other bodies with law enforcement or crime prevention functions should use P058.

Note 3: The Police will be agreeing more detailed descriptions of specific policing purposes with the Registrar. These will cover such applications as Crime Reporting, Fixed Penalties, Criminal Information and the various indexes of the Police National Computer.

P058 Crime Prevention & Prosecution of Offenders *

Crime prevention and detection and the apprehension and prosecution of offenders.

Typical activities are: maintaining details of offenders and suspected offenders, witnesses and other relevant persons; details of information received; details of resources directed towards this purpose; analysis for management purposes and statutory returns.

Note 1: If you use this purpose you *MUST* give further details in the space provided.

Note 2: This purpose should be used by organisations or agencies other than police forces which have statutory law enforcement powers, eg: the Post Office and H.M. Customs and Excise, and Local Authorities.

Note 3: This purpose may be used, in appropriate circumstances, by the investigating departments of private organisations such as banks and major retailers.

35

P059 Courts Administration

Internal administration and management of courts of law or tribunals.

Typical activities are: the scheduling of magistrates, judges or members rotas; maintaining records pertaining to judges, Justices of the Peace or members of a tribunal; related administrative matters; analysis for management purposes and statutory returns.

Note 1: This purpose applies to the Childrens Panels in Scotland.

P060 Discharge of Court Business

Carrying out the main functions of courts of law or tribunals.

Typical activities are: case scheduling; keeping fines and fees accounts; keeping maintenance records; enforcing fines; producing the court register; producing orders; managing legal aid, licensing and fixed penalties; analysis for management purposes and statutory returns.

Note 1: This purpose applies to the Childrens Panels in Scotland.

P061 Other Administration of Justice*

Note 1: If you use this purpose, you *MUST* give further details in the space provided.

P062 Provision of Health Care*

The provision of patient care in NHS hospitals or community services, family practice or in private health care institutions.

Typical activities are: the administration of patient records; the provision of general medical services; other medical, dental, pharmaceutical, nursing or opthalmic treatment or care; pathology or other investigative services; diagnosis, therapy, rehabilitation, preventative care, screening and follow up health services; analysis for management purposes and statutory returns.

Note 1: If you hold data for any of the following specific purposes, you *MUST* indicate this in the space provided:

Genetic services
Contraceptive services
Abortion services
Infertility services
Care/treatment of persons suffering from:
   —mental illness
   —addiction
   —sexually transmitted diseases.

36

P063 **Ambulance Services**

Provision of emergency and other transport where considered medically necessary.

Typical activities include analysis for management purposes and statutory returns.

P064 **Blood Transfusion Services**

Collection of blcod and blood products from voluntary donors, provision to hospitals and other users.

Typical activities are: organisation of collection and distribution; blood grouping, cross-matching and tissue typing for organ transplantation; routine testing of donated blood for diseases such as AIDS and hepatitis; analysis for management purposes and statutory returns.

P065 **Occupational Health Services**

Monitoring and surveillance of employees' health status; promotion of employee health and investigation of accident reports.

Typical activities include analysis for management purposes and statutory returns.

Note 1: This purpose should be used by private and public sector employers operating a full occupational health service beyond the narrow compliance with Health & Safety legislation covered by P001 (Personnel/Employee Administration).

P066 **Public Health**

Prevention and control of disease within the community, including reporting, surveillance and follow up of outbreaks of infectious diseases and food poisoning.

Typical activities are investigation, inspection and testing: analysis for management purposes and statutory returns.

37

P067 Health Care Administration

The administration of health care services in the NHS and private sector.

Typical activities are: organisation of in-patient, out-patient and family practitioner services; identification of patients; scheduling appointments and admissions; administration in connection with nursing; pharmacy, pathology and other investigative services; provision of health education information; financial administration including billing of patients and payment of fees; analysis for management purposes and statutory returns.

P068 Other Central Government*
Note 1: If you use this purpose, you *MUST* give further details in the space provided.

P069 Other Local Government*
Note 1: If you use this purpose, you *MUST* give further details in the space provided.

P070 Other Public Sector*
Note 1: If you use this purpose, you *MUST* give further details in the space provided.

38

Standard Descriptions — Data Classes

The standard descriptions of Data Classes, which appear in section B.2 of Form DPR.1, are expanded here in order to help you select those which are most appropriate. For each Class description, examples are given of the data items you *might* hold.

Code	Class Description	Example Data Items
	Identification Data	
C001	Personal Identifiers	Name, title, home address, work address, previous home address, home telephone number, work telephone number, any identification issued by the data user.
C002	Financial identifiers	Name and number of bank account(s), building society account(s), credit or charge card number(s), personal identification number(s)
C003	Identifiers issued by public bodies	NHS number, NI numbers, disabled persons number, pension book number, licence number(s), passport number
	Personal Characteristics	
C011	Personal details	Age, sex, date of birth, place of birth, nationality, legal status
C012	Physical description	Height, weight, colour of hair, colour of eyes, distinguishing characteristics
C013	Habits	Smoking, drinking habits
C014	Personality or Character	Opinions concerning personality or character

Family Circumstances

C021 Current marriage or partnership — Marital status, name of spouse or partner, maiden or previous name of spouse or partner, date of marriage, number of children

C022 Marital history — Details of previous marriages or partnerships, divorces, separations, names of previous partners

C023 Details of other family or household members — Children, dependants, other members of household, next of kin, parents

C024 Other social contacts — Friends, associates, relations other than immediate family

Social Circumstances

C031 Accommodation or housing — Residential address, type of accommodation, owned or rented, length of time at address, rent, rates, other expenditure on housing, housing classification, valuation details, names of key holders

C032 Property or possessions — Land, property, possessions owned or held

C033 Immigration status — Details of visa, work permit, residential or travel restrictions, entry details and conditions

C034 Travel and Movement Details — Information as to whereabouts, past movements, details of journeys, foreign travel visas and work permits

C035 Leisure activities or interests — Hobbies, sports, other interests

C036 Lifestyle — Details of consumption of goods or services. Personal or family behaviour

C037 Membership of voluntary or charitable bodies — Membership of clubs, societies, other voluntary organisations, offices held and record of participation

40

C038	Public offices held	Local councillor, school governor, magistrate, member of public committees, working parties
C039	Licences or permits held	Driving licence, vehicle excise licence, shotgun licence, fishing permit
C040	Complaint, incident or accident details	Details of accident, incident, or complaint involving data subject, nature of damage or injury, people involved, witnesses
C041	Court, tribunal or enquiry proceedings	Details of actions, criminal or civil, brought by or against data subject

Education, Skills, Profession

C051	Academic record	Details of schools, colleges, universities attended
C052	Qualifications and skills	Academic qualifications, trade or professional skills, special licences (HGV, PSV, Pilot's)
C053	Membership of professional bodies	Current membership type, membership record, special interests and record of participation
C054	Professional expertise	Professional interests, research interests, academic interests, specialist subjects, teaching experience, consultancies
C055	Membership of committees	Details of committee, working party, commission membership arising from professional expertise
C056	Publications	Books, articles, reports, audio-visual materials published
C057	Student record	Courses of study, qualifications sought, examination results, other progress reports
C058	Student financial records	Fees and charges due, source of finance, payment method, payment history

41

217

Employment Details

C061   Current employment

Employer, job title or job description, grade, date employed, location of employment, speciality or industry, terms and conditions or employment, previous duties and experience with current employer

C062   Recruitment details

Date recruited, method of recruitment, source of recruitment, references, details of probationary period

C063   Termination details

Date of leaving, reason for leaving, notice given, conditions of termination

C064   Career history

Previous employer(s), previous job, periods of unemployment, armed forces service

C065   Work record

Attendance record, reasons for absence, disciplinary record

C066   Health and Safety record

Occupational health, safety, accident record, first aid qualifications

C067   Trade union or staff association membership

Details of membership, offices held

C068   Payments and deductions

Salary, wages, commission, bonuses, expenses, allowances, benefits, loans, SSP details, tax, NI contributions, pension deductions, union dues, basis of earnings, method of payment, date of salary increment

C069   Property held by employee

Details of vehicle, tools, books, other property or equipment issued to employee

C070	Work management details	Current duties, responsibilities and projects, cost, charge or fee rate for employee, time and work allocation, time spent on job or assignment
C071	Work assessment details	Assessment of performance, potential
C072	Training record	Details of job-related training needs and training received, qualifications and skills gained
C073	Security details	Passwords, security codes and levels of authorisation

Financial Details

C081	Income, assets, investments	Total income, earned income, assets, investments, savings, dates of commencement and maturity, income from investments, charges on assets, covenants
C082	Liabilities and outgoings	Total outgoings, payments for rents loans, mortgages, HP and other credit facilities, covenants
C083	Creditworthiness	Credit rating, financial status or rating, income status or rating
C084	Loans, mortgages, credits	Type of loan etc, amount borrowed, amount outstanding, commencement date, duration, interest payable, payment record, details of securities
C085	Allowances, benefits, grants	
C086	Insurance details	Type of insurance, details of risk covered, amount insured, period of cover, date of maturity, payments made by or to data subject
C087	Pension details	Date of entry into scheme, type of scheme, date of leaving scheme, details of contributions to and payments from scheme, options under scheme, beneficiaries

C091   Goods or services provided to data subject   Details of goods or services supplied, loaned or hired to·data subject, details of goods or services withheld

C092   Goods or services obtained from data subject   Details of goods or services supplied by data subject, details of goods or services withheld

C093   Financial transactions   Amounts owed and paid to or by data subject, credit given, guarantors, method of payment, payment history, deposits and other security

C094   Compensation   Details of compensation claimed, amount paid or other compensation

Business Information

C101   Business activities of data subject   Type of business, goods or services used or provided, business contacts

C102   Agreements or contracts   Details of trading, commercial, legal, or other contracts of agreements, details of agents

C103   Trading licences held   On-licence, off-licence, market trader's licence, goods vehicle operator's licence

220

Health & Other

C111 Physical health record — Medical report, diagnostic information record of treatment, results of investigative tests

C112 Mental health record — Medical report, diagnostic information record of treatment, results of investigative tests

C113 Disabilities or infirmities

C114 Dietary or other special health requirements — Record of special requirements needed eg: for treatment, travel or accommodation

C115 Sexual Life

C116 Racial or ethnic origin

C117 Motoring convictions — Details of convictions, sentences, court orders relating to Road Traffic Act offences

C118 Other convictions — Details of convictions, sentences, court orders other than for Road Traffic Act offences

C119 Criminal intelligence — Suspected offences, association with known criminals, aliases, evidence supporting suspicions

C120 Political opinions — Political opinions, voting preferences

C121 Political party membership — Membership of political party, offices held

C122 Support for pressure groups — Membership of or support for pressure groups, campaigning bodies

C123 Religious beliefs

C124 Other beliefs

Miscellaneous Information

C131 References to manual files or records — Reference numbers, indices, codes etc referring to information not processed automatically

C132 Uncategorised Information — Correspondence, files, reports etc held as data but not organised by reference to any other specific data type. This applies to electronic mail or filing but should not be used to avoid registration of specific Data Classes known to be contained in the files

THE DATA PROTECTION REGISTRAR

Application for Registration

Data Protection Act 1984

Application No.

Form DPR. 1

Part A

About this form

Please read this section before completing the form

How to apply for Registration

The application form is in two separate parts:

This part (Part A) is for information about the applicant and other details covering the whole application.

Part B is for a description of a Purpose for which personal data are to be held or used, and a description of the data and associated details. You will need to complete one **Part B** in respect of each Purpose you wish to register.

You should read the accompanying **Notes** booklet before completing the form. The Notes contain rules and conditions which the Registrar will apply, as well as standard descriptions and definitions which you will need to consult. **It is important that you read the Notes booklet carefully.**

In completing form DPR 1, please use a typewriter or, if handwritten, use BLOCK CAPITALS

If your application is accepted, all the details given on this form, except for those in **A3** and the declaration, will appear in the Register and will be available for public inspection.

Do not use this form to:
Alter or remove an entry already on the Register   —use Form DPR.2
Renew an entry already on the Register   —in this case you will be sent a renewal reminder

Further registration packs, and extra copies of **Part B**, can be obtained from **Crown Post Offices** and from the **Office of the Data Protection Registrar, Springfield House, Water Lane, Wilmslow, Cheshire, SK9 5AX.**

Completed application forms, together with the appropriate fee, should be sent to the Registrar at **P.O.Box 66, Wilmslow, Cheshire, SK9 5AX.** This address must only be used for applications. Other correspondence should be sent to the full address given above — it may be seriously delayed if sent to P.O.Box 66.

Declaration

To be completed by all applicants

Please fill in the rest of the form before completing this declaration.

To the best of my knowledge and belief the particulars given in this application are correct and complete. I confirm that I am the Data User or Computer Bureau named in section **A2** or that I am authorised to act on behalf of that Data User or Computer Bureau

I have read the **Notes** booklet and understand the Registrar's conditions which it contains

I enclose the fee of £ _____ Date _____

Signature _____

Name _____

Position _____

It is an offence knowingly or recklessly to furnish the Registrar with information which is false or misleading in any material respect

Data Users Only

Write here the number of Parts B forming part of this application

For use by Registrar only

Exception No.

Receipt date

Registration No.

222

All applicants must complete sections **A1** and **A2** and where appropriate, **A3-A8**

A1 Type of application   Tick the appropriate box to indicate whether this
application is for registration as a Data User, a Computer
Bureau or both.

Data User and Bureau ☐

Bureau only ☐

Data User only ☐

A2 Name and address   Write here the name and address of the Data User or Computer Bureau for whom this
application is made

Name

Address

Post
Code:

A3 Contact name and address   You may wish to give the name and address of a contact person in your organisation with
whom the Registrar should discuss matters concerning this application. If you do, write it
here:

Name/Job title

Address (if different from that given in **A2**)

Post
Code   Phone No.   Extn

4 Company Registration Number   If the application is on behalf of a registered company, write the company registration number
here. Otherwise leave blank

A5 Other names   You may wish to associate other names (e.g. trading names) with this application. If you do, write the names here, starting each one on a new line

_____

_____

_____

_____

_____

_____

_____

A6 Organisation sub-division   You may wish to relate this application to a particular part or sub-division of your organisation. If you do, write the name here

_____

_____

A7 Period of registration   The initial period of registration will be 3 years unless you specify a shorter period by ticking one of these boxes   1 year: ☐

2 years: ☐

The remaining sections of this form (A8 and all of PART B) are for applicants wishing to register as Data Users. Applicants wishing to register as Computer Bureaux only should now complete the declaration on page 1.

A8 Subject access addresses   You must give at least one address for the receipt of requests from data subjects for access to the data described in this application.

If you wish to use one or both of the addresses already given in **A2** or **A3** — tick here: A2 ☐

A3 ☐

If you have not ticked one of the boxes above, you must write an address in the space below. If you have ticked one of the boxes, you may use the space below for a further subject access address:

Address

_____

_____

_____

Post Code

If you wish to give more addresses for subject access, turn to page 4

3   **224**

**Additional subject
access addresses (Optional)** If you wish to give additional addresses for subject access, use the spaces below:

Address

_____

_____

_____

Post Code

Address   :

_____

_____

_____

Post Code

Address

_____

_____

_____

Post Code

Address

_____

_____

_____

Post Code

Address

_____

_____

_____

Post Code

Form DPR.1 Part A 9/85   **Have you completed any related Parts B and signed the Declaration on page 1?**

4   225

Printed in the UK for HMSO Dd 8938926 8/85 1152

THE DATA PROTECTION REGISTRAR

Application for Registration

Data Protection Act 1984

Application No
(from Part A)

Please write in
this number before
proceeding

Form DPR 1 **Part B**

About this form This form is for use only in conjunction with form DPR 1 A

You should read the Notes on the back of this form and the accompanying **Notes** booklet

B.1 Purpose In this section you should describe a Purpose for which data are held or used

There are two methods of completing this section of the form

Method 1 By selecting one of the Standard Purposes listed and described in the Notes booklet

You may then relate the Purpose to a specific part of your organisation or particular business activity

Method 2 By describing the Purpose in your own words

You are likely to find registration simpler and easier under Method 1 and you are strongly advised to use this Method if it can meet your requirements.

Method 1 Select one of the Standard Purposes from those listed in the accompanying **Notes** booklet and write both the code number and the title in the spaces provided below

P	
code	title

If you are required to give further details of your Purpose (see **Notes** booklet) write these here

_____

_____

If you wish to relate this Purpose to a specific part or parts of your organisation or particular business activity enter details here

_____

_____

_____

_____

_____

Method 2 **(This method should only be used if Method 1 is inappropriate).**
Please describe the Purpose for which data are held or used, and, if you wish, the specific part or parts of your organisation or particular business activity to which it is related

_____

_____

_____

_____

_____

1

226

B.2 Description of Personal Data – Data Subjects

In this section you should describe the types of individual **(Data Subjects)** about whom personal data are to be held for the Purpose described in section B.1. Do this by ticking the appropriate boxes below

		Current	Past	Potential			Current	Past	Potential
Employees, trainees, voluntary workers	S001	☐	☐	☐	Offenders and suspected offenders	S021	☐	☐	☐
Employees of associated companies, organisations	S002	☐	☐	☐	Tenants	S022	☐	☐	☐
Employees of other organisations	S003	☐	☐	☐	Landlords, owners of property	S023	☐	☐	☐
Recipients, customers or clients for goods or services (direct or indirect)	S004	☐	☐	☐	Correspondents and enquirers	S024	☐	☐	☐
Suppliers of goods or services (direct or indirect)	S005	☐	☐	☐	Survey respondents, other persons assisting research	S025	☐	☐	☐
Claimants, beneficiaries, payees	S006	☐	☐	☐	Patients	S026	☐	☐	☐
Account holders	S007	☐	☐	☐	Self-employed persons	S027	☐	☐	☐
Share and stock holders	S008	☐	☐	☐	Unemployed persons	S028	☐	☐	☐
Partners, directors, other senior officers	S009	☐	☐	☐	Retired persons	S029	☐	☐	☐
Employers	S010	☐	☐	☐	Students	S030	☐	☐	☐
Competitors	S011	☐	☐	☐	Minors	S031	☐	☐	
Business or other contacts	S012	☐	☐	☐	Applicants for permits, licences, registration	S032	☐	☐	☐
Advisors, consultants, professional and other experts	S013	☐	☐	☐	Taxpayers, ratepayers	S033	☐	☐	☐
Agents, other intermediaries	S014	☐	☐	☐	Licence holders	S034	☐	☐	☐
Trustees	S015	☐	☐	☐	Vehicle keepers	S035	☐	☐	☐
Members, supporters of a club, society, institution	S016	☐	☐	☐	Elected representatives, other holders of public office	S036	☐	☐	☐
Assignees, guarantors, other parties with legitimate contractual or business interest	S017	☐	☐	☐	Authors, publishers, editors, artists, other creators	S037	☐	☐	☐
Donors and lenders	S018	☐	☐	☐	Immigrants, foreign nationals	S038	☐	☐	☐
Complainants	S019	☐	☐	☐	Relatives, dependants, friends, neighbours, referees, associates, contacts of any of those ticked above	S039	☐	☐	☐
Witnesses	S020	☐	☐	☐	Members of the public	S040	☐		

If you wish, you may write additional descriptions of Data Subjects here; start each description on a new line

_____

_____

_____

_____

_____

_____

_____

_____

2

B.2 Description of Personal Data — Data Classes

In this section, you should describe the **Classes** of personal data to be held for the Purpose described in B.1. Do this by ticking the appropriate boxes below. You should refer to the **Notes** booklet for examples of data items which might be covered by each Class.

Identification Data

Personal identifiers **C001** ☐

Financial identifiers **C002** ☐

Identifiers issued by public bodies **C003** ☐

Personal Characteristics

Personal details **C011** ☐

Physical description **C012** ☐

Habits **C013** ☐

Personality character **C014** ☐

Family Circumstances

Current marriage or partnership **C021** ☐

Marital history **C022** ☐

Details of other family, household members **C023** ☐

Other social contacts **C024** ☐

Social Circumstances

Accommodation or housing **C031** ☐

Property, possessions **C032** ☐

Immigration status **C033** ☐

Travel, movement details **C034** ☐

Leisure activities, interests **C035** ☐

Lifestyle **C036** ☐

Membership of voluntary, charitable bodies **C037** ☐

Public offices held **C038** ☐

Licences, permits held **C039** ☐

Complaint, incident, accident details **C040** ☐

Court, tribunal, enquiry proceedings **C041** ☐

Education, Skills, Profession

Academic record **C051** ☐

Qualifications and skills **C052** ☐

Membership of professional bodies **C053** ☐

Professional expertise **C054** ☐

Membership of committees **C055** ☐

Publications **C056** ☐

Student record **C057** ☐

Student financial records **C058** ☐

Employment Details

Current employment **C061** ☐

Recruitment details **C062** ☐

Termination details **C063** ☐

Career history **C064** ☐

Work record **C065** ☐

Health & safety record **C066** ☐

Trade union, staff association membership **C067** ☐

Payments, deductions **C068** ☐

Property held by employee **C069** ☐

Work management details **C070** ☐

Work assessment details **C071** ☐

Training record **C072** ☐

Security details **C073** ☐

Financial Details

Income, assets, investments **C081** ☐

Liabilities, outgoings **C082** ☐

Creditworthiness **C083** ☐

Loans, mortgages, credits **C084** ☐

Allowances, benefits, grants **C085** ☐

Insurance details **C086** ☐

Pension details **C087** ☐

Details of Transactions

Goods, services provided to the data subject **C091** ☐

Goods, services obtained from the data subject **C092** ☐

Financial transactions **C093** ☐

Compensation **C094** ☐

Business Information

Business activities of the data subject **C101** ☐

Agreements, contracts **C102** ☐

Trading licences held **C103** ☐

Health & Other Classes

Physical health record **C111** ☐

Mental health record **C112** ☐

Disabilities, infirmities **C113** ☐

Dietary, other special health requirements **C114** ☐

Sexual life **C115** ☐

Racial, ethnic origin **C116** ☐

Motoring convictions **C117** ☐

Other convictions **C118** ☐

Criminal intelligence **C119** ☐

Political opinions **C120** ☐

Political party membership **C121** ☐

Support for pressure groups **C122** ☐

Religious beliefs **C123** ☐

Other beliefs **C124** ☐

Miscellaneous Information

References to manual files, records **C131** ☐

Uncategorised information **C132** ☐

If you wish, you may describe additional Classes of data here; start each description on a new line:

_____

_____

_____

228

B.3 Sources and Disclosures

In this section, you should describe

In column A — The sources from which you intend or may wish to obtain any of the data you have described in section B.2
In column B — The person or persons to whom you intend or may wish to disclose these data

Do this by ticking the appropriate boxes below

Individuals or Organisations directly associated with the Data Subjects

A. Source / B. Disclosure

		A	B
The Data Subjects themselves	D101	☐	☐
Family, relatives, guardians, trustees	D102	☐	☐
Other members of their households, friends, neighbours	D103	☐	☐
Employers — past, current or prospective	D104	☐	☐
Employees, agents	D105	☐	☐
Colleagues, business associates	D106	☐	☐
Legal representatives	D107	☐	☐
Financial representatives	D108	☐	☐
Doctors, Dentists, other health advisers	D109	☐	☐
Social, spiritual, welfare, advice workers	D110	☐	☐
Other professional advisers	D111	☐	☐
Landlords	D112	☐	☐

Others — please specify here

_____   ☐ ☐

_____   ☐ ☐

Individuals or Organisations directly associated with the Data User

		A	B
Members, including shareholders	D201	☐	☐
Other companies in the same group	D202	☐	☐
Employees, agents	D203	☐	☐
Recipients, customers, clients for goods or services	D204	☐	☐
Claimants, beneficiaries, assignees, payees	D205	☐	☐
Suppliers, providers of goods or services	D206	☐	☐
Persons making an enquiry or complaint	D207	☐	☐
Tenants	D208	☐	☐

Others — please specify here

_____   ☐ ☐

_____   ☐ ☐

Organisations or Individuals (General Description)

Central Government

		A	B
Inland Revenue	D301	☐	☐
Customs & Excise	D302	☐	☐
Driver & Vehicle Licensing Centre (DVLC)	D303	☐	☐
Department of Education & Science (DES)	D304	☐	☐
Department of Health & Social Security (DHSS)	D305	☐	☐
Department of Employment	D306	☐	☐
Home Office	D307	☐	☐
Ministry of Defence, including armed forces	D308	☐	☐
Other central government, including Scottish, Welsh & Northern Ireland Offices*	D309		

Local Government

		A	B
Education department	D321	☐	☐
Housing department	D322	☐	☐
Social Services department	D323	☐	☐
Electoral registration, Assessment, Valuation departments	D324	☐	☐
Other local government*	D325		

Other Public Bodies

		A	B
Other public bodies not elsewhere specified*	D331		
Foreign governments or authorities*	D332		

Continued

229

4

B.3 Sources and Disclosures *Continued*

Justice

		A. Source	B. Disclosure
Police forces	D341	☐	☐
Prosecuting authorities	D342	☐	☐
Other statutory law enforcement agencies, investigating bodies *	D343		
The courts	D344	☐	☐
Judges, magistrates	D345	☐	☐
Prison service	D346	☐	☐
Probation service	D347	☐	☐

Health & Social Welfare

		A. Source	B. Disclosure
Health authorities, family practitioner committees	D351	☐	☐
Hospitals, nursing homes	D352	☐	☐
Registered medical practitioners	D353	☐	☐
Registered dental practitioners	D354	☐	☐
Nurses, midwives, health visitors	D355	☐	☐
Other health care agencies, practitioners *	D356		
Social welfare agencies, practitioners *	D357		

Other

		A. Source	B. Disclosure
Public utilities	D361	☐	☐
Banks	D362	☐	☐
Building societies	D363	☐	☐
Insurance companies	D364	☐	☐
Other financial organisations *	D365		
Accountants & auditors	D366	☐	☐
Lawyers	D367	☐	☐
Credit reference agencies	D368	☐	☐
Debt collection, tracing agencies	D369	☐	☐
Employment, recruitment agencies	D370	☐	☐
Private detective agencies, security organisations	D371	☐	☐
Trade, employers associations	D372	☐	☐
Trade unions, staff associations	D373	☐	☐
Professional bodies	D374	☐	☐
Voluntary, charitable, religious organisations or associations	D375	☐	☐
Political organisations	D376	☐	☐
Education or training establishments, examining bodies	D377	☐	☐
Survey or research organisations, workers	D378	☐	☐
Providers of publicly available information including public libraries, press and media	D379	☐	☐
Providers of privately available information and databanks	D380	☐	☐
Traders in personal data	D381	☐	☐
Other organisations or individuals *	D382		

You should use the space below to give further details if you wish to use one or more of the categories marked with an asterisk (*) above. You should give the code number for each category which you are explaining.

If you wish, you may also write here additional descriptions of Sources and Disclosures

If you are using the space below, start each description on a new line and indicate whether the item is a Source a Disclosure, or both

	A. Source	B. Disclosure
_____	☐	☐
_____	☐	☐
_____	☐	☐
_____	☐	☐
_____	☐	☐

B4 Overseas transfers

In this section you should name any countries or territories outside the United Kingdom to which you intend to transfer the data.

If none, you should tick this box
None **T000** ☐

If the nature of your business requires you to transfer the data to any country worldwide, you should tick this box, and indicate your business in the space below
Worldwide **T999** ☐

_____

_____

Otherwise, tick the appropriate box(es) below

Algeria	**T001**	☐	Indonesia	**T020**	☐	Norway	**T039**	☐
Argentina	**T002**	☐	Iran	**T021**	☐	Oman	**T040**	☐
Australia	**T003**	☐	Iraq	**T022**	☐	Pakistan	**T041**	☐
Austria	**T004**	☐	Republic of Ireland	**T023**	☐	Philippines	**T042**	☐
Belgium	**T005**	☐	Isle of Man	**T024**	☐	Poland	**T043**	☐
Brazil	**T006**	☐	Israel	**T025**	☐	Portugal	**T044**	☐
Canada	**T007**	☐	Italy	**T026**	☐	Saudi Arabia	**T045**	☐
Cyprus	**T008**	☐	Japan	**T027**	☐	Singapore	**T046**	☐
Denmark	**T009**	☐	Jersey	**T028**	☐	South Africa	**T047**	☐
Dubai	**T010**	☐	Kuwait	**T029**	☐	South Korea	**T048**	☐
Egypt	**T011**	☐	Libya	**T030**	☐	Spain	**T049**	☐
Finland	**T012**	☐	Liechtenstein	**T031**	☐	Sweden	**T050**	☐
France	**T013**	☐	Luxembourg	**T032**	☐	Switzerland	**T051**	☐
West Germany	**T014**	☐	Malaysia	**T033**	☐	Taiwan	**T052**	☐
Greece	**T015**	☐	Malta	**T034**	☐	Turkey	**T053**	☐
Guernsey	**T016**	☐	Mexico	**T035**	☐	USA	**T054**	☐
Hong Kong	**T017**	☐	Netherlands	**T036**	☐	USSR	**T055**	☐
Iceland	**T018**	☐	New Zealand	**T037**	☐	Venezuela	**T056**	☐
India	**T019**	☐	Nigeria	**T038**	☐			

If necessary, you may write additional names or descriptions here; start each on a new line:

_____

_____

_____

_____

_____

_____

_____

231

6

Continuation

The space below is reserved for continuation text from any of the sections of this form. You should only need to use this space in exceptional circumstances.

You should indicate clearly which section of the form (B.1, B.3 etc) is continued here. Please start each separate continuation on a new line.

How to apply for Registration   The application form is in two separate parts

Part A is for information about the applicant and other details covering the whole application.

This part (Part B) is for a description of a Purpose for which personal data are to be held or used, and a description of the data and associated details. You will need to complete one Part B in respect of each Purpose you wish to register

You should read the accompanying **Notes** booklet before completing the form. The Notes contain rules and conditions which the Registrar will apply, as well as standard descriptions and definitions which you will need to consult. **It is important that you read the Notes carefully.**

In completing form DPR 1, please use a typewriter or, if handwritten, use BLOCK CAPITALS.

Do not use this form to
 Alter or remove an entry already on the Register — use Form DPR.2
 Renew an entry already on the Register — in this case you will be sent a renewal reminder.

Further registration packs, and extra copies of Part B, can be obtained from **Crown Post Offices** and from the **Office of the Data Protection Registrar, Springfield House, Water Lane, Wilmslow, Cheshire, SK9 5AX.**

Completed application forms, together with the appropriate fee (see Notes Booklet), should be sent to the Registrar at **P.O.Box 66, Wilmslow, Cheshire, SK9 5AX.** This address must only be used for applications. Other correspondence should be sent to the full address given above — it may be seriously delayed if sent to P.O. Box 66

How to complete this form   In each section of Part B you may use standard descriptions to provide the detail required Although you also have the option of writing your own descriptions in free text, **you are strongly encouraged to use the standard description approach.** In most sections this is simply a matter of selecting the appropriate descriptions from the list printed on the form and ticking the corresponding boxes

The standard descriptions for **Purposes** are not printed on the form but are listed in the separate **Notes** booklet. You will need to read these before filling in the form. You should also refer to the booklet when selecting descriptions for **Data Classes.**

Before completing the rest of the form you should write the application number (copied from the front of Part A) in the box provided on the front of this Part B.

If your application is accepted, the details given in sections B.1 to B.4 will appear on the Register and will be available for public inspection

If you need more space than is provided for text in any Section, you may continue on page 7.

Appendix 3

Specimen registration application

Introduction to the organisation — Rapid Printing Services Ltd

This example organisation is a limited company trading under the name of 'Rapid Printing Services Ltd'. It is a wholly owned subsidiary of MLJP plc. Rapid Printing Services employ 500 people located in 20 retail outlets throughout the UK, in addition to 400 at the main factory/head office. The company is variously known as 'Rapid Duplicating' and 'Rapid Copies' by various groups of customers.

The company uses a mini computer at head office and a large micro in each retail outlet. The organisation very infrequently allows other data users to use their mini computer facilities. It is therefore also a bureau.

Sales are largely UK based, but the company employs agents in some 20 overseas countries: five of these are very large and sales details are despatched on floppy disc to these larger agents.

Marketing is a key aspect of business operations with substantial volumes of direct mail advertising.

The organisation operates five major systems/data bases. These are:

(a) A simple personnel/payroll system operating on a bureau. This system concerns current and past employees only: it is not involved with recruitment aspects. The content, sources of data and disclosures of data are quite usual for a typical personnel/payroll system.

(b) A marketing system containing details of past, current and prospective customers who may be individuals or organisations.

This system retains records on past customers and details of local organisations and individuals who may be customers in the future. This file is used extensively for direct mailing of flyers.

(c) Accounting — Sales and purchase ledgers. This system is a very simple sales and purchase ledger application that is also used for some aspects of customer administration, hence removing any possibility of claiming an exemption.

(d) Current jobs in progress. This system was purpose written and includes details of all printing jobs that are being processed or are awaiting processing in any of the organisation's units. Customers, employees and suppliers are all referenced and any of these may be individuals. The organisation's fourth generation development language allows, and the organisation uses, analysis by reference to any of the data subjects.

(e) Overseas agents file. This simple system keeps track of payments to agents and monitors their sales performances. It relates only to 20 individuals around the world. Of these, five receive their sales analysis records (running to some thousands of transactions) on floppy disc in Apple MacIntosh format.

The data protection application forms for this organisation run to some 44 pages and are reproduced here. The reasoning behind this does not form part of the application and, hence, would not be sent to the Registrar.

THE DATA PROTECTION REGISTRAR

Application for Registration
Data Protection Act 1984

Application No

0001

Form DPR. 1

Part A

About this form

Please read this section before completing the form

How to apply for Registration

The application form is in two separate parts

This part (Part A) is for information about the applicant and other details covering the whole application

Part B is for a description of a Purpose for which personal data are to be held or used, and a description of the data and associated details. You will need to complete one **Part B** in respect of each Purpose you wish to register.

You should read the accompanying **Notes** booklet before completing the form. The Notes contain rules and conditions which the Registrar will apply, as well as standard descriptions and definitions which you will need to consult. **It is important that you read the Notes booklet carefully.**

In completing form DPR.1, please use a typewriter or, if handwritten, use BLOCK CAPITALS

If your application is accepted, all the details given on this form, except for those in **A3** and the declaration, will appear in the Register and will be available for public inspection

Do not use this form to
Alter or remove an entry already on the Register   —use Form DPR 2
Renew an entry already on the Register   —in this case you will be sent a renewal reminder

Further registration packs, and extra copies of **Part B**, can be obtained from **Crown Post Offices** and from the **Office of the Data Protection Registrar, Springfield House, Water Lane, Wilmslow, Cheshire, SK9 5AX.**

Completed application forms, together with the appropriate fee, should be sent to the Registrar at **P.O.Box 66, Wilmslow, Cheshire, SK9 5AX.** This address must only be used for applications. Other correspondence should be sent to the full address given above — it may be seriously delayed if sent to PO Box 66

Declaration   **To be completed by all applicants**

Please fill in the rest of the form before completing this declaration

To the best of my knowledge and belief the particulars given in this application are correct and complete. I confirm that I am the Data User or Computer Bureau named in section **A2** or that I am authorised to act on behalf of that Data User or Computer Bureau

I have read the **Notes** booklet and understand the Registrar's conditions which it contains

I enclose the fee of £   XX   Date _____11.11.85_____

Signature _____A. J. Smith._____

Name _____A J SMITH_____

Position _____COMPANY SECRETARY_____

It is an offence knowingly or recklessly to furnish the Registrar with information which is false or misleading in any material respect

---

Data Users Only

Write here the number of Parts B forming part of this application

5

All applicants must complete sections **A1** and **A2** and where appropriate, **A3- A8**

A1 Type of application　　Tick the appropriate box to indicate whether this
application is for registration as a Data User, a Computer
Bureau or both.

Data User and Bureau ☑

Bureau only ☐

Data User only ☐

A2 Name and address　　Write here the name and address of the Data User or Computer Bureau for whom this
application is made

Name

RAPID PRINTING SERVICES LTD

Address
1 HIGH STREET

LEEDS

Post
Code:　LS10 1AX

A3 Contact name and address　　You may wish to give the name and address of a contact person in your organisation with
whom the Registrar should discuss matters concerning this application. If you do, write it
here:

Name/Job title
A F BYTE　　　DATA PROCESSING MANAGER

Address (if different from that given in **A2**)
AS A2

Post
Code　　　　Phone No.　LEEDS 818412　　　Extn 100

A4 Company Registration Number　　If the application is on behalf of a registered company, write the company registration number
here. Otherwise leave blank.

1234567

2　　　**237**

You may wish to associate other names (e.g. trading names) with this application. If you do, write the names here, starting each one on a new line

RAPID DUPLICATING

RAPID COPIES

A6 Organisation sub-division You may wish to relate this application to a particular part or sub-division of your organisation. If you do, write the name here

A7 Period of registration The initial period of registration will be 3 years unless you specify a shorter period by ticking one of these boxes

1 year: ☐

2 years: ☐

The remaining sections of this form (A8 and all of PART B) are for applicants wishing to register as Data Users. Applicants wishing to register as Computer Bureaux only should now complete the declaration on page 1.

A8 Subject access addresses You must give at least one address for the receipt of requests from data subjects for access to the data described in this application.

If you wish to use one or both of the addresses already given in **A2** or **A3** — tick here:

A2 ☑

A3 ☐

If you have not ticked one of the boxes above, you must write an address in the space below. If you have ticked one of the boxes, you may use the space below for a further subject access address:

Address

ANY OF OUR RETAIL SHOPS

Post Code

If you wish to give more addresses for subject access, turn to page 4

If you wish to give additional addresses for subject access, use the spaces below

Address

Post Code

Address

Post Code

Address

Post Code

Address

Post Code

Address

Post Code

Have you completed any related Parts B and signed the Declaration on page 1?

Application for Registration

Data Protection Act 1984

Form DPR 1

Part B

About this form

This form is for use only in conjunction with form DPR 1 A

You should read the Notes on the back of this form and the accompanying **Notes** booklet

---

B.1 Purpose

In this section you should describe a Purpose for which data are held or used

There are two methods of completing this section of the form:

Method 1   By selecting one of the Standard Purposes listed and described in the Notes booklet

You may then relate the Purpose to a specific part of your organisation or particular business activity

Method 2   By describing the Purpose in your own words

You are likely to find registration simpler and easier under Method 1 and you are strongly advised to use this Method if it can meet your requirements.

Method 1

Select one of the Standard Purposes from those listed in the accompanying **Notes** booklet and write both the code number and the title in the spaces provided below

P 001	PERSONNEL/EMPLOYEE ADMINISTRATION
code	title

If you are required to give further details of your Purpose (see **Notes** booklet) write these here

If you wish to relate this Purpose to a specific part or parts of your organisation or particular business activity enter details here

Method 2

(This method should only be used if Method 1 is inappropriate).
Please describe the Purpose for which data are held or used, and, if you wish, the specific part or parts of your organisation or particular business activity to which it is related

B.2 Description of Personal Data – Data Subjects

In this section you should describe the types of individual **(Data Subjects)** about whom personal data are to be held for the Purpose described in section B.1. Do this by ticking the appropriate boxes below

		Current	Past	Potential
Employees, trainees, voluntary workers	S001	☑	☑	☐
Employees of associated companies, organisations	S002	☐	☐	☐
Employees of other organisations	S003	☐	☐	☐
Recipients, customers or clients for goods or services (direct or indirect)	S004	☐	☐	☐
Suppliers of goods or services (direct or indirect)	S005	☐	☐	☐
Claimants, beneficiaries, payees	S006	☐	☐	☐
Account holders	S007	☐	☐	☐
Share and stock holders	S008	☐	☐	☐
Partners, directors, other senior officers	S009	☐	☐	☐
Employers	S010	☐	☐	☐
Competitors	S011	☐	☐	☐
Business or other contacts	S012	☐	☐	☐
Advisors, consultants, professional and other experts	S013	☐	☐	☐
Agents, other intermediaries	S014	☐	☐	☐
Trustees	S015	☐	☐	☐
Members, supporters of a club, society, institution	S016	☐	☐	☐
Assignees, guarantors, other parties with legitimate contractual or business interest	S017	☐	☐	☐
Donors and lenders	S018	☐	☐	☐
Complainants	S019	☐	☐	☐
Witnesses	S020	☐	☐	☐

		Current	Past	Potential
Offenders and suspected offenders	S021	☐	☐	☐
Tenants	S022	☐	☐	☐
Landlords, owners of property	S023	☐	☐	☐
Correspondents and enquirers	S024	☐	☐	☐
Survey respondents, other persons assisting research	S025	☐	☐	☐
Patients	S026	☐	☐	☐
Self-employed persons	S027	☐	☐	☐
Unemployed persons	S028	☐	☐	☐
Retired persons	S029	☐	☐	☐
Students	S030	☐	☐	☐
Minors	S031	☐	☐	☐
Applicants for permits, licences, registration	S032	☐	☐	☐
Taxpayers, ratepayers	S033	☐	☐	☐
Licence holders	S034	☐	☐	☐
Vehicle keepers	S035	☐	☐	☐
Elected representatives, other holders of public office	S036	☐	☐	☐
Authors, publishers, editors, artists, other creators	S037	☐	☐	☐
Immigrants, foreign nationals	S038	☐	☐	☐
Relatives, dependants, friends, neighbours, referees, associates, contacts of any of those ticked above	S039	☐	☐	☐
Members of the public	S040	☐		

If you wish, you may write additional descriptions of Data Subjects here, start each description on a new line

_____

_____

_____

_____

_____

_____

_____

_____

_____

2

B.2 Description of Personal Data – Data Classes

In this section, you should describe the **Classes** of personal data to be held for the Purpose described in B.1. Do this by ticking the appropriate boxes below. You should refer to the **Notes** booklet for examples of data items which might be covered by each Class.

Identification Data

Personal identifiers	C001	☑
Financial identifiers	C002	☑
Identifiers issued by public bodies	C003	☑

Personal Characteristics

Personal details	C011	☑
Physical description	C012	☐
Habits	C013	☐
Personality, character	C014	☐

Family Circumstances

Current marriage or partnership	C021	☑
Marital history	C022	☐
Details of other family, household members	C023	☑
Other social contacts	C024	☐

Social Circumstances

Accommodation or housing	C031	☐
Property, possessions	C032	☐
Immigration status	C033	☐
Travel, movement details	C034	☑
Leisure activities, interests	C035	☐
Lifestyle	C036	☐
Membership of voluntary, charitable bodies	C037	☑
Public offices held	C038	☐
Licences, permits held	C039	☐
Complaint, incident, accident details	C040	☐
Court, tribunal, enquiry proceedings	C041	☐

Education, Skills, Profession

Academic record	C051	☑
Qualifications and skills	C052	☑
Membership of professional bodies	C053	☑

Professional expertise	C054	☐
Membership of committees	C055	☐
Publications	C056	☐
Student record	C057	☐
Student financial records	C058	☐

Employment Details

Current employment	C061	☑
Recruitment details	C062	☑
Termination details	C063	☑
Career history	C064	☑
Work record	C065	☑
Health & safety record	C066	☐
Trade union, staff association membership	C067	☑
Payments, deductions	C068	☑
Property held by employee	C069	☐
Work management details	C070	☐
Work assessment details	C071	☐
Training record	C072	☑
Security details	C073	☐

Financial Details

Income, assets, investments	C081	☐
Liabilities, outgoings	C082	☐
Creditworthiness	C083	☐
Loans, mortgages, credits	C084	☐
Allowances, benefits, grants	C085	☐
Insurance details	C086	☐
Pension details	C087	☑

Details of Transactions

Goods, services provided to the data subject	C091	☐
Goods, services obtained from the data subject	C092	☐
Financial transactions	C093	☐
Compensation	C094	☐

Business Information

Business activities of the data subject	C101	☐
Agreements, contracts	C102	☐
Trading licences held	C103	☐

Health & Other Classes

Physical health record	C111	☑
Mental health record	C112	☐
Disabilities, infirmities	C113	☐
Dietary, other special health requirements	C114	☐
Sexual life	C115	☐
Racial, ethnic origin	C116	☐
Motoring convictions	C117	☐
Other convictions	C118	☐
Criminal intelligence	C119	☐
Political opinions	C120	☐
Political party membership	C121	☐
Support for pressure groups	C122	☐
Religious beliefs	C123	☐
Other beliefs	C124	☐

Miscellaneous Information

References to manual files, records	C131	☑
Uncategorised information	C132	☐

If you wish, you may describe additional Classes of data here, start each description on a new line

_____

_____

_____

B.3 Sources and Disclosures

In this section, you should describe:

In column A — The sources from which you intend or may wish to obtain any of the data you have described in section B.2
In column B — The person or persons to whom you intend or may wish to disclose these data.

Do this by ticking the appropriate boxes below

Individuals or Organisations directly associated with the Data Subjects

		A. Source	B. Disclosure			A. Source	B. Disclosure
The Data Subjects themselves	D101	☑	☐	Legal representatives	D107	☐	☐
Family, relatives, guardians, trustees	D102	☐	☐	Financial representatives	D108	☐	☐
Other members of their households, friends, neighbours	D103	☐	☐	Doctors, Dentists, other health advisers	D109	☐	☐
Employers — past, current or prospective	D104	☐	☐	Social, spiritual, welfare, advice workers	D110	☐	☐
Employees, agents	D105	☐	☐	Other professional advisers	D111	☐	☐
Colleagues, business associates	D106	☐	☐	Landlords	D112	☐	☐

Others — please specify here:

☐ ☐

☐ ☐

Individuals or Organisations directly associated with the Data User

		A. Source	B. Disclosure			A. Source	B. Disclosure
Members, including shareholders	D201	☐	☐	Claimants, beneficiaries, assignees, payees	D205	☐	☐
Other companies in the same group	D202	☐	☑	Suppliers, providers of goods or services	D206	☐	☑
Employees, agents	D203	☑	☑	Persons making an enquiry or complaint	D207	☐	☐
Recipients, customers, clients for goods or services	D204	☐	☐	Tenants	D208	☐	☐

Others — please specify here

COMPANY STAFF CLUB ☑ ☑

☐ ☐

Organisations or Individuals (General Description)

Central Government

		A. Source	B. Disclosure
Inland Revenue	D301	☑	☑
Customs & Excise	D302	☐	☐
Driver & Vehicle Licensing Centre (DVLC)	D303	☐	☐
Department of Education & Science (DES)	D304	☐	☐
Department of Health & Social Security (DHSS)	D305	☑	☑
Department of Employment	D306	☐	☐
Home Office	D307	☐	☐
Ministry of Defence including armed forces	D308	☐	☐
Other central government, including Scottish, Welsh & Northern Ireland Offices*	D309		

Local Government

		A. Source	B. Disclosure
Education department	D321	☐	☐
Housing department	D322	☐	☐
Social Services department	D323	☐	☐
Electoral registration, Assessment, Valuation departments	D324	☐	☐
Other local government*	D325		

Other Public Bodies

Other public bodies not elsewhere specified*	D331
Foreign governments or authorities*	D332

Continued

243

4

Justice		A. Source	B. Disclosure
Police forces	**D341**	☐	☐
Prosecuting authorities	**D342**	☐	☐
Other statutory law enforcement agencies, investigating bodies *	**D343**		
The courts	**D344**	☐	☐
Judges, magistrates	**D345**	☐	☐
Prison service	**D346**	☐	☐
Probation service	**D347**	☐	☐

Health & Social Welfare

		A. Source	B. Disclosure
Health authorities, family practitioner committees	**D351**	☐	☐
Hospitals, nursing homes	**D352**	☐	☐
Registered medical practitioners	**D353**	☐	☐
Registered dental practitioners	**D354**	☐	☐
Nurses, midwives, health visitors	**D355**	☐	☐
Other health care agencies, practitioners *	**D356**		
Social welfare agencies, practitioners *	**D357**		

Other		A. Source	B. Disclosure
Public utilities	**D361**	☐	☐
Banks	**D362**	☐	☐
Building societies	**D363**	☐	☐
Insurance companies	**D364**	☐	☑
Other financial organisations *	**D365**		
Accountants & auditors	**D366**	☐	☐
Lawyers	**D367**	☐	☐
Credit reference agencies	**D368**	☐	☐
Debt collection, tracing agencies	**D369**	☐	☐
Employment, recruitment agencies	**D370**	☑	☐
Private detective agencies, security organisations	**D371**	☐	☐
Trade, employers associations	**D372**	☐	☐
Trade unions, staff associations	**D373**	☐	☑
Professional bodies	**D374**	☐	☐
Voluntary, charitable, religious organisations or associations	**D375**	☐	☐
Political organisations	**D376**	☐	☐
Education or training establishments, examining bodies	**D377**	☐	☐
Survey or research organisations, workers	**D378**	☐	☐
Providers of publicly available information including public libraries, press and media	**D379**	☐	☐
Providers of privately available information and databanks	**D380**	☐	☐
Traders in personal data	**D381**	☐	☐
Other organisations or individuals *	**D382**		

You should use the space below to give further details if you wish to use one or more of the categories marked with an asterisk (*) above. You should give the code number for each category which you are explaining.

If you wish, you may also write here additional descriptions of Sources and Disclosures

If you are using the space below, start each description on a new line and indicate whether the item is a Source, a Disclosure, or both

	A. Source	B. Disclosure
	☐	☐
	☐	☐
	☐	☐
	☐	☐
	☐	☐

B.4 Overseas transfers

In this section you should name any countries or territories outside the United Kingdom to which you intend to transfer the data.

If none, you should tick this box   None **T000** ☑

If the nature of your business requires you to transfer the data to any country worldwide, you should tick this box, and indicate your business in the space below   Worldwide **T999** ☐

_____

_____

Otherwise, tick the appropriate boxes below

Country	Code		Country	Code		Country	Code	
Algeria	T001	☐	Indonesia	T020	☐	Norway	T039	☐
Argentina	T002	☐	Iran	T021	☐	Oman	T040	☐
Australia	T003	☐	Iraq	T022	☐	Pakistan	T041	☐
Austria	T004	☐	Republic of Ireland	T023	☐	Philippines	T042	☐
Belgium	T005	☐	Isle of Man	T024	☐	Poland	T043	☐
Brazil	T006	☐	Israel	T025	☐	Portugal	T044	☐
Canada	T007	☐	Italy	T026	☐	Saudi Arabia	T045	☐
Cyprus	T008	☐	Japan	T027	☐	Singapore	T046	☐
Denmark	T009	☐	Jersey	T028	☐	South Africa	T047	☐
Dubai	T010	☐	Kuwait	T029	☐	South Korea	T048	☐
Egypt	T011	☐	Libya	T030	☐	Spain	T049	☐
Finland	T012	☐	Liechtenstein	T031	☐	Sweden	T050	☐
France	T013	☐	Luxembourg	T032	☐	Switzerland	T051	☐
West Germany	T014	☐	Malaysia	T033	☐	Taiwan	T052	☐
Greece	T015	☐	Malta	T034	☐	Turkey	T053	☐
Guernsey	T016	☐	Mexico	T035	☐	USA	T054	☐
Hong Kong	T017	☐	Netherlands	T036	☐	USSR	T055	☐
Iceland	T018	☐	New Zealand	T037	☐	Venezuela	T056	☐
India	T019	☐	Nigeria	T038	☐			

If necessary, you may write additional names or descriptions here; start each on a new line.

_____

_____

_____

_____

_____

_____

_____

6

Continuation

The space below is reserved for continuation text from any of the sections of this form. You should only need to use this space in exceptional circumstances.

You should indicate clearly which section of the form (B.1, B.3 etc) is continued here. Please start each separate continuation on a new line.

_____

_____

_____

_____

_____

_____

_____

_____

_____

_____

_____

_____

_____

_____

_____

_____

_____

_____

_____

_____

_____

_____

_____

_____

_____

_____

_____

_____

_____

_____

_____

How to apply for Registration   The application form is in two separate parts.

Part A is for information about the applicant and other details covering the whole application.

This part (Part B) is for a description of a Purpose for which personal data are to be held or used, and a description of the data and associated details. You will need to complete one Part B in respect of each Purpose you wish to register.

You should read the accompanying **Notes** booklet before completing the form. The Notes contain rules and conditions which the Registrar will apply, as well as standard descriptions and definitions which you will need to consult. **It is important that you read the Notes carefully.**

In completing form DPR 1, please use a typewriter or, if handwritten, use BLOCK CAPITALS.

Do not use this form to
  Alter or remove an entry already on the Register — use Form DPR 2
  Renew an entry already on the Register — in this case you will be sent a renewal reminder

Further registration packs, and extra copies of Part B, can be obtained from **Crown Post Offices** and from the **Office of the Data Protection Registrar, Springfield House, Water Lane, Wilmslow, Cheshire, SK9 5AX.**

Completed application forms, together with the appropriate fee (see Notes Booklet) should be sent to the Registrar at **P.O.Box 66, Wilmslow, Cheshire, SK9 5AX.** This address must only be used for applications. Other correspondence should be sent to the full address given above — it may be seriously delayed if sent to P.O. Box 66.

How to complete this form   In each section of Part B you may use standard descriptions to provide the detail required. Although you also have the option of writing your own descriptions in free text, **you are strongly encouraged to use the standard description approach.** In most sections this is simply a matter of selecting the appropriate descriptions from the list printed on the form and ticking the corresponding boxes.

The standard descriptions for **Purposes** are not printed on the form but are listed in the separate **Notes** booklet. You will need to read these before filling in the form. You should also refer to the booklet when selecting descriptions for **Data Classes.**

Before completing the rest of the form you should write the application number (copied from the front of Part A) in the box provided on the front of this Part B.

If your application is accepted, the details given in sections B.1 to B.4 will appear on the Register and will be available for public inspection.

If you need more space than is provided for text in any Section, you may continue on page 7.

THE DATA PROTECTION REGISTRAR

Application for Registration

Data Protection Act 1984

Form DPR 1

Part B

About this form   This form is for use only in conjunction with form DPR 1 A

You should read the Notes on the back of this form and the accompanying **Notes** booklet

B.1 Purpose   In this section you should describe a Purpose for which data are held or used

There are two methods of completing this section of the form

Method 1   By selecting one of the Standard Purposes listed and described in the Notes booklet

You may then relate the Purpose to a specific part of your organisation or particular business activity

Method 2   By describing the Purpose in your own words

You are likely to find registration simpler and easier under Method 1 and you are strongly advised to use this Method if it can meet your requirements.

Method 1   Select one of the Standard Purposes from those listed in the accompanying **Notes** booklet and write both the code number and the title in the spaces provided below

P 002	WORK PLANNING AND MANAGEMENT
code	title

If you are required to give further details of your Purpose (see **Notes** booklet) write these here

If you wish to relate this Purpose to a specific part or parts of your organisation or particular business activity, enter details here

Method 2   **(This method should only be used if Method 1 is inappropriate).**
Please describe the Purpose for which data are held or used, and, if you wish, the specific part or parts of your organisation or particular business activity to which it is related

B.2 Description of Personal Data – Data Subjects

In this section you should describe the types of individual **(Data Subjects)** about whom personal data are to be held for the Purpose described in section B.1. Do this by ticking the appropriate boxes below

Data Subject	Code	Current	Past	Potential
Employees, trainees, voluntary workers	S001	☑	☑	☐
Employees of associated companies, organisations	S002	☐	☐	☐
Employees of other organisations	S003	☐	☐	☐
Recipients, customers or clients for goods or services (direct or indirect)	S004	☑	☑	☐
Suppliers of goods or services (direct or indirect)	S005	☑	☑	☐
Claimants, beneficiaries, payees	S006	☐	☐	☐
Account holders	S007	☐	☐	☐
Share and stock holders	S008	☐	☐	☐
Partners, directors, other senior officers	S009	☐	☐	☐
Employers	S010	☐	☐	☐
Competitors	S011	☐	☐	☐
Business or other contacts	S012	☐	☐	☐
Advisors, consultants, professional and other experts	S013	☐	☐	☐
Agents, other intermediaries	S014	☐	☐	☐
Trustees	S015	☐	☐	☐
Members, supporters of a club, society, institution	S016	☐	☐	☐
Assignees, guarantors, other parties with legitimate contractual or business interest	S017	☐	☐	☐
Donors and lenders	S018	☐	☐	☐
Complainants	S019	☐	☐	☐
Witnesses	S020	☐	☐	☐

Data Subject	Code	Current	Past	Potential
Offenders and suspected offenders	S021	☐	☐	☐
Tenants	S022	☐	☐	☐
Landlords, owners of property	S023	☐	☐	☐
Correspondents and enquirers	S024	☐	☐	☐
Survey respondents, other persons assisting research	S025	☐	☐	☐
Patients	S026	☐	☐	☐
Self-employed persons	S027	☐	☐	☐
Unemployed persons	S028	☐	☐	☐
Retired persons	S029	☐	☐	☐
Students	S030	☐	☐	☐
Minors	S031	☐	☐	☐
Applicants for permits, licences, registration	S032	☐	☐	☐
Taxpayers, ratepayers	S033	☐	☐	☐
Licence holders	S034	☐	☐	☐
Vehicle keepers	S035	☐	☐	☐
Elected representatives, other holders of public office	S036	☐	☐	☐
Authors, publishers, editors, artists, other creators	S037	☐	☐	☐
Immigrants, foreign nationals	S038	☐	☐	☐
Relatives, dependants, friends, neighbours, referees, associates, contacts of any of those ticked above	S039	☐	☐	☐
Members of the public	S040	☐		

If you wish, you may write additional descriptions of Data Subjects here, start each description on a new line

_____

_____

_____

_____

_____

_____

_____

_____

249

2

B.2 Description of Personal Data – Data Classes

In this section, you should describe the **Classes** of personal data to be held for the Purpose described in B.1 Do this by ticking the appropriate boxes below You should refer to the **Notes** booklet for examples of data items which might be covered by each Class

Identification Data

Personal identifiers	**C001**	☑
Financial identifiers	**C002**	☐
Identifiers issued by public bodies	**C003**	☐

Personal Characteristics

Personal details	**C011**	☐
Physical description	**C012**	☐
Habits	**C013**	☐
Personality character	**C014**	☐

Family Circumstances

Current marriage or partnership	**C021**	☐
Marital history	**C022**	☐
Details of other family, household members	**C023**	☐
Other social contacts	**C024**	☐

Social Circumstances

Accommodation or housing	**C031**	☐
Property, possessions	**C032**	☐
Immigration status	**C033**	☐
Travel, movement details	**C034**	☐
Leisure activities, interests	**C035**	☐
Lifestyle	**C036**	☐
Membership of voluntary charitable bodies	**C037**	☐
Public offices held	**C038**	☐
Licences, permits held	**C039**	☐
Complaint, incident, accident details	**C040**	☐
Court, tribunal, enquiry proceedings	**C041**	☐

Education, Skills, Profession

Academic record	**C051**	☐
Qualifications and skills	**C052**	☑
Membership of professional bodies	**C053**	☐
Professional expertise	**C054**	☐
Membership of committees	**C055**	☐
Publications	**C056**	☐
Student record	**C057**	☐
Student financial records	**C058**	☐

Employment Details

Current employment	**C061**	☑
Recruitment details	**C062**	☐
Termination details	**C063**	☐
Career history	**C064**	☐
Work record	**C065**	☐
Health & safety record	**C066**	☐
Trade union staff association membership	**C067**	☐
Payments, deductions	**C068**	☐
Property held by employee	**C069**	☐
Work management details	**C070**	☑
Work assessment details	**C071**	☑
Training record	**C072**	☐
Security details	**C073**	☐

Financial Details

Income assets, investments	**C081**	☐
Liabilities, outgoings	**C082**	☐
Creditworthiness	**C083**	☐
Loans, mortgages, credits	**C084**	☐
Allowances benefits, grants	**C085**	☐
Insurance details	**C086**	☐
Pension details	**C087**	☐

Details of Transactions

Goods services provided to the data subject	**C091**	☑
Goods services obtained from the data subject	**C092**	☑
Financial transactions	**C093**	☐
Compensation	**C094**	☐

Business Information

Business activities of the data subject	**C101**	☐
Agreements contracts	**C102**	☐
Trading licences held	**C103**	☐

Health & Other Classes

Physical health record	**C111**	☐
Mental health record	**C112**	☐
Disabilities infirmities	**C113**	☐
Dietary other special health requirements	**C114**	☐
Sexual life	**C115**	☐
Racial ethnic origin	**C116**	☐
Motoring convictions	**C117**	☐
Other convictions	**C118**	☐
Criminal intelligence	**C119**	☐
Political opinions	**C120**	☐
Political party membership	**C121**	☐
Support for pressure groups	**C122**	☐
Religious beliefs	**C123**	☐
Other beliefs	**C124**	☐

Miscellaneous Information

References to manual files records	**C131**	☐
Uncategorised information	**C132**	☐

If you wish, you may describe additional Classes of data here, start each description on a new line

_____

_____

_____

3

B.3 Sources and Disclosures

In this section, you should describe.

In column A — The sources from which you intend or may wish to obtain any of the data you have described in section B.2.
In column B — The person or persons to whom you intend or may wish to disclose these data.

Do this by ticking the appropriate boxes below.

Individuals or Organisations directly associated with the Data Subjects

A. Source / B. Disclosure

		A	B
The Data Subjects themselves	**D101**	☐	☐
Family, relatives, guardians, trustees	**D102**	☐	☐
Other members of their households, friends, neighbours	**D103**	☐	☐
Employers — past, current or prospective	**D104**	☐	☐
Employees, agents	**D105**	☑	☑
Colleagues, business associates	**D106**	☑	☑

		A	B
Legal representatives	**D107**	☐	☐
Financial representatives	**D108**	☐	☐
Doctors, Dentists, other health advisers	**D109**	☐	☐
Social, spiritual, welfare, advice workers	**D110**	☐	☐
Other professional advisers	**D111**	☐	☐
Landlords	**D112**	☐	☐

Others — please specify here

_____   ☐ ☐

_____   ☐ ☐

Individuals or Organisations directly associated with the Data User

		A	B
Members, including shareholders	**D201**	☐	☐
Other companies in the same group	**D202**	☐	☑
Employees, agents	**D203**	☑	☑
Recipients, customers, clients for goods or services	**D204**	☐	☑

		A	B
Claimants, beneficiaries, assignees, payees	**D205**	☐	☐
Suppliers, providers of goods or services	**D206**	☐	☑
Persons making an enquiry or complaint	**D207**	☐	☐
Tenants	**D208**	☐	☐

Others — please specify here

_____   ☐ ☐

_____   ☐ ☐

Organisations or Individuals (General Description)

Central Government

		A	B
Inland Revenue	**D301**	☐	☐
Customs & Excise	**D302**	☐	☐
Driver & Vehicle Licensing Centre (DVLC)	**D303**	☐	☐
Department of Education & Science (DES)	**D304**	☐	☐
Department of Health & Social Security (DHSS)	**D305**	☐	☐
Department of Employment	**D306**	☐	☑
Home Office	**D307**	☐	☐
Ministry of Defence, including armed forces	**D308**	☐	☐
Other central government, including Scottish, Welsh & Northern Ireland Offices*	**D309**		

Local Government

		A	B
Education department	**D321**	☐	☐
Housing department	**D322**	☐	☐
Social Services department	**D323**	☐	☐
Electoral registration, Assessment, Valuation departments	**D324**	☐	☐
Other local government*	**D325**		

Other Public Bodies

Other public bodies not elsewhere specified*	**D331**	
Foreign governments or authorities*	**D332**	

Continued

251

4

Justice	A. Source	B. Disclosure
Police forces **D341**	☐	☐
Prosecuting authorities **D342**	☐	☐
Other statutory law enforcement agencies, investigating bodies * **D343**		
The courts **D344**	☐	☐
Judges, magistrates **D345**	☐	☐
Prison service **D346**	☐	☐
Probation service **D347**	☐	☐

Health & Social Welfare

	A. Source	B. Disclosure
Health authorities, family practitioner committees **D351**	☐	☐
Hospitals, nursing homes **D352**	☐	☐
Registered medical practitioners **D353**	☐	☐
Registered dental practitioners **D354**	☐	☐
Nurses, midwives, health visitors **D355**	☐	☐
Other health care agencies, practitioners * **D356**		
Social welfare agencies, practitioners * **D357**		

Other	A. Source	B. Disclosure
Public utilities **D361**	☐	☐
Banks **D362**	☑	☐
Building societies **D363**	☐	☐
Insurance companies **D364**	☐	☐
Other financial organisations * **D365**		
Accountants & auditors **D366**	☐	☐
Lawyers **D367**	☐	☐
Credit reference agencies **D368**	☑	☐
Debt collection, tracing agencies **D369**	☐	☐
Employment, recruitment agencies **D370**	☐	☐
Private detective agencies, security organisations **D371**	☐	☐
Trade, employers associations **D372**	☐	☐
Trade unions, staff associations **D373**	☐	☐
Professional bodies **D374**	☐	☐
Voluntary, charitable, religious organisations or associations **D375**	☐	☐
Political organisations **D376**	☐	☐
Education or training establishments, examining bodies **D377**	☐	☐
Survey or research organisations, workers **D378**	☐	☐
Providers of publicly available information including public libraries, press and media **D379**	☐	☐
Providers of privately available information and databanks **D380**	☐	☐
Traders in personal data **D381**	☐	☐
Other organisations or individuals * **D382**		

You should use the space below to give further details if you wish to use one or more of the categories marked with an asterisk (*) above. You should give the code number for each category which you are explaining.

If you wish, you may also write here additional descriptions of Sources and Disclosures

If you are using the space below, start each description on a new line and indicate whether the item is a Source, a Disclosure, or both

	A. Source	B. Disclosure
_____		
_____	☐	☐
_____	☐	☐
_____	☐	☐
_____	☐	☐
_____	☐	☐

B.4 Overseas transfers

In this section you should name any countries or territories outside the United Kingdom to which you intend to transfer the data.

If none, you should tick this box .... None **T000** ☑

If the nature of your business requires you to transfer the data to any country worldwide, you should
tick this box, and indicate your business in the space below .... Worldwide **T999** ☐

_____

_____

Otherwise, tick the appropriate box(es) below

Country	Code		Country	Code		Country	Code	
Algeria	T001	☐	Indonesia	T020	☐	Norway	T039	☐
Argentina	T002	☐	Iran	T021	☐	Oman	T040	☐
Australia	T003	☐	Iraq	T022	☐	Pakistan	T041	☐
Austria	T004	☐	Republic of Ireland	T023	☐	Philippines	T042	☐
Belgium	T005	☐	Isle of Man	T024	☐	Poland	T043	☐
Brazil	T006	☐	Israel	T025	☐	Portugal	T044	☐
Canada	T007	☐	Italy	T026	☐	Saudi Arabia	T045	☐
Cyprus	T008	☐	Japan	T027	☐	Singapore	T046	☐
Denmark	T009	☐	Jersey	T028	☐	South Africa	T047	☐
Dubai	T010	☐	Kuwait	T029	☐	South Korea	T048	☐
Egypt	T011	☐	Libya	T030	☐	Spain	T049	☐
Finland	T012	☐	Liechtenstein	T031	☐	Sweden	T050	☐
France	T013	☐	Luxembourg	T032	☐	Switzerland	T051	☐
West Germany	T014	☐	Malaysia	T033	☐	Taiwan	T052	☐
Greece	T015	☐	Malta	T034	☐	Turkey	T053	☐
Guernsey	T016	☐	Mexico	T035	☐	USA	T054	☐
Hong Kong	T017	☐	Netherlands	T036	☐	USSR	T055	☐
Iceland	T018	☐	New Zealand	T037	☐	Venezuela	T056	☐
India	T019	☐	Nigeria	T038	☐			

If necessary, you may write additional names or descriptions here: start each on a new line

_____

_____

_____

_____

_____

_____

_____

253

Continuation

The space below is reserved for continuation text from any of the sections of this form. You should only need to use this space in exceptional circumstances.

You should indicate clearly which section of the form (B.1. B.3 etc) is continued here. Please start each separate continuation on a new line

How to apply for Registration   The application form is in two separate parts

Part A is for information about the applicant and other details covering the whole application

This part (Part B) is for a description of a Purpose for which personal data are to be held or used, and a description of the data and associated details. You will need to complete one Part B in respect of each Purpose you wish to register

You should read the accompanying **Notes** booklet before completing the form. The Notes contain rules and conditions which the Registrar will apply, as well as standard descriptions and definitions which you will need to consult. **It is important that you read the Notes carefully.**

In completing form DPR.1, please use a typewriter or if handwritten, use BLOCK CAPITALS

Do not use this form to
    Alter or remove an entry already on the Register — use Form DPR.2
    Renew an entry already on the Register — in this case you will be sent a renewal reminder

Further registration packs, and extra copies of Part B, can be obtained from **Crown Post Offices** and from the **Office of the Data Protection Registrar, Springfield House, Water Lane, Wilmslow, Cheshire, SK9 5AX.**

Completed application forms, together with the appropriate fee (see Notes Booklet) should be sent to the Registrar at **P.O.Box 66, Wilmslow, Cheshire, SK9 5AX.** This address must only be used for applications. Other correspondence should be sent to the full address given above — it may be seriously delayed if sent to P.O. Box 66

How to complete this form   In each section of Part B you may use standard descriptions to provide the detail required Although you also have the option of writing your own descriptions in free text, **you are strongly encouraged to use the standard description approach.** In most sections this is simply a matter of selecting the appropriate descriptions from the list printed on the form and ticking the corresponding boxes

The standard descriptions for **Purposes** are not printed on the form but are listed in the separate **Notes** booklet. You will need to read these before filling in the form. You should also refer to the booklet when selecting descriptions for **Data Classes.**

Before completing the rest of the form you should write the application number (copied from the front of Part A) in the box provided on the front of this Part B.

If your application is accepted, the details given in sections B.1 to B.4 will appear on the Register and will be available for public inspection

If you need more space than is provided for text in any Section, you may continue on page 7

THE DATA PROTECTION REGISTRAR

Application for Registration

Data Protection Act 1984

(from Part A)

0001

Please write in
this number before
proceeding

Form DPR 1

Part B

About this form   This form is for use only in conjunction with form DPR 1 A

You should read the Notes on the back of this form and the accompanying **Notes** booklet

---

B.1 Purpose   In this section you should describe a Purpose for which data are held or used

There are two methods of completing this section of the form

Method 1   By selecting one of the Standard Purposes listed and described in the Notes
               booklet

               You may then relate the Purpose to a specific part of your organisation or
               particular business activity

Method 2   By describing the Purpose in your own words

**You are likely to find registration simpler and easier under Method 1 and you
are strongly advised to use this Method if it can meet your requirements.**

Method 1   Select one of the Standard Purposes from those listed in the accompanying **Notes** booklet
               and write both the code number and the title in the spaces provided below

P 004	MARKETING AND SELLING	(including Direct Marketing to Individuals)
code	title	

If you are required to give further details of your Purpose (see **Notes** booklet) write these
here

If you wish to relate this Purpose to a specific part or parts of your organisation or particular
business activity enter details here

Method 2   **(This method should only be used if Method 1 is inappropriate).**
Please describe the Purpose for which data are held or used, and, if you wish, the specific
part or parts of your organisation or particular business activity to which it is related

B.2 Description of Personal Data – Data Subjects

In this section you should describe the types of individual **(Data Subjects)** about whom personal data are to be held for the Purpose described in section B.1 Do this by ticking the appropriate boxes below

		Current	Past	Potential
Employees, trainees, voluntary workers	S001	☐	☐	☐
Employees of associated companies, organisations	S002	☐	☐	☐
Employees of other organisations	S003	☐	☐	☐
Recipients, customers or clients for goods or services (direct or indirect)	S004	☑	☑	☑
Suppliers of goods or services (direct or indirect)	S005	☐	☐	☐
Claimants, beneficiaries, payees	S006	☐	☐	☐
Account holders	S007	☐	☐	☐
Share and stock holders	S008	☐	☐	☐
Partners, directors, other senior officers	S009	☐	☐	☐
Employers	S010	☐	☐	☐
Competitors	S011	☐	☐	☐
Business or other contacts	S012	☐	☐	☐
Advisors, consultants, professional and other experts	S013	☐	☐	☐
Agents, other intermediaries	S014	☐	☐	☐
Trustees	S015	☐	☐	☐
Members, supporters of a club, society, institution	S016	☐	☐	☐
Assignees, guarantors, other parties with legitimate contractual or business interest	S017	☐	☐	☐
Donors and lenders	S018	☐	☐	☐
Complainants	S019	☐	☐	☐
Witnesses	S020	☐	☐	☐

		Current	Past	Potential
Offenders and suspected offenders	S021	☐	☐	☐
Tenants	S022	☐	☐	☐
Landlords, owners of property	S023	☐	☐	☐
Correspondents and enquirers	S024	☐	☐	☐
Survey respondents, other persons assisting research	S025	☐	☐	☐
Patients	S026	☐	☐	☐
Self-employed persons	S027	☐	☐	☐
Unemployed persons	S028	☐	☐	☐
Retired persons	S029	☐	☐	☐
Students	S030	☐	☐	☐
Minors	S031	☐		
Applicants for permits, licences, registration	S032	☐	☐	☐
Taxpayers, ratepayers	S033	☐	☐	☐
Licence holders	S034	☐	☐	☐
Vehicle keepers	S035	☐	☐	☐
Elected representatives, other holders of public office	S036	☐	☐	☐
Authors, publishers, editors, artists, other creators	S037	☐	☐	☐
Immigrants, foreign nationals	S038	☐	☐	☐
Relatives, dependants, friends, neighbours, referees, associates, contacts of any of those ticked above	S039	☐	☐	☐
Members of the public	S040	☐		

If you wish, you may write additional descriptions of Data Subjects here, start each description on a new line

_____

_____

_____

_____

_____

_____

_____

_____

2

B.2 Description of Personal Data — Data Classes

In this section, you should describe the **Classes** of personal data to be held for the Purpose described in B.1. Do this by ticking the appropriate boxes below. You should refer to the **Notes** booklet for examples of data items which might be covered by each Class.

Identification Data

Personal identifiers	C001	☑
Financial identifiers	C002	☐
Identifiers issued by public bodies	C003	☐

Personal Characteristics

Personal details	C011	☐
Physical description	C012	☐
Habits	C013	☐
Personality, character	C014	☑

Family Circumstances

Current marriage or partnership	C021	☐
Marital history	C022	☐
Details of other family, household members	C023	☐
Other social contacts	C024	☐

Social Circumstances

Accommodation or housing	C031	☐
Property, possessions	C032	☐
Immigration status	C033	☐
Travel, movement details	C034	☐
Leisure activities, interests	C035	☐
Lifestyle	C036	☐
Membership of voluntary, charitable bodies	C037	☐
Public offices held	C038	☐
Licences, permits held	C039	☐
Complaint, incident, accident details	C040	☐
Court, tribunal, enquiry proceedings	C041	☐

Education, Skills, Profession

Academic record	C051	☐
Qualifications and skills	C052	☐
Membership of professional bodies	C053	☐
Professional expertise	C054	☐
Membership of committees	C055	☐
Publications	C056	☐
Student record	C057	☐
Student financial records	C058	☐

Employment Details

Current employment	C061	☐
Recruitment details	C062	☐
Termination details	C063	☐
Career history	C064	☐
Work record	C065	☐
Health & safety record	C066	☐
Trade union, staff association membership	C067	☐
Payments, deductions	C068	☐
Property held by employee	C069	☐
Work management details	C070	☐
Work assessment details	C071	☐
Training record	C072	☐
Security details	C073	☐

Financial Details

Income, assets, investments	C081	☐
Liabilities, outgoings	C082	☐
Creditworthiness	C083	☑
Loans, mortgages, credits	C084	☐
Allowances, benefits, grants	C085	☐
Insurance details	C086	☐
Pension details	C087	☐

Details of Transactions

Goods, services provided to the data subject	C091	☑
Goods, services obtained from the data subject	C092	☐
Financial transactions	C093	☐
Compensation	C094	☐

Business Information

Business activities of the data subject	C101	☑
Agreements, contracts	C102	☑
Trading licences held	C103	☐

Health & Other Classes

Physical health record	C111	☐
Mental health record	C112	☐
Disabilities, infirmities	C113	☐
Dietary, other special health requirements	C114	☐
Sexual life	C115	☐
Racial, ethnic origin	C116	☐
Motoring convictions	C117	☐
Other convictions	C118	☐
Criminal intelligence	C119	☐
Political opinions	C120	☐
Political party membership	C121	☐
Support for pressure groups	C122	☐
Religious beliefs	C123	☐
Other beliefs	C124	☐

Miscellaneous Information

References to manual files, records	C131	☐
Uncategorised information	C132	☐

If you wish, you may describe additional Classes of data here, start each description on a new line

_____

_____

_____

_____

B.3 Sources and Disclosures

In this section, you should describe

In column A — The sources from which you intend or may wish to obtain any of the data you have described in section B.2.
In column B — The person or persons to whom you intend or may wish to disclose these data

Do this by ticking the appropriate boxes below

Individuals or Organisations directly associated with the Data Subjects

A. Source / B. Disclosure

		A	B
The Data Subjects themselves	D101	☑	☐
Family, relatives, guardians, trustees	D102	☐	☐
Other members of their households, friends, neighbours	D103	☐	☐
Employers — past, current or prospective	D104	☐	☐
Employees, agents	D105	☑	☑
Colleagues, business associates	D106	☑	☑

		A	B
Legal representatives	D107	☐	☐
Financial representatives	D108	☐	☐
Doctors, Dentists, other health advisers	D109	☐	☐
Social, spiritual, welfare, advice workers	D110	☐	☐
Other professional advisers	D111	☐	☐
Landlords	D112	☐	☐

Others — please specify here

_____ ☐ ☐

_____ ☐ ☐

Individuals or Organisations directly associated with the Data User

		A	B
Members, including shareholders	D201	☐	☐
Other companies in the same group	D202	☐	☐
Employees, agents	D203	☑	☑
Recipients, customers, clients for goods or services	D204	☑	☐

		A	B
Claimants, beneficiaries, assignees, payees	D205	☐	☐
Suppliers, providers of goods or services	D206	☑	☐
Persons making an enquiry or complaint	D207	☐	☐
Tenants	D208	☐	☐

Others — please specify here

_____ ☐ ☐

_____ ☐ ☐

Organisations or Individuals (General Description)

Central Government

		A	B
Inland Revenue	D301	☐	☐
Customs & Excise	D302	☐	☐
Driver & Vehicle Licensing Centre (DVLC)	D303	☐	☐
Department of Education & Science (DES)	D304	☐	☐
Department of Health & Social Security (DHSS)	D305	☐	☐
Department of Employment	D306	☐	☐
Home Office	D307	☐	☐
Ministry of Defence, including armed forces	D308	☐	☐
Other central government, including Scottish, Welsh & Northern Ireland Offices*	D309		

Local Government

		A	B
Education department	D321	☐	☐
Housing department	D322	☐	☐
Social Services department	D323	☐	☐
Electoral registration, Assessment, Valuation departments	D324	☐	☐
Other local government*	D325		

Other Public Bodies

		A	B
Other public bodies not elsewhere specified*	D331		
Foreign governments or authorities*	D332		

Continued

259

4

B.3 Sources and Disclosures *Continued*

Justice		A. Source	B. Disclosure
Police forces	D341	☐	☐
Prosecuting authorities	D342	☐	☐
Other statutory law enforcement agencies, investigating bodies *	D343		
The courts	D344	☐	☐
Judges, magistrates	D345	☐	☐
Prison service	D346	☐	☐
Probation service	D347	☐	☐

Health & Social Welfare

		A. Source	B. Disclosure
Health authorities, family practitioner committees	D351	☐	☐
Hospitals, nursing homes	D352	☐	☐
Registered medical practitioners	D353	☐	☐
Registered dental practitioners	D354	☐	☐
Nurses, midwives, health visitors	D355	☐	☐
Other health care agencies, practitioners *	D356		
Social welfare agencies, practitioners *	D357		

Other		A. Source	B. Disclosure
Public utilities	D361	☐	☐
Banks	D362	☑	☐
Building societies	D363	☐	☐
Insurance companies	D364	☐	☐
Other financial organisations *	D365		
Accountants & auditors	D366	☐	☐
Lawyers	D367	☐	☐
Credit reference agencies	D368	☑	☐
Debt collection, tracing agencies	D369	☐	☑
Employment, recruitment agencies	D370	☐	☐
Private detective agencies, security organisations	D371	☐	☐
Trade, employers associations	D372	☐	☐
Trade unions, staff associations	D373	☐	☐
Professional bodies	D374	☐	☐
Voluntary, charitable, religious organisations or associations	D375	☐	☐
Political organisations	D376	☐	☐
Education or training establishments, examining bodies	D377	☐	☐
Survey or research organisations, workers	D378	☐	☐
Providers of publicly available information, including public libraries, press and media	D379	☐	☐
Providers of privately available information and databanks	D380	☐	☐
Traders in personal data	D381	☐	☐
Other organisations or individuals *	D382		

You should use the space below to give further details if you wish to use one or more of the categories marked with an asterisk (*) above. You should give the code number for each category which you are explaining.

If you wish, you may also write here additional descriptions of Sources and Disclosures

If you are using the space below, start each description on a new line and indicate whether the item is a Source, a Disclosure, or both

A. Source   B. Disclosure

_____

_____   ☐ ☐

_____

_____   ☐ ☐

_____

_____   ☐ ☐

_____   ☐ ☐

_____   ☐ ☐

260

B.4 Overseas transfers

In this section you should name any countries or territories outside the United Kingdom to which you intend to transfer the data.

If none, you should tick this box   None **T000** ☑

If the nature of your business requires you to transfer the data to any country worldwide, you should
tick this box, and indicate your business in the space below   Worldwide **T999** ☐

Otherwise tick the appropriate box(es) below

Algeria	**T001**	☐	Indonesia	**T020**	☐	Norway	**T039**	☐
Argentina	**T002**	☐	Iran	**T021**	☐	Oman	**T040**	☐
Australia	**T003**	☐	Iraq	**T022**	☐	Pakistan	**T041**	☐
Austria	**T004**	☐	Republic of Ireland	**T023**	☐	Philippines	**T042**	☐
Belgium	**T005**	☐	Isle of Man	**T024**	☐	Poland	**T043**	☐
Brazil	**T006**	☐	Israel	**T025**	☐	Portugal	**T044**	☐
Canada	**T007**	☐	Italy	**T026**	☐	Saudi Arabia	**T045**	☐
Cyprus	**T008**	☐	Japan	**T027**	☐	Singapore	**T046**	☐
Denmark	**T009**	☐	Jersey	**T028**	☐	South Africa	**T047**	☐
Dubai	**T010**	☐	Kuwait	**T029**	☐	South Korea	**T048**	☐
Egypt	**T011**	☐	Libya	**T030**	☐	Spain	**T049**	☐
Finland	**T012**	☐	Liechtenstein	**T031**	☐	Sweden	**T050**	☐
France	**T013**	☐	Luxembourg	**T032**	☐	Switzerland	**T051**	☐
West Germany	**T014**	☐	Malaysia	**T033**	☐	Taiwan	**T052**	☐
Greece	**T015**	☐	Malta	**T034**	☐	Turkey	**T053**	☐
Guernsey	**T016**	☐	Mexico	**T035**	☐	USA	**T054**	☐
Hong Kong	**T017**	☐	Netherlands	**T036**	☐	USSR	**T055**	☐
Iceland	**T018**	☐	New Zealand	**T037**	☐	Venezuela	**T056**	☐
India	**T019**	☐	Nigeria	**T038**	☐			

If necessary, you may write additional names or descriptions here, start each on a new line

---

Continuation

The space below is reserved for continuation text from any of the sections of this form. You should only need to use this space in exceptional circumstances

You should indicate clearly which section of the form (B1 B3 etc) is continued here. Please start each separate continuation on a new line

How to apply for Registration

The application form is in two separate parts

Part A is for information about the applicant and other details covering the whole application

This part (Part B) is for a description of a Purpose for which personal data are to be held or used, and a description of the data and associated details. You will need to complete one Part B in respect of each Purpose you wish to register

You should read the accompanying **Notes** booklet before completing the form. The Notes contain rules and conditions which the Registrar will apply, as well as standard descriptions and definitions which you will need to consult. **It is important that you read the Notes carefully.**

In completing form DPR 1, please use a typewriter or, if handwritten, use BLOCK CAPITALS

Do not use this form to
    Alter or remove an entry already on the Register — use Form DPR 2
    Renew an entry already on the Register — in this case you will be sent a renewal reminder

Further registration packs, and extra copies of Part B, can be obtained from **Crown Post Offices** and from the **Office of the Data Protection Registrar, Springfield House, Water Lane, Wilmslow, Cheshire, SK9 5AX.**

Completed application forms, together with the appropriate fee (see Notes Booklet), should be sent to the Registrar at **P.O.Box 66, Wilmslow, Cheshire, SK9 5AX.** This address must only be used for applications. Other correspondence should be sent to the full address given above — it may be seriously delayed if sent to P.O. Box 66.

How to complete this form

In each section of Part B you may use standard descriptions to provide the detail required. Although you also have the option of writing your own descriptions in free text, **you are strongly encouraged to use the standard description approach.** In most sections this is simply a matter of selecting the appropriate descriptions from the list printed on the form and ticking the corresponding boxes

The standard descriptions for **Purposes** are not printed on the form but are listed in the separate **Notes** booklet. You will need to read these before filling in the form. You should also refer to the booklet when selecting descriptions for **Data Classes.**

Before completing the rest of the form you should write the application number (copied from the front of Part A) in the box provided on the front of this Part B.

If your application is accepted, the details given in sections B 1 to B 4 will appear on the Register and will be available for public inspection

If you need more space than is provided for text in any Section, you may continue on page 7

THE DATA PROTECTION REGISTRAR

Application for Registration

Data Protection Act 1984

(from Part A)

0001

Please write in
this number before
proceeding

Form DPR 1

Part B

About this form   This form is for use only in conjunction with form DPR 1 A

You should read the Notes on the back of this form and the accompanying **Notes** booklet

---

B.1 Purpose   In this section you should describe a Purpose for which data are held or used

There are two methods of completing this section of the form

Method 1   By selecting one of the Standard Purposes listed and described in the Notes
booklet

You may then relate the Purpose to a specific part of your organisation or
particular business activity

Method 2   By describing the Purpose in your own words

**You are likely to find registration simpler and easier under Method 1 and you
are strongly advised to use this Method if it can meet your requirements.**

Method 1   Select one of the Standard Purposes from those listed in the accompanying **Notes** booklet
and write both the code number and the title in the spaces provided below

P 007	MANAGEMENT OF AGENTS AND INTERMEDIARIES
code	title

If you are required to give further details of your Purpose (see **Notes** booklet) write these
here

If you wish to relate this Purpose to a specific part or parts of your organisation or particular
business activity, enter details here

THIS PURPOSE RELATES ONLY TO OVERSEAS AGENTS

Method 2   **(This method should only be used if Method 1 is inappropriate).**
Please describe the Purpose for which data are held or used, and, if you wish, the specific
part or parts of your organisation or particular business activity to which it is related

1

264

B.2 Description of Personal Data — Data Subjects

In this section you should describe the types of individual **(Data Subjects)** about whom personal data are to be held for the Purpose described in section B1. Do this by ticking the appropriate boxes below

		Current	Past	Potential				Current	Past	Potential
Employees, trainees, voluntary workers	**S001**	☐	☐	☐	Offenders and suspected offenders	**S021**	☐	☐	☐
Employees of associated companies, organisations	**S002**	☐	☐	☐	Tenants	**S022**	☐	☐	☐
Employees of other organisations	**S003**	☐	☐	☐	Landlords, owners of property	**S023**	☐	☐	☐
Recipients, customers or clients for goods or services (direct or indirect)	**S004**	☐	☐	☐	Correspondents and enquirers	**S024**	☐	☐	☐
Suppliers of goods or services (direct or indirect)	**S005**	☐	☐	☐	Survey respondents, other persons assisting research	**S025**	☐	☐	☐
Claimants, beneficiaries, payees	**S006**	☐	☐	☐	Patients	**S026**	☐	☐	☐
Account holders	**S007**	☐	☐	☐	Self-employed persons	**S027**	☐	☐	☐
Share and stock holders	**S008**	☐	☐	☐	Unemployed persons	**S028**	☐	☐	☐
Partners, directors, other senior officers	**S009**	☐	☐	☐	Retired persons	**S029**	☐	☐	☐
Employers	**S010**	☐	☐	☐	Students	**S030**	☐	☐	☐
Competitors	**S011**	☐	☐	☐	Minors	**S031**	☐	☐	
Business or other contacts	**S012**	☐	☐	☐	Applicants for permits, licences, registration	**S032**	☐	☐	☐
Advisors, consultants, professional and other experts	**S013**	☐	☐	☐	Taxpayers, ratepayers	**S033**	☐	☐	☐
Agents, other intermediaries	**S014**	☑	☑	☐	Licence holders	**S034**	☐	☐	☐
Trustees	**S015**	☐	☐	☐	Vehicle keepers	**S035**	☐	☐	☐
Members, supporters of a club, society, institution	**S016**	☐	☐	☐	Elected representatives, other holders of public office	**S036**	☐	☐	☐
Assignees, guarantors, other parties with legitimate contractual or business interest	**S017**	☐	☐	☐	Authors, publishers, editors, artists, other creators	**S037**	☐	☐	☐
Donors and lenders	**S018**	☐	☐	☐	Immigrants, foreign nationals	**S038**	☐	☐	☐
Complainants	**S019**	☐	☐	☐	Relatives, dependants, friends, neighbours, referees, associates, contacts of any of those ticked above	**S039**	☐	☐	☐
Witnesses	**S020**	☐	☐	☐	Members of the public	**S040**	☐		

If you wish, you may write additional descriptions of Data Subjects here; start each description on a new line:

_____

_____

_____

_____

_____

_____

_____

_____

2

B.2 Description of Personal Data – Data Classes

In this section, you should describe the **Classes** of personal data to be held for the Purpose described in B.1. Do this by ticking the appropriate boxes below. You should refer to the **Notes** booklet for examples of data items which might be covered by each Class.

Identification Data

Personal identifiers	C001	☑
Financial identifiers	C002	☑
Identifiers issued by public bodies	C003	☑

Personal Characteristics

Personal details	C011	☑
Physical description	C012	☑
Habits	C013	☐
Personality, character	C014	☐

Family Circumstances

Current marriage or partnership	C021	☐
Marital history	C022	☐
Details of other family, household members	C023	☐
Other social contacts	C024	☐

Social Circumstances

Accommodation or housing	C031	☐
Property, possessions	C032	☐
Immigration status	C033	☐
Travel, movement details	C034	☑
Leisure activities, interests	C035	☐
Lifestyle	C036	☐
Membership of voluntary, charitable bodies	C037	☐
Public offices held	C038	☐
Licences, permits held	C039	☐
Complaint, incident, accident details	C040	☐
Court, tribunal, enquiry proceedings	C041	☐

Education, Skills, Profession

Academic record	C051	☐
Qualifications and skills	C052	☐
Membership of professional bodies	C053	☐
Professional expertise	C054	☐
Membership of committees	C055	☐
Publications	C056	☐
Student record	C057	☐
Student financial records	C058	☐

Employment Details

Current employment	C061	☐
Recruitment details	C062	☑
Termination details	C063	☑
Career history	C064	☐
Work record	C065	☐
Health & safety record	C066	☐
Trade union, staff association membership	C067	☐
Payments, deductions	C068	☑
Property held by employee	C069	☐
Work management details	C070	☐
Work assessment details	C071	☑
Training record	C072	☐
Security details	C073	☐

Financial Details

Income, assets, investments	C081	☐
Liabilities, outgoings	C082	☐
Creditworthiness	C083	☐
Loans, mortgages, credits	C084	☐
Allowances, benefits, grants	C085	☐
Insurance details	C086	☐
Pension details	C087	☐

Details of Transactions

Goods, services provided to the data subject	C091	☐
Goods, services obtained from the data subject	C092	☑
Financial transactions	C093	☑
Compensation	C094	☐

Business Information

Business activities of the data subject	C101	☐
Agreements, contracts	C102	☐
Trading licences held	C103	☐

Health & Other Classes

Physical health record	C111	☐
Mental health record	C112	☐
Disabilities, infirmities	C113	☐
Dietary, other special health requirements	C114	☐
Sexual life	C115	☐
Racial, ethnic origin	C116	☐
Motoring convictions	C117	☐
Other convictions	C118	☐
Criminal intelligence	C119	☐
Political opinions	C120	☐
Political party membership	C121	☐
Support for pressure groups	C122	☐
Religious beliefs	C123	☐
Other beliefs	C124	☐

Miscellaneous Information

References to manual files, records	C131	☐
Uncategorised information	C132	☐

If you wish, you may describe additional Classes of data here, start each description on a new line

_____

_____

_____

B.3 Sources and Disclosures

In this section, you should describe:

In column A — The sources from which you intend or may wish to obtain any of the data you have described in section B.2.
In column B — The person or persons to whom you intend or may wish to disclose these data

Do this by ticking the appropriate boxes below

Individuals or Organisations directly associated with the Data Subjects

		A. Source	B. Disclosure
The Data Subjects themselves	D101	☑	☐
Family, relatives, guardians, trustees	D102	☐	☐
Other members of their households, friends, neighbours	D103	☐	☐
Employers — past, current or prospective	D104	☐	☐
Employees, agents	D105	☐	☐
Colleagues, business associates	D106	☐	☐

		A. Source	B. Disclosure
Legal representatives	D107	☐	☐
Financial representatives	D108	☐	☐
Doctors, Dentists, other health advisers	D109	☐	☐
Social, spiritual, welfare, advice workers	D110	☐	☐
Other professional advisers	D111	☐	☐
Landlords	D112	☐	☐

Others — please specify here

_____

_____   ☐ ☐

_____   ☐ ☐

Individuals or Organisations directly associated with the Data User

		A. Source	B. Disclosure
Members, including shareholders	D201	☐	☐
Other companies in the same group	D202	☐	☐
Employees, agents	D203	☐	☑
Recipients, customers, clients for goods or services	D204	☐	☐

		A. Source	B. Disclosure
Claimants, beneficiaries, assignees, payees	D205	☐	☐
Suppliers, providers of goods or services	D206	☐	☑
Persons making an enquiry or complaint	D207	☐	☐
Tenants	D208	☐	☐

Others — please specify here

_____

_____   ☐ ☐

_____   ☐ ☐

**Organisations or Individuals
(General Description)**

Central Government

		A. Source	B. Disclosure
Inland Revenue	D301	☐	☐
Customs & Excise	D302	☐	☑
Driver & Vehicle Licensing Centre (DVLC)	D303	☐	☐
Department of Education & Science (DES)	D304	☐	☐
Department of Health & Social Security (DHSS)	D305	☐	☐
Department of Employment	D306	☐	☐
Home Office	D307	☐	☐
Ministry of Defence, including armed forces	D308	☐	☐
Other central government, including Scottish, Welsh & Northern Ireland Offices*	D309		

Local Government

		A. Source	B. Disclosure
Education department	D321	☐	☐
Housing department	D322	☐	☐
Social Services department	D323	☐	☐
Electoral registration, Assessment, Valuation departments	D324	☐	☐
Other local government*	D325		

Other Public Bodies

Other public bodies not elsewhere specified*	D331	
Foreign governments or authorities*	D332	

Continued

267

4

B.3 Sources and Disclosures *Continued*

		A. Source	B. Disclosure
Justice			
Police forces	**D341**	☐	☐
Prosecuting authorities	**D342**	☐	☐
Other statutory law enforcement agencies, investigating bodies *	**D343**		
The courts	**D344**	☐	☐
Judges, magistrates	**D345**	☐	☐
Prison service	**D346**	☐	☐
Probation service	**D347**	☐	☐
Health & Social Welfare			
Health authorities, family practitioner committees	**D351**	☐	☐
Hospitals, nursing homes	**D352**	☐	☐
Registered medical practitioners	**D353**	☐	☐
Registered dental practitioners	**D354**	☐	☐
Nurses, midwives, health visitors	**D355**	☐	☐
Other health care agencies, practitioners *	**D356**		
Social welfare agencies, practitioners *	**D357**		

		A. Source	B. Disclosure
Other			
Public utilities	**D361**	☐	☐
Banks	**D362**	☐	☐
Building societies	**D363**	☐	☐
Insurance companies	**D364**	☐	☐
Other financial organisations *	**D365**		
Accountants & auditors	**D366**	☐	☐
Lawyers	**D367**	☐	☐
Credit reference agencies	**D368**	☑	☐
Debt collection, tracing agencies	**D369**	☐	☐
Employment, recruitment agencies	**D370**	☐	☐
Private detective agencies, security organisations	**D371**	☐	☐
Trade, employers associations	**D372**	☐	☐
Trade unions, staff associations	**D373**	☐	☐
Professional bodies	**D374**	☐	☐
Voluntary, charitable, religious organisations or associations	**D375**	☐	☐
Political organisations	**D376**	☐	☐
Education or training establishments, examining bodies	**D377**	☐	☐
Survey or research organisations, workers	**D378**	☐	☐
Providers of publicly available information, including public libraries, press and media	**D379**	☐	☐
Providers of privately available information and databanks	**D380**	☐	☐
Traders in personal data	**D381**	☐	☐
Other organisations or individuals *	**D382**		

You should use the space below to give further details if you wish to use one or more of the categories marked with an asterisk (*) above. You should give the code number for each category which you are explaining.

If you wish, you may also write here additional descriptions of Sources and Disclosures

If you are using the space below, start each description on a new line and indicate whether the item is a Source, a Disclosure, or both

	A. Source	B. Disclosure
_____	☐	☐
_____	☐	☐
_____	☐	☐
_____	☐	☐
_____	☐	☐

B.4 Overseas transfers

In this section you should name any countries or territories outside the United Kingdom to which you intend to transfer the data.

If none, you should tick this box

None **T000** ☐

If the nature of your business requires you to transfer the data to any country worldwide, you should tick this box, and indicate your business in the space below

Worldwide **T999** ☐

Otherwise, tick the appropriate box(es) below

Country	Code		Country	Code		Country	Code	
Algeria	T001	☐	Indonesia	T020	☐	Norway	T039	☐
Argentina	T002	☐	Iran	T021	☐	Oman	T040	☐
Australia	T003	☐	Iraq	T022	☐	Pakistan	T041	☐
Austria	T004	☐	Republic of Ireland	T023	☐	Philippines	T042	☐
Belgium	T005	☐	Isle of Man	T024	☐	Poland	T043	☐
Brazil	T006	☐	Israel	T025	☐	Portugal	T044	☐
Canada	T007	☐	Italy	T026	☐	Saudi Arabia	T045	☑
Cyprus	T008	☐	Japan	T027	☑	Singapore	T046	☐
Denmark	T009	☐	Jersey	T028	☐	South Africa	T047	☐
Dubai	T010	☐	Kuwait	T029	☐	South Korea	T048	☐
Egypt	T011	☐	Libya	T030	☐	Spain	T049	☐
Finland	T012	☐	Liechtenstein	T031	☐	Sweden	T050	☐
France	T013	☐	Luxembourg	T032	☐	Switzerland	T051	☐
West Germany	T014	☐	Malaysia	T033	☐	Taiwan	T052	☐
Greece	T015	☐	Malta	T034	☐	Turkey	T053	☐
Guernsey	T016	☐	Mexico	T035	☐	USA	T054	☑
Hong Kong	T017	☑	Netherlands	T036	☐	USSR	T055	☐
Iceland	T018	☐	New Zealand	T037	☐	Venezuela	T056	☐
India	T019	☐	Nigeria	T038	☐			

If necessary, you may write additional names or descriptions here, start each on a new line.

SRI LANKA

Continuation

The space below is reserved for continuation text from any of the sections of this form. You should only need to use this space in exceptional circumstances

You should indicate clearly which section of the form (B1 B3 etc) is continued here. Please start each separate continuation on a new line

How to apply for Registration   The application form is in two separate parts

Part A is for information about the applicant and other details covering the whole application

This part (Part B) is for a description of a Purpose for which personal data are to be held or used, and a description of the data and associated details. You will need to complete one Part B in respect of each Purpose you wish to register

You should read the accompanying **Notes** booklet before completing the form. The Notes contain rules and conditions which the Registrar will apply, as well as standard descriptions and definitions which you will need to consult. **It is important that you read the Notes carefully.**

In completing form DPR 1, please use a typewriter or, if handwritten, use BLOCK CAPITALS

Do not use this form to
   Alter or remove an entry already on the Register — use Form DPR 2
   Renew an entry already on the Register — in this case you will be sent a renewal reminder

Further registration packs, and extra copies of Part B, can be obtained from **Crown Post Offices** and from the **Office of the Data Protection Registrar, Springfield House, Water Lane, Wilmslow, Cheshire, SK9 5AX.**

Completed application forms, together with the appropriate fee (see Notes Booklet), should be sent to the Registrar at **P.O.Box 66, Wilmslow, Cheshire, SK9 5AX.** This address must only be used for applications. Other correspondence should be sent to the full address given above — it may be seriously delayed if sent to P.O. Box 66

How to complete this form   In each section of Part B you may use standard descriptions to provide the detail required. Although you also have the option of writing your own descriptions in free text, **you are strongly encouraged to use the standard description approach.** In most sections this is simply a matter of selecting the appropriate descriptions from the list printed on the form, and ticking the corresponding boxes

The standard descriptions for **Purposes** are not printed on the form but are listed in the separate **Notes** booklet. You will need to read these before filling in the form. You should also refer to the booklet when selecting descriptions for **Data Classes.**

Before completing the rest of the form you should write the application number (copied from the front of Part A) in the box provided on the front of this Part B.

If your application is accepted, the details given in sections B 1 to B 4 will appear on the Register and will be available for public inspection

If you need more space than is provided for text in any Section, you may continue on page 7

Application for Registration

Data Protection Act 1984

THE DATA PROTECTION REGISTRAR

Form DPR 1

Part B

About this form This form is for use only in conjunction with form DPR 1 A

You should read the Notes on the back of this form and the accompanying **Notes** booklet

B.1 Purpose In this section you should describe a Purpose for which data are held or used

There are two methods of completing this section of the form

Method 1 By selecting one of the Standard Purposes listed and described in the Notes booklet

You may then relate the Purpose to a specific part of your organisation or particular business activity

Method 2 By describing the Purpose in your own words

You are likely to find registration simpler and easier under Method 1 and you are strongly advised to use this Method if it can meet your requirements.

Method 1 Select one of the Standard Purposes from those listed in the accompanying **Notes** booklet and write both the code number and the title in the spaces provided below

p 013	CUSTOMER/CLIENT ADMINISTRATION
code	title

If you are required to give further details of your Purpose (see **Notes** booklet) write these here

If you wish to relate this Purpose to a specific part or parts of your organisation or particular business activity, enter details here

Method 2 **(This method should only be used if Method 1 is inappropriate).**
Please describe the Purpose for which data are held or used, and, if you wish, the specific part or parts of your organisation or particular business activity to which it is related.

B.2 Description of Personal Data – Data Subjects

In this section you should describe the types of individual (**Data Subjects**) about whom personal data are to be held for the Purpose described in section B1. Do this by ticking the appropriate boxes below

		Current	Past	Potential				Current	Past	Potential
Employees trainees voluntary workers	S001	☐	☐	☐	Offenders and suspected offenders	S021	☐	☐	☐
Employees of associated companies organisations	S002	☐	☐	☐	Tenants	S022	☐	☐	☐
Employees of other organisations	S003	☐	☐	☐	Landlords owners of property	S023	☐	☐	☐
Recipients customers or clients for goods or services (direct or indirect)	S004	☑	☑	☐	Correspondents and enquirers	S024	☐	☐	☐
Suppliers of goods or services (direct or indirect)	S005	☑	☑	☐	Survey respondents other persons assisting research	S025	☐	☐	☐
Claimants beneficiaries payees	S006	☐	☐	☐	Patients	S026	☐	☐	☐
Account holders	S007	☐	☐	☐	Self-employed persons	S027	☐	☐	☐
Share and stock holders	S008	☐	☐	☐	Unemployed persons	S028	☐	☐	☐
Partners directors other senior officers	S009	☐	☐	☐	Retired persons	S029	☐	☐	☐
Employers	S010	☐	☐	☐	Students	S030	☐	☐	☐
Competitors	S011	☐	☐	☐	Minors	S031	☐	☐	
Business or other contacts	S012	☐	☐	☐	Applicants for permits licences registration	S032	☐	☐	☐
Advisors consultants professional and other experts	S013	☐	☐	☐	Taxpayers ratepayers	S033	☐	☐	☐
Agents other intermediaries	S014	☐	☐	☐	Licence holders	S034	☐	☐	☐
Trustees	S015	☐	☐	☐	Vehicle keepers	S035	☐	☐	☐
Members supporters of a club society institution	S016	☐	☐	☐	Elected representatives other holders of public office	S036	☐	☐	☐
Assignees guarantors other parties with legitimate contractual or business interest	S017	☐	☐	☐	Authors publishers editors artists other creators	S037	☐	☐	☐
Donors and lenders	S018	☐	☐	☐	Immigrants foreign nationals	S038	☐	☐	☐
Complainants	S019	☐	☐	☐	Relatives dependants friends neighbours referees associates contacts of any of those ticked above	S039	☐	☐	☐
Witnesses	S020	☐	☐	☐	Members of the public	S040	☐		

If you wish you may write additional descriptions of Data Subjects here start each description on a new line

_____

_____

_____

_____

_____

_____

_____

_____

273

2

B.2 Description of Personal Data – Data Classes

In this section, you should describe the **Classes** of personal data to be held for the Purpose described in B.1. Do this by ticking the appropriate boxes below. You should refer to the **Notes** booklet for examples of data items which might be covered by each Class

Identification Data

Personal identifiers	**C001**	☑
Financial identifiers	**C002**	☐
Identifiers issued by public bodies	**C003**	☐

Personal Characteristics

Personal details	**C011**	☐
Physical description	**C012**	☐
Habits	**C013**	☐
Personality, character	**C014**	☐

Family Circumstances

Current marriage or partnership	**C021**	☐
Marital history	**C022**	☐
Details of other family/household members	**C023**	☐
Other social contacts	**C024**	☐

Social Circumstances

Accommodation or housing	**C031**	☐
Property, possessions	**C032**	☐
Immigration status	**C033**	☐
Travel, movement details	**C034**	☐
Leisure activities, interests	**C035**	☐
Lifestyle	**C036**	☐
Membership of voluntary charitable bodies	**C037**	☐
Public offices held	**C038**	☐
Licences, permits held	**C039**	☐
Complaint, incident, accident details	**C040**	☐
Court, tribunal, enquiry proceedings	**C041**	☐

Education, Skills, Profession

Academic record	**C051**	☐
Qualifications and skills	**C052**	☐
Membership of professional bodies	**C053**	☐
Professional expertise	**C054**	☐
Membership of committees	**C055**	☐
Publications	**C056**	☐
Student record	**C057**	☐
Student financial records	**C058**	☐

Employment Details

Current employment	**C061**	☐
Recruitment details	**C062**	☐
Termination details	**C063**	☐
Career history	**C064**	☐
Work record	**C065**	☐
Health & safety record	**C066**	☐
Trade union, staff association membership	**C067**	☐
Payments, deductions	**C068**	☐
Property held by employee	**C069**	☐
Work management details	**C070**	☐
Work assessment details	**C071**	☐
Training record	**C072**	☐
Security details	**C073**	☐

Financial Details

Income, assets, investments	**C081**	☐
Liabilities, outgoings	**C082**	☐
Creditworthiness	**C083**	☑
Loans, mortgages, credits	**C084**	☐
Allowances, benefits, grants	**C085**	☐
Insurance details	**C086**	☐
Pension details	**C087**	☐

Details of Transactions

Goods, services provided to the data subject	**C091**	☑
Goods, services obtained from the data subject	**C092**	☑
Financial transactions	**C093**	☑
Compensation	**C094**	☐

Business Information

Business activities of the data subject	**C101**	☑
Agreements, contracts	**C102**	☐
Trading licences held	**C103**	☐

Health & Other Classes

Physical health record	**C111**	☐
Mental health record	**C112**	☐
Disabilities, infirmities	**C113**	☐
Dietary, other special health requirements	**C114**	☐
Sexual life	**C115**	☐
Racial, ethnic origin	**C116**	☐
Motoring convictions	**C117**	☐
Other convictions	**C118**	☐
Criminal intelligence	**C119**	☐
Political opinions	**C120**	☐
Political party membership	**C121**	☐
Support for pressure groups	**C122**	☐
Religious beliefs	**C123**	☐
Other beliefs	**C124**	☐

Miscellaneous Information

References to manual files, records	**C131**	☐
Uncategorised information	**C132**	☐

If you wish, you may describe additional Classes of data here; start each description on a new line

B.3 Sources and Disclosures

In this section, you should describe

In column A — The sources from which you intend or may wish to obtain any of the data you have described in section B.2
In column B — The person or persons to whom you intend or may wish to disclose these data

Do this by ticking the appropriate boxes below

Individuals or Organisations directly associated with the Data Subjects

		A. Source	B. Disclosure
The Data Subjects themselves	**D101**	☑	☐
Family relatives, guardians, trustees	**D102**	☐	☐
Other members of their households, friends, neighbours	**D103**	☐	☐
Employers — past, current or prospective	**D104**	☐	☐
Employees, agents	**D105**	☑	☑
Colleagues, business associates	**D106**	☐	☐

		A. Source	B. Disclosure
Legal representatives	**D107**	☐	☐
Financial representatives	**D108**	☐	☐
Doctors, Dentists, other health advisers	**D109**	☐	☐
Social, spiritual, welfare, advice workers	**D110**	☐	☐
Other professional advisers	**D111**	☐	☐
Landlords	**D112**	☐	☐

Others — please specify here

☐ ☐

☐ ☐

Individuals or Organisations directly associated with the Data User

		A. Source	B. Disclosure
Members, including shareholders	**D201**	☐	☐
Other companies in the same group	**D202**	☐	☑
Employees, agents	**D203**	☑	☑
Recipients, customers, clients for goods or services	**D204**	☑	☑

		A. Source	B. Disclosure
Claimants, beneficiaries, assignees, payees	**D205**	☐	☐
Suppliers, providers of goods or services	**D206**	☐	☐
Persons making an enquiry or complaint	**D207**	☐	☐
Tenants	**D208**	☐	☐

Others — please specify here

☐ ☐

☐ ☐

Organisations or Individuals (General Description)

Central Government

		A. Source	B. Disclosure
Inland Revenue	**D301**	☐	☐
Customs & Excise	**D302**	☐	☐
Driver & Vehicle Licensing Centre (DVLC)	**D303**	☐	☐
Department of Education & Science (DES)	**D304**	☐	☐
Department of Health & Social Security (DHSS)	**D305**	☐	☐
Department of Employment	**D306**	☐	☐
Home Office	**D307**	☐	☐
Ministry of Defence, including armed forces	**D308**	☐	☐
Other central government, including Scottish, Welsh & Northern Ireland Offices*	**D309**		

Local Government

		A. Source	B. Disclosure
Education department	**D321**	☐	☐
Housing department	**D322**	☐	☐
Social Services department	**D323**	☐	☐
Electoral registration, Assessment, Valuation departments	**D324**	☐	☐
Other local government *	**D325**		

Other Public Bodies

		A. Source	B. Disclosure
Other public bodies not elsewhere specified *	**D331**		
Foreign governments or authorities *	**D332**		

Continued

Justice		A. Source	B. Disclosure
Police forces	**D341**	☐	☐
Prosecuting authorities	**D342**	☐	☐
Other statutory law enforcement agencies, investigating bodies *	**D343**		
The courts	**D344**	☐	☐
Judges, magistrates	**D345**	☐	☐
Prison service	**D346**	☐	☐
Probation service	**D347**	☐	☐

Health & Social Welfare

		A. Source	B. Disclosure
Health authorities, family practitioner committees	**D351**	☐	☐
Hospitals, nursing homes	**D352**	☐	☐
Registered medical practitioners	**D353**	☐	☐
Registered dental practitioners	**D354**	☐	☐
Nurses, midwives, health visitors	**D355**	☐	☐
Other health care agencies, practitioners *	**D356**		
Social welfare agencies, practitioners *	**D357**		

Other		A. Source	B. Disclosure
Public utilities	**D361**	☐	☐
Banks	**D362**	☐	☐
Building societies	**D363**	☐	☐
Insurance companies	**D364**	☐	☐
Other financial organisations *	**D365**		
Accountants & auditors	**D366**	☐	☐
Lawyers	**D367**	☐	☐
Credit reference agencies	**D368**	☐	☐
Debt collection, tracing agencies	**D369**	☐	☑
Employment, recruitment agencies	**D370**	☐	☐
Private detective agencies, security organisations	**D371**	☐	☐
Trade, employers associations	**D372**	☐	☐
Trade unions, staff associations	**D373**	☐	☐
Professional bodies	**D374**	☐	☐
Voluntary, charitable, religious organisations or associations	**D375**	☐	☐
Political organisations	**D376**	☐	☐
Education or training establishments, examining bodies	**D377**	☐	☐
Survey or research organisations, workers	**D378**	☐	☐
Providers of publicly available information, including public libraries, press and media	**D379**	☐	☐
Providers of privately available information and databanks	**D380**	☐	☐
Traders in personal data	**D381**	☐	☐
Other organisations or individuals *	**D382**		

You should use the space below to give further details if you wish to use one or more of the categories marked with an asterisk (*) above. You should give the code number for each category which you are explaining.

If you wish, you may also write here additional descriptions of Sources and Disclosures

If you are using the space below, start each description on a new line and indicate whether the item is a Source, a Disclosure, or both

	A. Source	B. Disclosure
_____		
_____	☐	☐
_____	☐	☐
_____	☐	☐
_____	☐	☐
_____	☐	☐

5

B.4 Overseas transfers

In this section you should name any countries or territories outside the United Kingdom to which you intend to transfer the data.

If none, you should tick this box — None **T000** ☑

If the nature of your business requires you to transfer the data to any country worldwide, you should tick this box, and indicate your business in the space below — Worldwide **T999** ☐

_____

_____

Otherwise tick the appropriate boxes below

Algeria **T001** ☐	Indonesia **T020** ☐	Norway **T039** ☐
Argentina **T002** ☐	Iran **T021** ☐	Oman **T040** ☐
Australia **T003** ☐	Iraq **T022** ☐	Pakistan **T041** ☐
Austria **T004** ☐	Republic of Ireland **T023** ☐	Philippines **T042** ☐
Belgium **T005** ☐	Isle of Man **T024** ☐	Poland **T043** ☐
Brazil **T006** ☐	Israel **T025** ☐	Portugal **T044** ☐
Canada **T007** ☐	Italy **T026** ☐	Saudi Arabia **T045** ☐
Cyprus **T008** ☐	Japan **T027** ☐	Singapore **T046** ☐
Denmark **T009** ☐	Jersey **T028** ☐	South Africa **T047** ☐
Dubai **T010** ☐	Kuwait **T029** ☐	South Korea **T048** ☐
Egypt **T011** ☐	Libya **T030** ☐	Spain **T049** ☐
Finland **T012** ☐	Liechtenstein **T031** ☐	Sweden **T050** ☐
France **T013** ☐	Luxembourg **T032** ☐	Switzerland **T051** ☐
West Germany **T014** ☐	Malaysia **T033** ☐	Taiwan **T052** ☐
Greece **T015** ☐	Malta **T034** ☐	Turkey **T053** ☐
Guernsey **T016** ☐	Mexico **T035** ☐	USA **T054** ☐
Hong Kong **T017** ☐	Netherlands **T036** ☐	USSR **T055** ☐
Iceland **T018** ☐	New Zealand **T037** ☐	Venezuela **T056** ☐
India **T019** ☐	Nigeria **T038** ☐	

If necessary you may write additional names or descriptions here, start each on a new line

_____

_____

_____

_____

_____

_____

_____

6

Continuation

The space below is reserved for continuation text from any of the sections of this form. You should only need to use this space in exceptional circumstances.

You should indicate clearly which section of the form (B.1. B.3 etc) is continued here. Please start each separate continuation on a new line.

How to apply for Registration   The application form is in two separate parts

Part A is for information about the applicant and other details covering the whole application.

This part (Part B) is for a description of a Purpose for which personal data are to be held or used, and a description of the data and associated details. You will need to complete one Part B in respect of each Purpose you wish to register

You should read the accompanying **Notes** booklet before completing the form. The Notes contain rules and conditions which the Registrar will apply, as well as standard descriptions and definitions which you will need to consult. **It is important that you read the Notes carefully.**

In completing form DPR 1, please use a typewriter or, if handwritten, use BLOCK CAPITALS

Do not use this form to
   Alter or remove an entry already on the Register — use Form DPR 2
   Renew an entry already on the Register — in this case you will be sent a renewal reminder.

Further registration packs, and extra copies of Part B, can be obtained from **Crown Post Offices** and from the **Office of the Data Protection Registrar, Springfield House, Water Lane, Wilmslow, Cheshire, SK9 5AX.**

Completed application forms, together with the appropriate fee (see Notes Booklet) should be sent to the Registrar at **P.O.Box 66, Wilmslow, Cheshire, SK9 5AX.** This address must only be used for applications. Other correspondence should be sent to the full address given above — it may be seriously delayed if sent to PO Box 66

How to complete this form   In each section of Part B you may use standard descriptions to provide the detail required Although you also have the option of writing your own descriptions in free text, **you are strongly encouraged to use the standard description approach.** In most sections this is simply a matter of selecting the appropriate descriptions from the list printed on the form and ticking the corresponding boxes

The standard descriptions for **Purposes** are not printed on the form but are listed in the separate **Notes** booklet. You will need to read these before filling in the form. You should also refer to the booklet when selecting descriptions for **Data Classes.**

Before completing the rest of the form you should write the application number (copied from the front of Part A) in the box provided on the front of this Part B.

If your application is accepted, the details given in sections B 1 to B 4 will appear on the Register and will be available for public inspection

If you need more space than is provided for text in any Section, you may continue on page 7

Brief notes on compilation of the application forms

Listed below are the noteworthy points on the registration documents. Not every item is explained as by far the majority are either self-explanatory, or understandable by referring to the Registrar's notes.

Form A

Field A1 — note the organisation is also a bureau.
Field A5 — note the trading names of the organisation.
Field A8 — note multiple subject access points.

Form B — Purpose 001 — refers to the personnel/payroll system

Field B2/data classes — C023
The details of the number of children and their birthdates are maintained for issuing christmas party invitations.

Field B2/data classes — C034
The system pays travelling expenses and maintains a simple analysis of an individual's movements.

File B2/data classes — C037
This relates to membership by some staff members of a hospital sickness scheme.

File B2/data classes — C111
In some parts of the plant ink is used which may cause irritation to the hands of printers. This field simply records such outbreaks of irritation.

File B2/data classes — C131
This is the cross reference number to the application forms and other extremely private documents.

File B3/disclosures — D202
Very occasionally disclosures of personnel records are made to the parent company.

File B3/disclosures — D206
The data user's lawyer provides continuing services and in the course of that relationship personal data relating to employees are disclosed. Note that sources/disclosure in respect of lawyers not directly associated with the data user should be indicated at D367.

File B3/sources and disclosures — added item.
The company staff club is constitutionally independent from the company and personal data about members of the club/employees of the company is derived from and disclosed to the staff club. (Note the staff club may themselves be a data user see para. 5.3).

File B3/disclosures — D364
The company's insurers use information from this file in determining the premiums.

File B3/disclosures — D373
Lists of members from whom union deductions are made and sent to the union branch secretary each month.

Form B — Purpose 002 — refers to the current jobs in progress system

Field B2/data subjects — S001, S004 and S005
This database contains details of customers, suppliers (that is subcontractors) and employees. The system allows analysis by any of these data subjects. Orders are only added to the file when the order has been specified and agreed: hence, 'potential' data subjects are excluded.

Field B2/data classes — C052
Skills of employees are specified on the database.

Field B2/data classes — C070 and C071
The prime purpose of this system is work management and assessment and many details of this kind are retained.

Field B3/sources and disclosures — D105 and D106
Data are both collected from and disclosed to employees of non-corporated bodies (that is the other employee or partner in a two-man business or partnership).

Field B3/disclosures — D204 and D206
Data are occasionally disclosed about customer A in respect of orders placed to our supplier B and vice versa.

Field B3/disclosures — D206
Data may often be disclosed to the company lawyer in the context of personal injury and other work related disputes.

Form B — Purpose 004 — marketing and selling
(including direct marketing to individuals).

Field B2/data classes — C014
Data are retained on any 'awkward' characteristics of the customers.

Field B3/sources — D362 and D368
Data on customers' creditworthiness are obtained both from banks and credit agencies.

Form B — Purpose 007 — management of agents

Field B1/purpose — note the limiting comment

Field B2/data clases — C034
Data are retained on agent's travel movements for purposes of remuneration of expenses.

Field B4/transfers — T017, T027, T045, T054
Data are transferred in machine readable form to the countries listed and that added.

Form B — Purpose 013 — customer/client administration

Field B3/sources and disclosures — D105
This is selected to cater for the small non-incorporated organisations who nevertheless have employees. Information may come from these employees or be disclosed to them.

Field B3/sources and disclosures — D202
This allows disclosure to our parent company.

Field B3/disclosure — D369
The data are disclosed to a debt collecting agency.

Index

Accounting data
  exemption 32–5, 43–4
  permitted disclosures 33–4
Accounting services 65–6
Adopted persons, access to birth
  certificates 41
Ancillary and support function 59–60
Audit process 34, 66
Automatic data processing 25–8
  see also Computers

Back-up files, exemption 42–3
Bank of England, supervision of banks 40
Banking 64
Borrower account administration 63, 64
Business and technical intelligence 58–9

Census information, confidentiality 3
Charity and voluntary organisation 62
Chief Registrar of Friendly Societies,
  supervisory function 40
Club membership details, exemption 35–7
Coded information 92
Codes of practice 11, 12, 85, 86, 110
Committee on Data Protection, Report of
  (Lindop Report) (Cmnd 7341) 11, 26,
  86
Complaints 85
  Registrar's powers and functions 76–84,
  102–3
Computer bureaux
  and obligations of data users 13
  definition 13, 23–4
  failure to assist Registrar 78–9
  registration 50–1
    information required 53–5
  services provided outside UK 119–21
Computer databanks
  not discouraged by Act 21
  principles to regulate access 10
  rectification of errors 15
  threats to privacy 9–11
Computer programs 6
Computers
  no specific mention in Act 26
  see also Automatic data processing
Computers and Privacy (Cmnd 6353) 10–11

Confidential information disclosure
  defining 'confidential information' 6
  distinguished from data protection
    legislation 7–8
  elements of action 5–6
  legal protection 4
  legal sanctions 3–4
  remedies 6–7
Confidentiality
  duty of employees 5–6
  recognition of existence 5
Consultancy services 66
Consumer Credit Act (1974) 3
  s. 158 42
Corporate bodies
  data on 45
  information excluded from Act 24
  liability of directors 80
Council of Europe Data Protection
  Convention 9
  Act's compliance 116
  countries covered 115–16
  objectives 115
  Registrar's obligations 86–7
  transborder data flows 116–17
Court of Session (Scotland) 91
Courts
  actions brought under Act 101
  powers under Act 13
Credit reference agencies 65
  files 3–4
    fees for access 94
  licensing 40
Crime data, exemption from subject
  access 38–9
Customer/client administration 60

Data Protection Act (1984)
  background 9–12
  compliance with Convention 116
  dissemination of information on 85
  distinguished from law regulating breaches
    of confidence 7–8
  exclusion of legal persons 24
  exemptions 18, 31–45
    limits on Registrar's powers 78
    types 31–2

Index

Data Protection Act (1984)—*continued*
  groups affected 22–4
  major procedures 13–15
  penalties 79
  persons and activities regulated 21
  persons and agencies involved 12–13
  text 124–73
  timescale for action 122–3
  underlying principles 15–18
  see also Confidential information
    disclosure
Data Protection Authority 11
Data Protection Committee 11
Data Protection Convention, *see* Council of
  Europe Data Protection Convention
Data Protection Tribunal 13, 85
  appeals from 91
  composition 88
    when hearing appeals 89
  dealing with obstructive persons 90
  possible decisions 90–1
  practice and procedure 90
  rights of persons to appeal to 89–90
Data subjects
  access to courts 101
  access to data 14–15, 17–18, 92–7
    back-up files exempt 42–3
    barred from crime data 38–9
    checking identity 93–4, 112
    exemptions 31
    failure to comply with request 96
    form of request 93
    frivolous, etc. requests 96
    influence on registration 52–3
    overridden by other prohibitions 41
    processing requests 111–13
    time limit for file production 95
  access to Registrar 102–3
  affected by Act 24
  basic rights 92
  compensation for inaccuracy 97–9
  compensation for loss or unauthorised
    access 99–100
  definition 12, 24
  inaccuracy of third party
    information 98–9
  rectification and erasure of data 100–1
  redress against inaccuracies 15
  remedies for damage 18
  types 68
  see also Personal data
Data users
  conditions of holding data 22
  coordinating policy within organisation
    107–8

Data users—*continued*
  data collection not a function 26
  data held outside UK 119–21
  definition 12–13, 22
  duty to supply information 13–14
  failure to assist Registrar 78–9
  policy decisions 107–8
  preparation for registration 109–10
  procedures with requests for
    access 111–13
  Registrar's access rights 76–7
  registration 13–14, 50–1
    information required 53–71
  rights of appeal against Registrar 88–91
Decision tables 6
Deposit account administration 64
De-registration notices 80, 82–3
  right of appeal 89–90
Directors, liability of 80
Domestic data 41–2
Duchess of Argyll v *Duke of Argyll* 6

Education and training administration 63
Electronic mail systems 35
Employees, duty of confidentiality 5–6
Enforcement notices 80–2
  right of appeal 89–90
Examination results 95–6

Factoring 65
Fees for access to data 93, 94
Financial services 66
Flow charts 6
Franks Committee 3
Fund raising 58

Government departments 22–3

Health data, exemption 40–1
High Court
  appeals from Data Protection Tribunal
    91
  see also Courts
Home Office, registration of data bases 52
Housing management 63

Identity checks 93–4, 112
Immigration Department data bases 52
Information and data bank
    administration 62
Inland Revenue *see* Taxation data
Insurance administration 65
Insurance against liability 114
Insurance companies, licensing 40
Intention, statements of 29–30

Investment account administration 64
Investment management 65

Judicial appointments, information relevant
to 42

Legal professional advice, limit of Registrar's
powers 78
Legal professional privilege 42
Legal services 66
Lending and hire service
administration 60–1
Limited company information 43
Lindop, Sir Norman 11
Lindop Report 11, 26, 86

Mail order lists 36–7
Management of agents and
intermediaries 58
Manually processed data 18, 25, 45
Marketing and selling 57
Medical records, confidentiality 3
Membership administration 59

Name and address files, exemption 35–7
National Police Computer 52
National security data 42
exemption 18
Non-personal data 45

Official Receiver, statutory responsibilities
40
Official Secrets Act (1911) 3
Ombudsman 38
Opinion, statements of 28–9

Parliamentary Commissioner for
Administration (Ombudsman) 38
Parole Board indexes 52
Payroll data
exemption 32–5, 43–4
limits on use 34–5
permitted disclosures 34–5
Penalties 79
Pension data
exemption 32–5
limits on use 35
Personal data
access see Data subjects: access
adequacy and relevance 17
at date of Act coming into force 114
available to public by law 43
back-up files 42–3
categories 28–30
classes 68–70

Personal data—continued
coded information 92
collection not covered by Act 26
conditions for disclosure 43–4
control 22
correction and erasure rights 100–1
action by data user 113
criteria for protection by Act 25
disclosure to prevent damage to
health 44
disclosure to third parties 17, 70
factual 28
for statutory functions 39–40
held outside UK 119–21
including information on second person
94
information handling methods 26
intention data 29
judgmental 28–9
length of retention 17, 38
manually processed 18, 25, 45
overseas transfers 70–1
principles of obtaining 16
security measures 18
sources 70
specified purposes for holding 17
transborder flows 116–19
types of protection under Act 21
see also Confidential information
disclosure; Data subjects
Personal information, trading in 62
Personnel administration 56
Police Complaints Board 39
Property management 62–3
Public relations 58
Public sector standard purposes 66–8
Purchase/supplier administration 58

Registrar of Data Protection 11
accountability 86
action after inspection of data users 79
advice to data users 110
and exemptions 31–2
clarification from 30
complaints procedure 102–3
data users' rights of appeal 88–91
de-registration notices 80, 82–3
appeals 89–90
duties 50, 85–7
enforcement notices 80–2
appeals 89–90
enforcement powers 15
ensuring compliance with principles 80
functions 13, 76

Index

Registrar of Data Protection—*continued*
obligations in respect of Convention
86–7
obstruction 78–9
powers 76–7
limits 78
regulation of transborder data
flows 117–19
transfer prohibition notices 80, 84, 117–
19
appeals 89–90
Registration
activities pending outcome of application
72–3
alterations 71, 111
appeal against refusal 89–90
application form structuring 51–2
computer bureaux, information required
53–5
data users, information required 53–71
group of companies 71
implications of non-registration 74
maintaining currency of
registration 110–11
maintenance of register 50, 85
of new systems 111
number of entries 52–3
period in force 54–5
preparation by companies 109–10
procedure 49–75
public access to register 85
purpose 49–50
refusal of application 72
appeals against 72–3, 89–90
removal of defunct systems 111
renewals 73–4
requirements 13–14
standard purposes 56–68
undertaking activities not covered by
74–5

Rent administration 62–3
Research purposes 37–8, 61–2
Reservations, bookings and ticket issue 61

Saltman Engineering Co. Ltd v *Campbell
Engineering Co. Ltd* 4, 6
Secretary of State
licensing insurance companies 40
powers under Act 13
Security of databanks 18
see also National security data
Seager v *Copydex Ltd (No.2)* 6–7
Share and stockholding registration 59
Sick days, use of data on 33
Social work data 97
exemption 40–1
Statistical information 37–8
Statutory functions, data required
for 39–40

Taxation information
confidentiality 3
exemption 38–9
Text processed data 45
Trading lists 36–7
Transborder data flows 116–19
Registrar's powers 117–19
Transfer prohibition notices 80, 84, 117–19
right of appeal 89–90
Triplex Safety Glass Co. Ltd v *Scorah* 5
Trustees, information disclosure to
beneficiaries 43

Warrants
categories of material excluded 78
for access to data user's premises 76–9
Word processors 41
Work planning and management 56–7

Younger Report on Privacy (Cmnd
5012) 9–10